CRE

GATEWAY TO THE HIGHER REALMS

A COMPREHENSIVE GUIDE TO RECREATION, HIKING TRAILS, CAMPGROUNDS, TRAILHEADS, JEEP ROADS, ACTIVITIES, LOCAL HISTORY, MOTELS AND B&Bs, RESTAURANTS, MUSEUMS, AND SPIRITUAL CENTERS

JAMES MCCALPIN

CRESTONE SCIENCE CENTER
GUIDEBOOK NO. 7
2011

Front Cover: The Fourteeners above Crestone burn with fiery light at sunset, mimicking the burning zeal of spiritual practitioners seeking enlightenment. Photo by Bill Ellzey.

Frontispiece: Clouds blast forth from behind the Sangre de Cristo Mountains above Crestone, a purported vortex of cosmic alignments. Photo by Bill Ellzey.

Base maps for the Color Trail Maps (Plates 1-5) were made from National Geographic Society Topo! Maps, digitized from U.S. Geological Survey 1:24,000-scale topographic maps.

Quotations from THE DHARMA BUMS by Jack Kerouac, © 1958 by Jack Kerouac, renewed 1986 by Stella Kerouac and Jan Kerouac. Used by permission of Penguin, a division of Penguin Group (USA) Inc.

Quotations from the works of Wallace Stegner (p. 43, 131, 169) courtesy of Random House, Inc., New York, NY. Quotation on p. 256 courtesy of the University of Michigan Press, Ann Arbor, MI.

Quotations from PINON COUNTRY by Haniel Long courtesy of the University of Nebraska Press and University of California, Los Angeles.

Crestone: Gateway to the Higher Realms

Copyright © 2011 by James P. McCalpin

Published by Crestone Science Center, Inc., P. O. Box 837, Crestone, CO 81131 www.crestonescience.org; Guidebook No. 7

ISBN 978-0-9835382-0-2
Library of Congress Control No. 2011906021

Printed by B&B Printing, 220 Spencer Ave., Gunnison, CO 81230; (888) 500-7746; www.bbprinters.com

TABLE OF CONTENTS

PART 1—THE PHYSICAL REALM

3

FOREWARD

Dear fortunate reader who has discovered this guide book to Crestone, a hidden Shangri-la where the outer lands are the gateway to mystery and wonder. People come to Crestone for the natural beauty and mountain adventures but stay because of community. A coming together of diverse folk; from 4th generation mining families who remember the wild and wooly days, to solitary

spiritual practitioners that live in old mine shafts and trees, from the monks and nuns of various spiritual traditions, to families that have chosen Crestone as the place to raise their children, we are a wide ranging, international lot. Crestone the town serves as the commercial center for the surrounding community, a total population of about 1500. The town is going through a renaissance with three new restaurants, and the reopening of our "saloon", hardware, lumber yard, and grocery stores. The greater Crestone area includes 22 spiritual retreat centers where teachers and students gather from all over the world to deepen their spiritual awareness.

At 8000 feet we are a high desert community, but the runoff of mountain snows replenishes the huge aquifer lying beneath our feet. Crestone is a presentation o opposites; the vast flat valley offers pristine views of the surrounding mountain ranges, our hippy folk mix with wealthy land owners, dedicated spiritual practitioners shop at our stores mingling with the company of tourists from the coasts. Crestone welcomes everyone with a secret test. Some people come and fall in love with the land and set up their homestead, others run screaming into the night saying things like "the energy is too powerful here". It's really up to you, dear reader to discover what Crestone might have to offer you. Are you looking for a retirement home, or a short adventure into the mountains, a spiritua pilgrimage, or hunting, fishing expedition, a week to get away from it all, or a lifetime to change ones' self? All possibilities await. Whatever happens, we wis you well.

Ralph Abrams, Mayor
Town of Crestone

1. INTRODUCTION: CRESTONE AS A GATEWAY

Hikers and climbers have long known Crestone, Colorado as the physical gateway to recreation in the northern Sangre de Cristo Mountains. It is the only town on the western side of the northern Sangres, nestled at the foot of the highest peaks of the Crestone Group, beneath five of the Range's nine Fourteeners. From the town of Crestone, trails radiate into the rugged backcountry of the Sangre de Cristo Wilderness (and since 2004, into the newly-expanded Great Sand Dunes National Park & Preserve). Climbers aiming at the Fourteeners just east town (Challenger Point, Kit Carson Mountain, Crestone Peak, Crestone Needle) find Crestone a convenient base camp.

However, if that is all Crestone is, yet another gateway town to yet another Colorado mountain range, this guidebook would not be necessary. The fact is, over the past three decades Crestone has evolved into another, more ethereal type of gateway. It has become a metaphysical gateway to religious retreats, monasteries, yoga ashrams, nature-based fine art, and natural (alternative) building. The town and its adjacent Baca Grande subdivision encompass a smorgasbord of world religions, counter-cultural residents, spiritual retreatants, cowboys and carpenters. Sometimes it is hard to separate the physical lure from the metaphysical lure. Between the otherworldy physical setting and the pervasive New Age spirituality, a visit to Crestone can be a bit different than your average Colorado tourist experience. You may take more than pictures, and leave more than footprints.

Fig. 1-1. *Left*; Hikers overlook Willow Creek Park on their way to Willow Lake, on the area's most popular trail. *Right;* A wintery scene frames the Enlightenment Stupa of the Pundarika Foundation in the Baca subdivision.

Crestone's unique combination of a physical and metaphysical gateway has attracted attention in some unexpected places. For example, how many other Colorado towns with a population of 127, and at the end of a dead-end road, have been the subject of feature articles in major newspapers (Los Angeles Times, Rubin, 1989; New York Times, Jones, 2008; Minneapolis Star-Tribune, Welsch, 2009), and magazines (US News & World Report, Paine, 2007; Four Corners Magazine, Rae, 2002; Sunset Magazine, Grudowski, 2011)? Or had a Grammy-winning CD produced here and named after it? (*Crestone*; Paul Winter Consort, Best New Age Album, 2007).

There are two other aspects of the Crestone area that are generally under-appreciated, even by local residents. These are the mute story of the mountains themselves as expressed in their natural history, and the human history beginning with the Baca Land Grant and the El Dorado and Crestone Mining Districts. Professor Arthur Lakes (a founder of the Colorado School of Mines) visited in 1901 and declared *"Crestone is one of the prettiest and most beautifully situated mining camps in Colorado"* (Lakes, 1902, p. 467). As a geologist, I find the natural history equally as compelling as the outdoor recreation and spiritual aspects of the area, and therefore it is a topic interwoven throughout this guidebook.

> *The elevation and dryness of the atmosphere gives to it an elastic, exhilarating, tonic quality never found in sea level air, except it may be right on the ocean beach. One feels "braced up," strengthened and stimulated by inhaling the prevailing breezes, especially in the morning, when it is so cool and refreshing.... Of course with such an atmosphere, clear, light, electrical, and the snowcapped mountains all around, there are gorgeous sun-rises and sun-sets, and innumerable scenic effects produced by clouds and sunshine.*

Pelton, *San Luis Valley Illustrated,* 1891

Likewise, the human history of the area, (described from 1860 to present in Part 3), has left its mark on the landscape. Starting with the discovery of gold near Pole Creek in 1870, the first 68 years of Crestone's history are represented today by mines, shafts, tunnels, spoil piles, mining roads, ghost mining camps, and old buildings in Crestone that can still be seen (and some of which are still occupied). Many historical artifacts are located in the Baca Grant south of Crestone and are well preserved because the Grant was closed to the public from 1900 until 2004. However, the former Grant is now public land and is easily accessible from Crestone, opening the area's "time capsule" of the mining days to amateur historians and visitors alike

Fig. 1-2. Evening light penetrates sheets of virga in front of Kit Carson Mountain, making a magical rainbow. Zoe Shipton, late of Trinity College Dublin, is smiling because she knows how Murphy's Law works: *"If I traveled to the end of the rainbow as Dame Fortune did intend, Murphy would be there to tell me the pot's at the other end."*

To various user groups Crestone may appear to be a different entity, like the elephant in the Indian parable of the five blind men. This guidebook is an attempt to illuminate "the whole elephant." It is mainly for visitors to the Crestone-Baca area and the surrounding Federal lands (Fig. 1-3), to assist in their pursuit of happiness, whether that be hiking, camping, mountain climbing, mountain biking, wildlife watching, hunting, fishing, adventure travel, spiritual journey, or simply to get away from it all.

SCOPE OF THIS GUIDEBOOK

This guidebook covers the western side of the Sangre de Cristo Mountains between San Isabel Creek and Sand Creek, a stretch of 15 miles. Centered within the area are the Town of Crestone (population 73), the Baca Grande subdivision (population about 1000), and the Crestone Group of high peaks.

The book begins by describing trails and camping in the Sangre de Cristo Wilderness. Historically visitors have used Crestone as a jumping-off spot for the rugged Sangre de Cristo Mountains. However, since 2006 two additional wildland attractions have developed (Fig. 1-3). The land between the Baca Grande subdivision and the old Great Sand Dunes National Monument is now part of Great Sand Dunes National Park & Preserve. The land southwest of Crestone is now part of the 78,697-acre Baca National Wildlife Refuge.

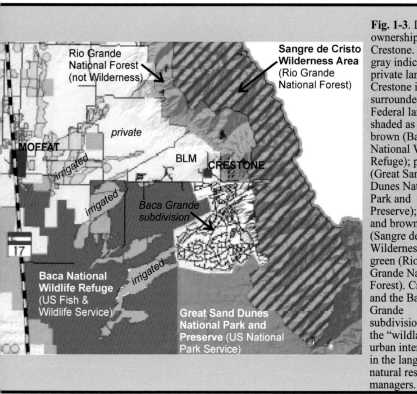

Fig. 1-3. Land ownership around Crestone. Light gray indicates private land. Crestone is surrounded by Federal land, shaded as follows: brown (Baca National Wildlife Refuge); pink (Great Sand Dunes National Park and Preserve); green and brown stripes (Sangre de Cristo Wilderness); and green (Rio Grande National Forest). Crestone and the Baca Grande subdivision lie on the "wildland-urban interface", in the language of natural resource managers.

Abbreviations:
BLM—U.S. Bureau of Land Management (Dept. of the Interior)
BNWR—Baca National Wildlife Refuge (Dept. of the Interior)
CO 17—Colorado State Highway 17
CR T—County Road T
FR-- Forest Road (in National Forest)
FT—Forest Trail (in National Forest)
GRSA—Great Sand Dunes National Park & Preserve
NPS—National Park Service (Dept. of the Interior)
SLV—San Luis Valley
USFS—U.S. Forest Service (Dept. of Agriculture)
US 285—US Highway 285

GETTING HERE

Crestone is not the easiest place to get to, not being served by direct air service, trains, or buses. Perhaps that is part of its appeal, and one reason it's not a typical tourist town. You can get CLOSE to Crestone by several modes of public transportation, but then you need to either rent a car to make it those last few miles, or have someone drive from Crestone to come get you.

Via Air: The closest airport with regularly scheduled commercial flights is the San Luis Valley Regional Airport (airport code ALS) in Alamosa, 50 miles by road south of Crestone. All flights are by Great Lakes Airlines, which operates turbo-prop flights under its own name (airline code ZK) and under United Express (airline code UA). All flights into Alamosa originate at Denver International Airport (airport code DEN) in Denver, Colorado. In 2010 there were three flights per day in and out of Alamosa on weekdays and one flight per day in and out on weekends.
Two rental car companies operate out of the airport.
Budget Car Rental (800) 527-0700 or (719) 589-0103(www.budget.com).
L&M Car Rental (719) 589-4651. Open limited hours during weekdays, by prior reservation only on weekends.
Alternatively, you can arrange for someone from Crestone to pick you up in Alamosa. Windhorse Transportation (719) 256-4091 will bring you to Crestone for a fee; call for prices or visit www.windhorse.crestonecolorado.com.

The next closest major airport is in Colorado Springs (airport code COS), 150 road miles from Crestone. It takes about 3 hours to drive from COS to Crestone via US 50, US 285, and CO 17. All major car rental companies are at COS.

Via Train: The closest AMTRACK station to Crestone is Denver Union Station, 1701 Wynkoop Street, Denver CO 80202. Unfortunately, AMTRACK passenger trains in the Rockies run only east-west, and Crestone is south of Denver. So, from the AMTRACK station you would have to catch a bus to Moffat, Colorado, 12 miles west of Crestone (see below).

Via Bus: Bus service does not come to Crestone, but it now comes within 12 miles (Moffat, CO). Starting in January of 2010, the Arrow/Black Hills Stage Lines (www.blackhillsstagelines.com) instituted a "road stop" at Moffat for southbound buses (from Denver) and northbound buses (from Alamosa). There are no agents at the road stop and tickets are not sold. Buses depart Denver at the Denver Bus Center (Greyhound Station; at 1:40 pm) and Denver Union Station (AMTRACK train station; at 1:50 pm) and arrive in Moffat at 5:45 pm (4 hour ride). Call Arrow/Black Hills at (877) 779-2999 for fare information. Buses depart Alamosa (Greyhound Bus Terminal, 1924 Stockton St., Alamosa, CO 81101, 719-589-4948) at 6:20 am and arrive in Moffat at 7:00 am (40 minute ride). NOTE: the bus from Alamosa leaves before any incoming flights arrive at the Alamosa Airport (San Luis Valley Regional Airport)! Bummer.

Via Auto:
To drive to Crestone, you must first enter the San Luis Valley. Highways enter the San Luis Valley from five points of the compass; N, NW, SW, S, and SE (Fig. 1-3). The latter three approaches utilize US Highway 160, the major east-west highway that passes through Alamosa, Colorado, the largest town in the San Luis Valley.

UPDATED INFORMATION

With the passage of time, some of the information in this book will inevitably become outdated. For updated information, check the Kiosk at the entrance to the Baca subdivision (Fig. 1-4); the Town of Crestone website (www.townofcrestone.org); or the latest edition of the *Crestone Eagle* newspaper (www.crestoneeagle.com).

Fig. 1-4. The information "Kiosk" at the bend in County Road T, ¼ mile south of Crestone, near the entrance to the Baca Grande subdivision. Check here for current information about lodging, services, and events. The tops of Mt. Adams (left) and Challenger Point (right) peek over the roof.

11

From the NORTHWEST: enter the SLV via CO 114 from Gunnison, This road (paved) goes over Cochetopa Pass (shown, but not labeled) and enters the SLV at Saguache, the County seat of Saguache County. *As you enter Saguache from the west, the entire width of the Sangres appear before you, lying 40 miles away across the San Luis Valley.* Continue to Moffat in one of two ways: (1) east on US 285 and then south on CO 17, or (2) drive south of Saguache 2 miles and turn left (east) onto County Road X. Continue on this paved road for 18 zig-zag miles to Moffat. Once you intersect CO 17, turn right and drive ½ mile to County Road T. Turn left onto T and drive 12 miles east to Crestone

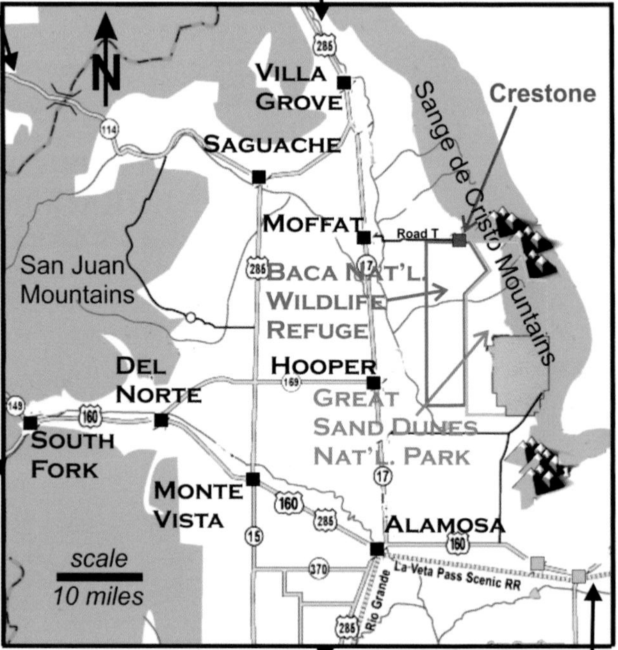

How To Get To CRESTONE

From the NORTH: enter the San Luis Valley via US 285 and Poncha Pass. Drive south 15 miles to Villa Grove. Five miles south of Villa Grove turn left (east) onto CO 17 and continue 12 miles to Moffat. Turn left (east) at Moffat onto County Road T and drive 12 miles to Crestone.

From the SOUTHWEST: enter the SLV from the west on US 160 from Pagosa Springs and points west. At Del Norte turn left (north) onto CO 112 and drive 13 miles east to US 285. Cross 285 and continue east 2 miles to Center. Continue east on CO 112 through Center and drive 12.5 miles to Hooper. At Hooper turn left (north) onto CO 17 and drive 16 miles to Moffat. Turn right (east) at Moffat onto County Road T and drive 12 miles to Crestone.

FROM THE SOUTH: enter the SLV from the south on US 285 from New Mexico. At Alamosa turn right (east) onto US 160 and drive through downtown, and over the bridge across the Rio Grande (about 1 mile total). About 0.3 miles east of the river, turn left (north) onto CO 17 and drive 38 miles to Moffat. Turn right (east) at Moffat onto County Road T and drive 12 miles to Crestone.

FROM THE SOUTHEAST: enter the SLV from the east on US 160. This is the route people take to access the SLV from Interstate 25. On the eastern outskirts of Alamosa turn right (north) onto CO 17 and drive 38 miles to Moffat. Turn right (east) at Moffat onto County Road T and drive 12 miles to Crestone.

Fig. 1-5. Roads leading to the San Luis Valley and Crestone.

2. THE NATURAL ENVIRONMENT OF CRESTONE AND VICINITY

GEOGRAPHY

Fig. 2-1. Satellite view of the northern Sangre de Cristo Mountains and Crestone (right center). Green circles at lower left are 160-acre fields irrigated by wells.

13

Crestone lies on the eastern margin of the San Luis Valley (Fig. 2-1), or the "San Luis Park" (or parc) as it was called in the early-to-mid 1800s. The San Luis Valley (or SLV for short) lies astride the 38th North parallel of Latitude, and the valley floor in Colorado (not counting adjacent ranges) encompasses an area of 3230 square miles, an area larger than the states of Rhode Island or Delaware. The Sangre de Cristo Range draining into the SLV adds another 710 square miles, and that part of the San Juan Mountains in the watershed adds another 3466 square miles. The total area of the valley floor and its watershed is thus 7406 square miles, larger than Connecticut.

The San Luis Valley occupies the down-dropped axis of the Rio Grande rift zone, with the volcanic foothills of the San Juans visible on the west. The western San Luis Valley is dominated by potato farming (the small dots at lower left are 160-acre irrigated fields). The eastern SLV and the Wet Mountain Valley are dominated by ranching and hay production in irrigated meadows (irregular light green areas north and south of Crestone).

> "T*he San Luis parc is then an immense elliptical bowl, the bed of a primeval sea which has been drained; its bottom, smooth as a water surface, and concave..... An extraordinary symmetry of configuration is its prominent feature. The scenery, everywhere sublime, has the ever-changing variety of the kaleidoscope.*
> William Gilpin, *Mission of the North American People*, 1860

WILLIAM GILPIN, SHAMELESS PROMOTER OF THE SAN LUIS VALLEY

William Gilpin was the first Governor of the Territory of Colorado, appointed by Abraham Lincoln in 1861. However, his association with Crestone is more direct, because in 1877 he purchased the Baca Grant south of Crestone and held it until 1885. He first passed through Colorado on his way to Oregon in 1843, and then met John C. Fremont on the latter's First Expedition ("*On the Fourth of July, 1843, I was here; on this present site of Denver: one of a small, but resolute and intrepid camp. Here were Carson Fremont, Fitzpatrick, Talbot. The American flag floated over us*" [Gilpin, 1873, p. 212]).

Based on his early experiences in Colorado, in 1860 Gilpin wrote a flattering description of Colorado and particularly the San Luis Valley in his book *Mission of the North American People* (Gilpin, 1860). He predicted the discovery of gold in the Sangre de Cristos, a full 14 years before the formation of the earliest mining district. In 1863, he bought the Beaubien Land Grant in Costilla County (now known as the Sangre de Cristo Grant) as a development investment; 1 million acres of plains, mountains, and forests. To publicize his development he wrote new glowing descriptions of the San Luis Valley (Gilpin, 1869) and reissued his 1860 book in 1873.

Gilpin's enthusiasm for the SLV arose partly out of his Isothermal Axis Theory, which stated that the mid-latitude temperate zones of the earth are the "natural enabling and controlling zones of robust, vigorous civilizations." This latitudinal belt lies between 30° and 50° North Latitude, encompassing the USA, Western Europe, Japan, and China. The San Luis Valley lies in its center. In honor of his boosterism of the SLV I have scattered many of his picturesque descriptions and flowery Victorian language throughout this guidebook.

CLIMATE

In meteorology the atmospheric condition of the San Luis parc, like its scenery, is one of constant brilliancy, both by day and night; obeying steady laws, yet alternating with a playful methodical fickleness.
William Gilpin; *Mission of the North American People*, 1860

PRECIPITATION; HIGH AND DRY

The farmers and ranchers of the SLV don't always appreciate the playful fickleness of climate, especially in regards to precipitation. The San Luis Valley is the driest part of Colorado, despite its high elevation (valley floor at 7500-8000 ft). The valley averages only 7-8 inches of precipitation (rain plus snow) per year (Fig. 2-2), because it lies in the rain shadow created by high mountain ranges to the west, north, and east. Values this low classify as an *arid climate (or high desert)*, the only such area within Colorado. Only by relying on streamflow from the neighboring mountains, and on groundwater from the last ce Age, can agriculture survive in the Valley.

Precipitation increases with elevation on the valley margins, as can be seen in the close contours shown in the Sangre de Cristo Range. At range-front locations like Crestone, total precipitation is only 12-16 inches/year (*305-405 mm/year*), which classifies as a semi-arid climate (defined as 10-20" precip/year). In contrast, at the crest of the Sangre de Cristo Mountains total precipitation (mostly snow) increases to more than 40 inches/year (*1015 mm/year*).

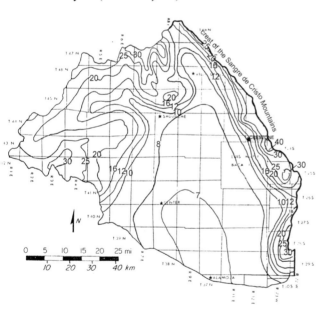

Fig. 2-2. Contour map of mean annual precipitation (inches) in the San Luis Valley and west half of the Sangre de Cristo Mountains (far right). From McCalpin, 1982

Crestone Precipitation Records (based on local station data, 1982-2009 (Source: www.keno.org)
Mean Annual Precipitation ....13.4 inches (340 mm)
Highest Annual Precipitation (1990) ....19.2 inches (488 mm)
Lowest Annual Precipitation (2002).............. 4.9 inches (124 mm)

15

Mean Annual Snowfall...................................65.1 inches (1.65 m)
Highest Annual Snowfall (2008-2009) ....99.0 inches (2.5 m)
Highest Snowstorm Series (Apr. 12-17, 2009); 45 inches in 5 days
Lowest Annual Snowfall (1999-2000) ....22.5 inches (0.6 m)

Fig. 2-3. A summer thunderstorm pummels the Sangres east of Crestone. Towering cumulus clouds can rise to heights of 40,000 feet, fueled by updrafts of hot air rising from the valley floor. Summer hail is a common result. Such storms are welcomed in this semi-arid zone, but can cause erosion problems in foothill areas such as the Crestone-Baca. Photo by Bill Ellzey

WHO OWNS THE RAIN?

One of the challenges to sustaining any community in the high desert is… WATER. Yes Crestone does receive 65" of snow annually, but it is a dry powder snow containing only about 10% water by volume. Residents push it off their decks and porches with brooms rather than shovels. The snowpack contains about 6.5" of liquid water, or about half of the mean annual precipitation amount; the remainder falls as rain.

An obvious way to collect water for home use is from the roof via gutters and cisterns. Surprisingly, that practice has been illegal in Colorado for more than 100 years. The State Engineer has ruled that the rain that falls on your roof actually belongs to whoever owns the water rights to the watershed (surface streams) in which your house sits. Thus, a homeowner who collects rainwater from his roof is stealing water from the owner of that water right.

Thus situation was partly modified in 2009 when Governor Bill Ritter signed the "Rooftop Precipitation Capture" bill (Senate Bill 09-080). (http://water.state.co.us/RainWaterBills.pdf). That bill permits homeowners who have a valid "domestic well permit" to collect the water that falls on their roofs. However, the bill does not apply to houses served by a municipal or community water system. Nor does it apply to homeowners who own less than 35 acres and have a "Household Use Only" well permit. The bill only applies to those who own 35 acres or more and have a well permit that allows inside water use and outside water use for up to 1 acre of garden (limit 1 acre-ft/yr). Because of these restrictions, homeowners in the Crestone-Baca area still cannot (legally) collect the water that falls on their roofs.

TEMPERATURE: *FREEZE OR BAKE? (YOUR CHOICE)*
The temperature regime of Crestone is seriously bipolar. Early promoters of the area glossed over that fact with poetic language, as seen below:

> *... One can hardly conceive of a greater luxury than to hie away to a mountainous region, so far heavenward as to be above the reach of the dense miasmas and fogs of the low lands, and the heavy, dull, heated atmosphere of those only a few hundred feet above sea level; to enjoy by day the cool breezes of mid-air which have not been raised to oven heat by the caloric absorbed from the sun-scorched soil; and to sleep at night under blankets where the thermometer seldom stays above 45 or 50 degrees, and never above 60 degrees during 10 good hours.*
>
> *... The rarified air, comparatively free from vapor, does not absorb these* [sun] *rays, and so does not reach a high figure on the thermometer scale, seldom above 80 to 85 degrees in the house or in any shade, in the hottest hours of the day. The ground, cooled by the airwaves descending from high peaks or ridges, often snowclad in summer, does not get so warm during the day as to send up hot currents. Then, the freer perspiration in the dryer atmosphere carries away the surplus heat of the body and keeps the skin at a comfortable temperature.*
>
> Pelton, *San Luis Valley Illustrated,* 1891

Due to its elevation, the atmosphere in the SLV is thin and the humidity is low. Such a thin, dry atmosphere can't hold heat very well. It's rather like living on Mars or the Moon; when the sun goes down, the temperature plummets. On a typical day the high temperature may be 35° to 40°F warmer than the low temperature. Extreme variations in daily temperature are typical of areas far from the moderating effects of oceans (the nearest ocean is 750 miles away), and are called *continental climates.* What this means for outdoor clothing is "dress in layers;" as the day inevitably warms up, you will need to shed those layers.

For the same reason, season-to-season temperatures also vary widely. In the winter, the daily low might be 0°F and the high 35 to 40°F. In the heat of the summer, the daily low might be 50°F and the high 85 to 90°F. In both times of year, after sunset cool air moves down off the mountains (cold air drainage) into the San Luis Valley. During the day, warm air rises from the valley up onto the mountains, reversing the air flow.

Crestone Temperature Records (based on local station data, 1982-2009) (Source: www.keno.org)
Mean Annual Temperature .... 41°F (5°C)
Highest Temperature (July 2005) .... 98°F (37°C)
Lowest temperature (Feb. 1985) .... -26°F (-32°C)

> *The meridian sun retains its vitalizing heat around the year; at midnight prevails a corresponding tonic coolness. The clouds are wafted away by steady atmospheric currents coming from the west. They rarely interrupt the sunshine, but, refracting his rays, imbue the canopy with a shining silver light, at once intense and brilliant.*
>
> William Gilpin; *Mission of the North American People,* 1860

17

THE ADIABATIC LAPSE RATE

This arcane term refers to the decrease of temperature as one travels to higher elevations. The lapse rate for dry air is 3.5°F per 1000 ft of elevation gain. Thus on a day when it is 50°F in Crestone (8000 ft elevation), on the summit of Challenger Point (6000 ft higher) it will be 21° cooler, or 29°F. It's something to remember when hiking…

WEIRD WEATHER; *THE TORNADO OF 2005*

At 5:15 pm on April 24, 2005, a tornado (Fig. 2-4) was observed over Crestone (no, this was not a UFO sighting). It hit the range front above town at about 8700 ft, and was accompanied by 1" of hail with hailstones up to ½" in diameter. A Crestone resident videotaped the funnel cloud for 5 minutes and reported that "it was spinning real fast." Weather experts speculated that it was probably a rare *cold air funnel tornado*, rather than a more common and powerful supercell tornado (the air temperature was 42°F at the time; Keno, 2005a).

Fig. 2-4. The funnel cloud of the Crestone tornado of April 24, 2005. The hill in center distance, just to the right of the funnel cloud, is "Banner Mountain", the ridge separating North Crestone Creek from Burr Gulch. Photo was taken looking north from the Baca subdivision. Photo by Jeanne Sullivan.

MORE WEIRD WEATHER; *THE DUST STORM OF 2005*

Spring and early-summer sandstorms and duststorms are rather common in the SLV. Brisk southwest winds whip up the freshly-plowed soil in thousands of agricultural fields in the western and central Valley, sending it heavenward. A good example is the June 3, 2005 sandstorm. Its front was a 1000 foot-high "wall" of sand and dust that swept rapidly across the valley from west to east (Fig. 2-5), reminiscent of the awesome Dust Bowl storms of the midwestern USA in the 1930s. Accompanying winds ripped the roof off of the school at Moffat and sent pieces of it flying into town and onto Highway 17. See Keno (2005b).

Fig. 2-5. The front of the June 2005 sand storm approaching the Baca subdivision from the west. Much of this dark cloud is topsoil (and associated chemicals) deflated from agricultural fields between Alamosa and Center. Such storms are part of the "playful (!) methodical fickleness" of weather referred to by Gilpin (1860). Photo by Michael Dennett; see also Keno, 2005b.

18

FLORA and LIFE ZONES

From the floor of the San Luis Valley to the crest of the Sangres 6700 feet above, the microclimate and vegetation (flora) change drastically. In less than five miles you can hike from the high desert to the tundra, a progression that at sea level would require a several-thousand-mile walk northward. But in the Sangres the vegetation zones (life zones) have been "telescoped" into narrow bands by the abrupt rise from 7500 feet to 14,200 feet elevation (Fig. 2-6).

The flanks of the great mountains, bathed by the embrace of these irrigating clouds, are clad with great forests of pine, fir, spruce, hemlock, aspen, oak, cedar, pinyon, and a variety of smaller fruit-trees and shrubs, which protect the sources of the springs and rivulets. Among the forests, alternate mountain meadows of luxuriant and nutritious grass. [photo by Bill Ellzey]
　　　William Gilpin; *Mission of the North American People*, 1860

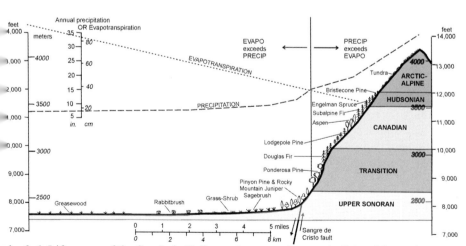

Fig. 2-6. Life zones of the San Luis Valley and western Sangre de Cristo Mountains, using the definitions of Merriam and Steineger, 1890 (http://en.wikipedia.org/wiki/Life_zone). Redrawn from McCalpin, 1982.

19

The vegetation of the valley floor and mountain range is ultimately determined by the ratio of precipitation to potential *evapotranspiration* (rainfall directly evaporated from leaf surfaces, or transpired from leaves during photosynthesis). With increasing elevation precipitation increases (Fig. 2-6) and temperature decreases by 3.5°F/1000 ft (the adiabatic lapse rate). Conversely, evapotranspiration is greatest on the valley floor where it's warmer, and steadily decreases at higher (and cooler) elevations. (*Potential* evapotranspiration is the amount of water that theoretically could be evaporated or transpired, if there was enough water available all the time, and it wasn't frozen).

THE *UPPER SONORAN* LIFE ZONE

As shown by the evapotranspiration and precipitation curves in Fig. 2-6, on the valley floor potential evapotranspiration is greater than precipitation (that is, there is a moisture deficit). Accordingly, the vegetation is that of a high desert characterized by greasewood, rabbitbrush (Fig. 2-7), grass, and shrubs. This plant community belongs to the *Upper Sonoran* life zone of Merriam and Steineger (1890).

Fig. 2-7. Rabbitbrush *(Ericameria nauseosa)* in bloom on the valley floor south of the Great Sand Dunes. Rabbitbrush is the dominant plant on dry parts of the valley floor. Photo by NPS/Patrick Myers.

As the ground begins to rise in the forested apron at the foot of the mountains, precipitation increases a bit and begins to approach the magnitude of potential evapotranspiration. Because of the increased moisture, the piedmont slopes are covered by a dense pinyon-juniper woodland, comprised exclusively of two low tree species, Pinyon Pine and Rocky Mountain Juniper. This close-packed dwarf forest is very susceptible to forest fires (pinyon is a very hot-burning wood), and tends to experience stand-replacing fires about every century or so. The upper limit of the pinyon-juniper woodland and the Sonoran life zone falls approximately where precipitation equals potential evapotranspiration. Upslope of this elevation there is a moisture surplus, and the transition from desert vegetation to true forest.

Two additional plant communities in the Upper Sonoran life zone are not shown on Fig. 2-6, but they are very important on the valley floor. The first is the long ribbons of narrowleaf cottonwoods along the perennial streams which flow out of the mountains and onto the valley floor. The second is the wetlands that occupy the downstream reaches of those perennial streams.

20

THE BURNING BUSH

Bill Moyers, famous author and commentator, visited the Baca Ranch in 1981 to film a seminar at the Aspen Institute campus (see Ch. 9), which had its headquarters at the Baca from 1980 to 1984. The seminar ("Six Great Ideas: Truth, Goodness, Beauty, Liberty, Equality, Justice" by Mortimer Adler) was later broadcast on public television. While walking with Maurice and Hanne Strong back to his car on the valley floor, he reported that a "sagebrush" in front of him spontaneously burst into flames. (Note: there are no sagebrush in the Baca Ranch; it was probably a rabbitbrush]) Later, Moyers reported that this episode of the "burning bush" was the only truly mystical and unexplained experience in his life (McDonald, 1994; Torkelson, 2001).

VALLEY FLOOR MEADOWS & WETLANDS (summarized from Sovell, 2006)

Long before gold was discovered in the Crestone area, the main attraction of the area was the natural meadows on the valley floor. Gilpin (1860) rhapsodized about these meadows as *"immense saturated savannas of luxuriant grass."* He continues *"These delicate grasses, growing rapidly during the annual melting of the snows, cure into hay as the aridity of the atmosphere returns. They form perennial pastures, and supply the winter food of the aboriginal cattle, everywhere indigenous and abundant."* It was these meadows that led the Baca family to choose this 100,000 acres for their Land Grant, out of all the land in the western United States (Fig. 2-8; also see Part 3).

Fig. 2-8. The "luxuriant grass" described by Gilpin grows as high as a horse's tail along lower Deadman Creek. From the Baca Grant Development Company, 1909.

Spanish Creek Wetland in the Baca Grande subdivision is one of two accessible examples of wetlands on the valley floor. (The other, Oxbow Wetlands, is described on page 155).The Wetland is a 120-acre wet meadow at the far western edge of the Baca subdivision. To reach it, drive south from the entrance to the Baca 1.6 (paved) miles on Camino Baca Grande to Badger Road and turn right; proceed 1.0 (paved) miles on Badger to Wagon Wheel and turn right (west); proceed 2.4 (gravel) miles west to Camino

21

del Rey, and turn left (south) and drive 1.1 (gravel) miles south on Camino Real to the wetland.

Spanish Wetland is located where Spanish Creek exits the Baca and enters the Baca National Wildlife Refuge (BNWR). Groundwater and spring runoff fill a natural wetland bisected by the Camino Del Rey road berm. The wetland is dominated by Baltic rush, wild irises, and stands of woolly sedge (*Carex pellita*). It is characterized as a *Juncus balticus* Herbaceous Meadow (or, Baltic Rush Western Slope Wet Meadow). The wetland and surrounding area is rich in plant and animal life with numerous rare species including Mountain Plover (*Charadrius Montana*), Wilson's phalarope (*Phalaropus tricolor*), the Brazilian free-tailed bat (*Tadarida brasiliensis*), and the northern pocket gopher *agrestis* subspecies. The are probably foraging individuals from the colony at the Orient Mine, approximately 20 miles (32 km) north of the wetland. Other common species observed at the wetland include the western chorus frog (*Pseudacris triseriata*) and tiger salamander (*Amblystoma tigrimum*).

THE PINYON-JUNIPER WOODLAND (FIG. 2-9)
The upper half of the Sonoran life zone is the Pinyon-Juniper Woodland. In this carpet-like woodland live most of the residents of the Crestone-Baca area. Fortunately for residents of the Baca Grande subdivision, the woodland is sufficiently dense that houses even on adjacent ½ acre lots are scarcely visible to each other. Trees in this dwarf forest average only 15-25 feet tall. To prevent buildings from rising too far out of the forest canopy and becoming visually obtrusive, they are limited to 30 feet high.

Fig. 2-9. *Left:* The carpet-like forest of pinyon-juniper woodland, looking north from FR 949 east of Crestone; *Right:* a stocky Pinyon Pine (*Pinus edulis Engelmann*) on the left intergrows with a more open and lacy Rocky Mountain Juniper (*Juniperus scopulorum*) on the right.

THE NARROWLEAF COTTONWOOD – ROCKY MOUNTAIN JUNIPER WOODLAND; A UNIQUE AND GLOBALLY-RARE PLANT COMMUNITY
The creeks flowing through Crestone and out onto the valley floor are bordered by a unique plant community, the narrowleaf cottonwood (*Populus angustifolia*)--Rocky Mountain juniper woodland community. The plant community is characterized by an open canopy of narrowleaf cottonwood and Rocky Mountain juniper, often with grasses and wildflowers growing in the shady understory (Fig. 2-10).

Fig. 2-10. On a hot summer day, the ribbon-like cottonwood-juniper forest offers a cool and shady streamside retreat. Don't be surprised to see a family of deer or the odd pheasant taking advantage of the shade too. As inviting as these streamside groves are, they are also vulnerable to overgrazing, human disturbance, and drought. The multi-year drought that peaked in 2002 killed many of the cottonwoods along County Road T at the entrance to Crestone.

This rare tree assemblage is imperiled both in Colorado (38 occurrences) and globally, and in the USA has been documented only in Colorado, north-central Wyoming and northern New Mexico. In Saguache County, there are eight known occurrences of this community and four of those are in the Baca Grande subdivision. Newly-mapped occurrences of this plant community are found along all four creeks (South Crestone, Willow, Spanish and Cottonwood) that cross the Baca.

THE *TRANSITION* LIFE ZONE

Where precipitation equals and then exceeds potential evapotranspiration, the forest grows thicker with taller pines and firs. On the lower mountain slopes Ponderosa pine is the first to appear, with Douglas fir on the moister north-facing slopes. This is the *transition life zone* of Merriam and Steineger (1890). In its native habitat of the Transition Zone, the Ponderosa pine (also called Western Yellow Pine) inhabits an open woodland interspersed with grassy openings (Fig. 2-11, left). These openings range from small to many acres, and the larger ones were called "parks" by early settlers of Colorado. As a result, many early Colorado towns sited in the Ponderosa forest were named after these parks (Estes Park, Bergen Park, Woodland Park, etc.). Standing in a park surrounded by Ponderosas on a warm summer day, you can close your eyes and let your senses reach out; to the whisper of the wind through the long needles, the smell of warm pine-sap faintly reminiscent of vanilla.

23

Fig. 2-11. *Left:* The stately Ponderosa Pine (*Pinus ponderosa*) towers over the lower tree of the juniper pinyon-woodland. This asymmetrical, older Ponderosa, was probably topped by a windstorm in years past; height= 59 ft; diameter at breast height (DBH)= 36". Based on its DBH, this tree is probably 150-200 years old. *Right:* A culturally-peeled Ponderosa Pine (right) growing next to Burnt Gulch east of Crestone; DBH= 23". Height= 30 ft. The Ponderosa to the left is slightly larger (DBH= 30") but twice as tall, suggesting that the right-hand tree was significantly stunted by the peeling.

"PEELED" PONDEROSAS: THE LEGACY OF HARD TIMES

Throughout the Ponderosa forests of the western Sangre de Cristo, one may find large Ponderosas (normally thicker than 24" DBH) that carry unusual scars. The scars are 6" to 12" or more wide, and extend up from ground level to about the height of a man's outstretched reach (Fig. 2-11, right). There are at least 72 such trees along Medano Creek in the Great Sand Dunes National Park, concentrated in Indian Grove (Winger and Winger, 2003, p. 59). Most of the scars there have been dated between 1816 and 1848, based on counting tree rings. Tree rings show that much of that period was a drought (Grissino-Mayer et al., 1998), suggesting that other foods might have been scarce.

According to Gulliford (2009), Ute Indians refer to these as "medicine trees". The Utes removed areas of bark on Ponderosas to expose the protein-rich cambium (sapwood) layer beneath the bark. They then cut into the cambium at the base of the tree, grasped the sapwood and pulled it upward, "peeling" off long thin strips of the sapwood.

The cambium was used as a food source in times of drought or food scarcity; supposedly it tastes like cookie dough. Gulliford (2009) states that the cambium "is high in fiber, calcium, protein, carbohydrates, magnesium, iron, zinc, vitamin C, and equal in

24

ood value to nine glasses of milk." Such peeled trees have been found east of Crestone, and they presumably exist in the Baca subdivision as well. Jim Erdman cored a peeled Ponderosa and dated the peeling to the period 1860-1865 (Erdman, 2004). According to Crestone 'old timers', the Ute Indians still roamed the area at that time, 5-10 years before the discovery of gold south of Crestone.

DOUGLAS FIR (*PSEUDOTSUGA MENZIESII*) (called the Douglas Spruce in the late 1800s). This tree (Fig. 2-12) dominates north-facing slopes in the Transition Zone, between elevations of 8500 and 10,000 feet. John Muir called it "the king of the spruces" and remarked:

> *"This vigorous spruce is ever beautiful, welcoming the mountain winds and snow as well as the mellow summer light, and maintaining its youthful freshness undiminished from century to century through a thousand storms."*
> John Muir, *The Mountains of California*, 1894

Douglas fir was evidently much more numerous near Crestone before the mining era, as evidenced by many large (up to 3 feet in diameter), decayed stumps scattered throughout the piedmont and foothills. The stumps' abundance on a piedmont now occupied almost exclusively by pinyon and juniper trees, indicates that the piedmont forest had quite a different composition when the miners appeared in the 1870s.

Fig. 2-12. Old-growth Douglas Fir rising out of the pinyon-juniper woodland on the Burnt Gulch alluvial fan. The tree is rooted in the active channel of Burnt Gulch, which flows 4-6 weeks each year in May and June. Height= 63 ft, DBH= 38". Based on its DBH, this tree is probably 150-200 years old. In Colorado this tree grows to a maximum height of about 100 feet and often lives to be 300-400 years old.

For use as mine timbers and lumber, Douglas Fir was *"frequently preferred to all other available species, because of its durability and strength, and because of the desirable*

25

sizes in which it may be obtained" (Kempfer, 1911). In the early mining era (1870-1910), the foothills east of Crestone were totally denuded of trees, as occurred near almost every Colorado mining town (Fig. 2-13).

Fig. 2-13. Panoramic photo of the Sangres from the Baca Grant, ca. 1908. The foothills appear to have been totally denuded of trees, except for a few dark-tones groves on high ridges. All the rest of the forest had been cut down between 1870 and 1910, to furnish firewood, lumber, and mine timbers to the El Dorado and Crestone Mining Districts. These same foothills are now covered by a dense forest of second-growth timber. At righ center, cattle of the famous Baca Herd graze contentedly. From Baca Grant Developmen Company, Inc., 1909.

THE *CANADIAN* LIFE ZONE
With increasing elevation precipitation increases even more and mean annual temperatur drops. In response to these changes **Lodgepole pine** forests appear along with **aspen** (Fig. 2-14) and **subalpine fir** . This is the *Canadian* life zone of Merriam and Steineger (1890), or the mixed conifer forest of modern terminology. In forest openings, subalpine meadows are rich in summer wildflowers.

Fig. 2-14. Aspen (*Populus tremuloides*). *Left,* Typical aspen forest in the Canadian life zone, just below timberline on the north side (middle ground) and south side (distance) c San Isabel Creek. The long aspen-covered ridge in the middle ground is a lateral morain favored by aspens due to its thick, moisture-retaining soil. *Right,* typical aspen grove in summer, with an understory of lush grass and wildflowers.

26

The Colorado Blue Spruce (*Picea pungens*) has the distinction of being the State Tree of both Colorado and Utah, selected by the former in a vote of school children on April 15, 1892. The Blue Spruce requires more moisture than other spruces and firs, and is most often found near watercourses. It is treasured for its unique silver or blue-green color and symmetrical, tapering shape, and is a common ornamental tree in towns. Peattie (1991, p. 38) mentions that the Colorado Blue Spruce has become a popular landscape tree throughout the United States, planted in suburban lawns by the working classes, or lining the driveways of wealthy estates.

THE *HUDSONIAN* LIFE ZONE

The highest and wettest forests are dominated by fir and **Englemann spruce** (Fig. 2-15), **bristlecone pine** (Figs. 2-16, -17), and **limber pine** on exposed, windy slopes. This assemblage is the *Hudsonian* life zone of Merriam, or Spuce-fir or Subalpine conifer forest of modern terminology.

Fig. 2-15. *Left*: The spruce-fir forest near timberline on a north-facing slope. The spruces struggle to grow amid the thin, rocky soil and winds near treeline. Note how the trees decrease in height toward the top of the ridge, ending in a strip of krumholz at the ridgeline. *Right*: The "Methuselah Tree" on the slopes above Wild Cherry Lake. This bristlecone Pine had only one live branch on it when I visited in 1979; many others had clearly been cut or broken off by campers. It may have been nearly 1000 years old in 1979, but may no longer be living.

The easiest Engelmann Spruce to see are those planted in the town of Crestone by the pioneers 130 years ago. These trees have grown to nearly 100 feet high and tower over the lower cottonwoods and aspens. One such spruce guards the entrance to Crestone at the Elephant Cloud Tea House (west end of Golden Avenue).

    Bristlecones as old as 715 years were documented on the east side of the Sangres, north of Hermit Lake in the headwaters of Middle Taylor Creek (LaMarche and Stockton, 1974; their Hermit Lake site). At Great Sand Dunes National Park, at 10,500 ft elevation in the head of Morris Gulch, the oldest living tree (a limber pine) was dated as 412 years old by Grissino-Mayer et al. (1998).

27

KRUMHOLZ
As the forest approaches treeline, its spruce, fir, bristlecone, and limber pines become progressively more stunted and shrublike; this is the zone of "krumholz." Wherever a natural timber line occurs, in any mountain range of the world, the trees grow more and more stunted as they approach timberline. Their shapes are crushed and bowed down by the long-lasting weight of winter's snow, while simultaneously being starved at the roots for nutrients in the brief growing season. Over the decades and centuries these gnarled spruces attain a natural bonsai-like shape. Such trees were called the Krummholz in the European Alps, a German word meaning "crooked wood." In Colorado it is sometimes called "wind timber" (Peattie, 1991, p. 59).

THE *ARCTIC-ALPINE* LIFE ZONE
On the western side of the Sangres trees stop between about 11,800 and 12,000 ft elevation, above which is **tundra** vegetation (the *Arctic-Alpine* life zone of Merriam, and Alpine Tundra zone of modern terminology). The low carpet of tundra plants includes stunted grasses and groundcover plants, such as Alpine phlox, Dwarf clover, Alpine forget-me-nots, Fairy primrose, and Alpine avens.

HYDROLOGY

Hydrology, the study of water, is not just an academic topic in the San Luis Valley. Life and livelihood in our high desert depend on it. Of the all the resources in the Valley (space, soil, sunshine), water is the "limiting resource" whose scarcity places limits on both agricultural and urban development. This basic fact has long been recognized, although often glossed over by promoters:

> *The San Luis parc… is watered by thirty-five mountain streams, which, descending from the encircling crest of snow, converge nineteen into San Luis Lake, the rest into the Rio del Norte…. The San Luis Lake, extending south from the point of the foot-hills, occupies the center of the parc for sixty miles. It forms a bowl without any outlet to its waters. It is encircled by immense saturated savannas of luxuriant grass…Its water surface expands over this savanna during the season of the melting snows upon the Sierras, and shrinks when the season of evaporation returns.*
> William Gilpin; *Mission of the North American People*, 1860.

SURFACE WATER
The Crestone-Baca area is a valley-margin oasis in an otherwise dry valley, being blessed by five perennial streams flowing off the highest peaks of the Sangres. These streams pick up flow as they descend from the valley heads to the canyon mouths. Hydrologists call such streams "gaining streams", because they gain flow downvalley, from both surface flow from tributaries, and from groundwater seeping into the channel walls. The majority of streamflow comes in May and June as the snowpack melts. Once past the canyon mouths, the streams flatten out on the valley floor and wander through long, linear groves of cottonwood and juniper, which can be seen from a distance crossing the

alley floor like green ribbons. At the end of these ribbons the streams feed giant meadows and wetlands of grass and sedges.

The local farmers and ranchers know well that streams crossing the valley floor lose flow as they travel across the valley floor. Many of the streams never make it to the valley center, but lose their entire flow by leakage into the stream bed, where the water becomes shallow groundwater. In such reaches the streams are known as "losing streams", that is, they lose their surface flow to the groundwater table. It is this phenomenon of streamflow loss that keeps the water table high beneath the valley floor, and keeps the aquifers "topped up."

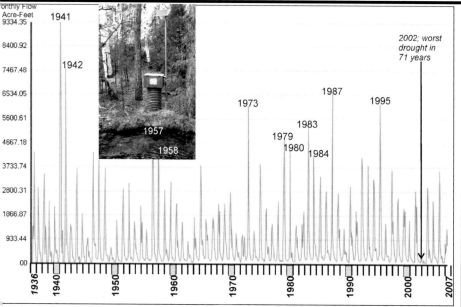

ig. 2-16. Stream flow measurements from the gaging station located in the North restone Campground. Years of higher-than-average flow are labeled; of the 11 years, ght form pairs of successive years (1941-42; 1957-58; 1979-80; 1983-84). Fortunately, accessive years of very low flows (droughts) are rare. But note the three years of nearly-accessive low flows (1971, 72, and 74). The 2002 drought, which killed many ottonwoods on the valley floor, was (fortunately for us) flanked by normal-runoff years. set photo: The Colorado Division of Water Resources measures streamflow volumes ith unattended stream gages, such as this one on Willow Creek in the Baca subdivision. ater depth is measured by a float gage inside the corrugated pipe, and the data are ansmitted to Denver via satellite.

an average year, North Crestone Creek sends 8557 *acre-feet* of water past the gaging ation in North Crestone Campground (an acre-foot of water is the volume required to ver an acre 1 foot deep, or 43,560 cubic feet). With an area of 8165 acres and an erage precipitation of about 30"/yr, the North Crestone watershed above the gage ould receive about 20,400 acre-feet of precipitation per year. What this means is that ly 42% of the precipitation that falls on the watershed in a given year exits the Range as streamflow at the canyon mouth. The remaining 58% either evaporates, is transpired by forest trees during photosynthesis, or infiltrates as recharge to deep groundwater. Most of the "lost" water is probably transpired, since direct evaporation is low in mountains (due to cool temperatures) and deep infiltration through rock is limited. Hydrologists and valley irrigators may refer to this 58% as "lost water", since it is not available to them, but to a forester the water transpired is what keeps the forest growing, so it is hardly "lost"…The same type of water balance comparison can be done for the other streams in the Sangres.

WHEN IT RAINS IT POURS; THUNDERSTORMS AND FLASH FLOODS
Although Crestonians love rain, sometimes it comes down a bit harder than desired. Crestone's wettest months are July (2.3") and August (2.1"), when summer thunderstorms drift in from the southwest as part of the "North American monsoon." Convective thunderstorms may drop as much as 1.5" of rain (a typical monthly total) in as little as 20 minutes. When this happens on terrain such as the steep alluvial fans of the Baca subdivision, runoff is quick and extreme. For example, the storm on July 3, 2006 (Keno, 2006) eroded gullies up to 6 feet deep and ate up a few cars (Fig. 2-17).

Fig. 2-17. Effects of the rainstorm of July 3, 2006 in the Baca subdivision. *Left*, looking east up Panorama Way after the storm; *Right*, a car, which was parked in front of the owner's house (background), undermined by gully erosion. From www.keno.org

Torrential rainstorms tend to cause recurrent erosion in the Baca subdivision, for two reasons. The first is the high gradient of the alluvial fan surface east of Camino Baca Grande, which averages about 10% , or 6°. The second reason is that many of the roads on this surface were designed by the developers to run straight down the fall line, which is the steepest gradient and the one on which runoff will accelerate fastest. The longest such road is Panorama Way at 1.33 miles long, oriented straight down the fall line; it is not surprising that erosion occurs repeatedly on the lower parts of Panorama.

GROUND WATER
The Crestone-Baca area lies in the important zone of groundwater recharge. Creeks flowing down from the Sangres begin to lose water to infiltration as soon as they exit the mountains *(losing streams)*, and this water infiltrates downward to the groundwater table. Over most of the Valley there are two groundwater aquifers, an upper **unconfined**

30

quifer and a series of lower **confined aquifers**, separated by a 100 ft-thick clay layer called the "Blue Clay."

Another Artesian Well   This Well was Put Down for $150.00

Fig. 2-18. Historic photo of a flowing artesian well on the Baca Grant. The depth of the well was not given, but Pelton (1891) states that Baca artesian wells were between 150 and 400 feet deep. Because this well still has considerable pressure, and there are no water tanks at the site, the well was probably drilled shortly before the photo was taken). From Baca Grant Development Company, 1909.

In the approximately 100 ft-thick unconfined aquifer, the groundwater level is close to the surface and the water is not under pressure, so has to be pumped to the surface. In the confined aquifer(s) water pressure increases with increasing depth, so at sufficient depths it will flow above the ground surface (artesian pressure; see Fig. 2-18). Importantly, water infiltrating from streams into the unconfined aquifer generally cannot continue downward into the confined aquifer, due to the impermeability of the Blue Clay.

Since the early 1900s the artesian pressure in the upper confined aquifer beneath the Grant has slowly declined, as the result of many flowing wells reducing the pressure. Today [2011] most artesian wells barely flow above the top of surface casing, about 2-3 feet above ground surface level. Fortunately for the confined aquifers, the Blue Clay pinches out about 4 miles from the range front of the Sangres. That means there is a four-mile-wide strip, called the *recharge zone* (Fig. 2-19), where infiltrating water from creeks can "bypass" the Blue Clay and recharge the confined aquifers directly.

The Crestone-Baca area sits squarely on this recharge zone, and the creeks (North Crestone, South Crestone, Willow, Spanish, Cottonwood) all infiltrate large quantities of water every year to the unconfined and confined aquifers. This is a good thing, since without this natural recharge from stream infiltration, the water pumped from the confined aquifer by wells would not be "replaced", and thus the aquifer would eventually become depleted. Pumping more groundwater per year than is recharged is sometimes called "groundwater mining", and of course is unsustainable in the long term. This has been demonstrated since about 1950 in the large desert cities of the American Southwest (Phoenix, Tucson, Las Vegas) where groundwater levels have dropped hundreds of feet due to pumping.

31

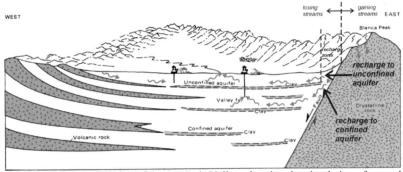

Fig. 2-19. Schematic cross-section of the San Luis Valley, showing the circulation of groundwater (squiggly arrows). Precipitation falling on the Sangre de Cristo Mountains either runs off in stream or infiltrates to groundwater through fractured rock. When streams cross the Sangre de Cristo fault and become *losing streams*, part of their flow infiltrates downward. In the narrow *recharge zone* o the Crestone-Baca area, the confined aquifer obtains most of its needed recharge.

"Katie Snider Teaches Me to Dowse"

In the summer of 1979 I visited Katie Snider at her home in downtown Crestone [now the Town Center Building]. The conversation somehow drifted to geology, then mining, and eventually to groundwater and then to dowsing. She was visibly shocked when I said I did not know how to dowse, and yet considered myself a geologist! [I should explain here that geologists are taught that dowsing is a bunch of superstitious poppycock practiced by charlatans]. But belief in dowsing is firm in rural areas and cannot be eradicated by any amount of scientific arguments. Katie propose a solution; she would teach me how to dowse, saying "it's so simple even a man can do it."

She ducked into the house and returned with two pieces of solid copper rod, about 1/8" i diameter. Each rod was bent into a L-shape of unequal length, about 18" on the long side and 10" on the short side. First, she said, hold the rods in an upright fist with the long side horizontal and pointed forward, and the short side hanging straight down through your closed fist. The hands should be 6"-8" apart. The trick is to balance the bend of the rod on your side of your index finger so the long end (which is pointed forward and horizontal) is free to swivel on its own to right or left. Begin walking forward, with the rods out in front of you. As you walk over a water source, the long ends of the rods will swivel of their own accord, pivoting on your index fingers, and move toward each other, eventually crossing when you are directly atop the water. When you continue past the water source, the rods will magically swivel away from each other until they are parallel again and pointed forward. At least, that's the theory.

Her grassy back yard contained two small springs, so my first dowsing traverse was directly uphill of the two springs. Starting about 20 feet from the springs, I began walking forward holding the rods in front of me parallel and level, balanced loosely on my index fingers. As I approached the first spring, the two rods began to swivel toward each other, as if some force was attracting them. I was astonished. They crossed over each other as I reached the head of the spring As I continued walking past the spring, the rods slowly uncrossed until they were parallel and pointing forward again. Highly suspicious, I turned around and reversed course. The rods did the same thing again, at the same location. This was distressing.

I returned the rods and mumbled my thanks to Katie, but soon left. Turning over in my mind what had just happened. I definitely did not twist or turn those rods, they had swiveled on their own accord. Could my professors at the Colorado School of Mines have been wrong? I wondered, had they ever actually tried dowsing themselves? Maybe they had never met anyone li Katie, who could show them. Hmmm...... Perhaps there were more things in heaven and earth, Horatio, than were dreamt of in my philosophy.....

GEOLOGY

HOW THE MOUNTAIN RANGE CAME TO BE

The Sangre de Cristo Mountains are not like most mountain ranges in Colorado, which formed about 65 million years ago (Front Range) or 25-35 million years ago (San Juans). Instead, the Sangres are among Colorado's youngest mountain range (along with the Sawatch, Mosquito, Tenmile, and Gore Ranges), created within the past 20 million years by crustal stretching along the (still expanding) Rio Grande rift zone. The young rift-flanking ranges differ from Colorado's other ranges in that: (1) they are straight and narrow, and (2) they have no foothills, but rise straight up from base to summit elevations. For example, an older mountain range like the Front Range is 43 miles wide at the latitude of I-70, and it takes 25 miles to rise from 5000 ft to its 14,000 ft crest (an average of 360 feet per mile). By comparison, the Sangres are just as high but only 8 miles wide, rising from 8000 ft to 14,000 ft in a mere 4 miles. That represents an average rise of 1500 feet per mile, or four times steeper than the Front Range.

The San Luis Valley is part of a 600 mile-long tear in the Earth's crust named the Rio Grande rift (Fig. 2-20). The rift is a series of pull-apart basins, flanked by mountain ranges, marking where states west of the Rocky Mountains are slowly pulling westward from the stable center of the North American continent. The rift began spreading about 20 million years ago, and is still slowly spreading today according to precise GPS measurements. However, the rate of east-west spreading is very slow, about 1/50 inch per year. This is much slower than the spreading rate measured across oceanic spreading centers such as the Mid-Atlantic Ridge, which spreads about 7/8 inch per year.

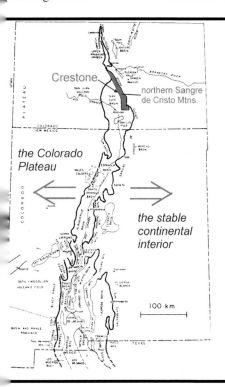

Fig. 2-20. Map of the Rio Grande rift zone, showing the northern Sangre de Cristo Mountains at its northern end. The rift is a giant crustal pull-apart zone, formed where the Colorado Plateau and Basin and Range Province are being pulled westward away from the stable continental interior of North America. The rift is wider at the south end because the Colorado Plateau is not only pulling away westward, but is rotating clockwise at the same time, which creates more extension in the southern rift. From McCalpin, 1982.

A side-effect of stretching the crust is thinning it and allowing the hot mantle material beneath to rise closer to the earth's surface. The thin crust explains the high heat flow in the San Luis Valley, and its high geothermal gradients (the rate at which temperature increases with depth in wells; browse to: geosurvey.state.co.us/Default.aspx?tabid=504)). Numerous warm and hot wells provide geothermal heat for facilities such as the Sand Dunes Swimming Pool (Hooper), Joyful Journey Hot Springs (Villa Grove), the Colorado Gators alligator farm (Mosca), and the Splashland pool (Alamosa). Valley View Hot Springs, in contrast, is a natural spring on the Sangre de Cristo fault.

When the earth's crust is pulled apart horizontally it normally breaks along steep fault lines into a central downdropped crustal block (called a *graben* by geologists), flanked by fault-bounded uplifts (called *horsts*). The San Luis Valley is such a graben and the Sangre de Cristo Mountains is a horst (Fig. 2-21). The boundary between the valley and mountains is formed by the Sangre de Cristo fault, which runs along the base of the range just east of Crestone. Rift faults provide pathways for the ascent of hot geothermal water such as Valley View Hot Springs (on the Sangre de Cristo fault) and Joyful Journey Hot Springs and Sand Dunes Swimming Pool (between 4 and 5 on the drawing below).

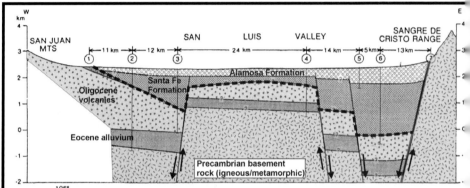

Fig. 2-21. East-west subsurface cross-section through the northern San Luis Valley (a complex graben) and flanking horsts. This is what you would see if you had X-ray vision and could see through all the sand and gravel beneath the valley floor. The vertical scale is greatly exaggerated in this drawing for clarity; note the location of sea level (zero on the vertical scale). The valley floor underlain by a central buried horst block that separates a shallow, western sub-graben (the Monte Vista graben) and a deeper, eastern sub-graben (the Baca graben). Bedrock formations below the thick dashed line predate the formation of the Rio Grande rift. These formations were faulted as the rift formed (about 20 million years ago) and the rift axis subsided downward. Over the past 20 million years the rift basin has continued to subside and to fill up with sediments (formations above the dashed line) washed in from the neighboring mountain ranges, with each process keeping pace with the other. These rift-filling gravels, sands, silts, and lake clays are up to 8,000 feet thick in the deepest part of the rift basin, between Crestone and the Great Sand Dunes, which puts their bottom below sea level. Without these sediments, the Rio Grande rift would be an arm of the Gulf of Mexico.

THE SANGRE DE CRISTO FAULT

The Sangre de Cristo Fault is Colorado's most active fault, having moved as recently as about 7500 years ago in a Magnitude 7 to 7.5 earthquake. Do we have your attention now?.........We know this because the fault has displaced alluvial fan surfaces as young as 10,000 years old (Holocene) and has created small "fault scarps" where the fault cuts the fan (McCalpin, 1982). Where older alluvial fans are displaced by the fault, the fault scarps are progressively higher with increasing age, indicating that the fault has continued moving throughout at least the past 400,000 years, earthquake by earthquake.

Geologists have mapped the recent fault scarps in the Crestone area (Fig. 2-22) and have determined they were created during Magnitude 7.0-7.5 earthquakes that occur roughly every 10,000 to 15,000 years. During the earthquake, the faults "breaks loose" in the subsurface and the displacement rapidly propagates up the fault plane to the ground surface, where it displaces the east side of the fault up 5-8 feet relative to the west side.

34

his means that anything straddling the fault trace (a fence, a road, a buried water line, a uilding) is also displaced vertically by 5-8 feet. The extreme displacement is enough to estroy roads, pipelines, and buildings. Fault scarps produced by past M7+ earthquakes xist at the mouths of San Isabel, North Crestone, Spanish, Cottonwood, Deadman, and ole Creeks. At some trailheads, you may be parking your car right next to one and not ealize it!

g. 2-22. Map of the recent fault scarps of the Sangre de Cristo fault (thick dark lines, ks on downthrown side) in the Crestone-Baca area. Most of the traces pass through cant land, except for selected spots in the Baca subdivision (lots and roads shown in ack) and spiritual retreat lands (polygons outlined with lighter gray lines, no ticks). hen the next Big One occurs on the fault, the vertical surface breaks, 5 to 8 feet high, ill follow these scarps.

THE NEXT "BIG ONE"

It is a question of when, not if, for the next M 7.5 earthquake (The Big One). But there Is some good news… The probability of a large earthquake in the near future is low, according to the geologic evidence. Paleoseismic trenching studies (McCalpin, 1982) have shown that the typical repeat time between such earthquakes is 10,000-15,000 years and the previous large earthquake occurred about 7500 years ago. Thus, if the fault remains on its same "time clock" for stress release, the next large earthquake will not occur for another 2,500 to 7,500 years. Technical information on this section of the Sangre de Cristo fault is contained in US Geological Survey's Quaternary fault and Fold Database: http://gldims.cr.usgs.gov/webapps/cfusion/Sites/qfault/index.cfm.

THE "BONES" OF A MOUNTAIN RANGE

To make a high mountain range like the Sangres, it is not enough to merely uplift the range at a fast rate. The rocks in the range must also resist the power of *erosion*, a force which increases exponentially as the mountains grow higher. In other words, to become high like the Sangres, a Range needs "good bones." In that regard, the Sangres are lucky to be composed of hard rocks that resist erosion, which explains why they are so high and so steep (see Lindsey, 2010).

The Igneous and Metamorphic Rocks

In the Crestone area the western part of the range is made of very old (Precambrian) igneous and metamorphic rocks, mainly granites and gneisses. These are the crustal "basement rocks" that underlie sedimentary rocks everywhere in the USA (Fig. 2-23).

Fig. 2-23. A high-grade biotite gneiss (metamorphic rock) from the Deadman Creek area. This rock became so heated and pressured during its metamorphism that it became plastic like toothpaste, and the white quartz vein was squeezed into a serpentine shape.

From a 1-mile-wide band of granite at the range front north of Crestone, the proportion of the Sangres composed of basement rocks progressively increases to the south, ultimately underlying more than half the width of the range These basement granites and gneisses are separated from the sedimentary rocks of the Sangres by a fault named the Crestone Thrust. Back 65 million years ago, long before the present Sangres existed, plate tectonic forces from the west pushed and shoved the basement rocks up an over the sedimentary rocks in this area, using the Crestone Thrust as the gliding plane. This west-to-east thrusting folded the layered sedimentary rocks ahead of the Thrust into broad folds (Fig. 2-24).

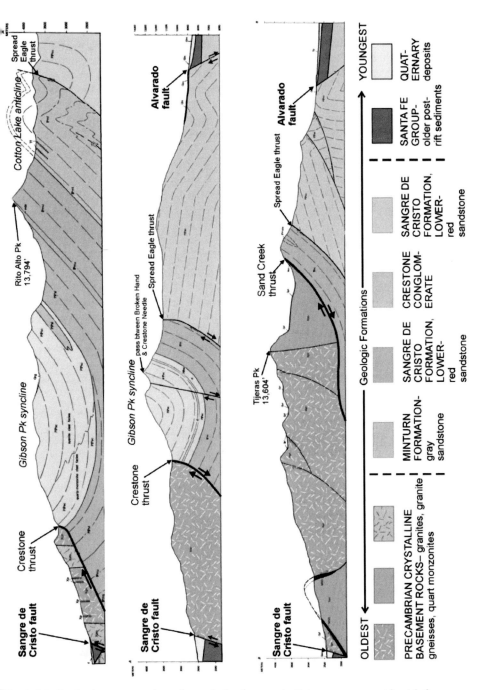

ig. 2-24. Geologic cross sections through the Sangre de Cristo range; west is at left. op, latitude of Rito Alto Peak (adapted from Lindsey et al., 1985). Middle, latitude of restone Needle; bottom, latitude of Tijeras Peak (adapted from Lindsey et al., 1986).

37

The Sedimentary Rocks
Most of the high peaks and valleys in the Sangres are underlain by well-stratified sedimentary rocks of the Sangre de Cristo Formation (well-bedded reddish sandstones) and the Crestone Conglomerate (massive green-to-red conglomerate). Although the Sangre de Cristo sandstones are moderately hard, the Crestone Conglomerate is much harder, even harder than granite. The Conglomerate is a hodgepodge of subangular clasts of many different rock types, including granite (large salt-and-pepper colored rocks), quartzite (smooth gray rocks, above the granite in the photo), metamorphic rocks (dark), and others, all contained in a red to green matrix of sand and silt (Fig. 2-25).

Fig. 2-25. The Crestone Conglomerate, with a 6 inch-long pencil for scale. For details on this fascinating rock, see Smith (2005).

Fig. 2-26. The head of the Lake Fork of North Crestone Creek and Mount Adams (right) are composed of well-stratified beds of the Sangre de Cristo Formation, mainly sandstones with some minor conglomerates. All the rock strata here tilt 35° to 45° to the right (west). The smooth bedding-plane surfaces at left are called "boilerplate" slabs, smooth like giant tilted pool tables. North Crestone Lake in the foreground. Photo by Bill Ellzey.

38

THE CRESTONE CONGLOMERATE (COULD'A BEEN A CONTENDER)

The official "State Rock" of Colorado (chosen only in 2004) is the Yule Marble http://geosurvey.state.co.us/Default.aspx?tabid=284). Now admittedly, the Yule Marble s an OK rock, not bad for a somewhat bland, white rock. It's the rock equivalent of (say) wine like a mass-produced Chardonnay. But many geologists would have lobbied for he State Rock to be the Crestone Conglomerate instead, a rock more the equivalent of say) a 1961 Chateau Margaux. That is, a rich, complex rock with a story to tell……..

The Crestone Conglomerate epitomizes what geologists call the "rock cycle." That is, the concept that mountain chains are uplifted, become eroded, the eroded ediments are transported away and deposited in nearby subsiding basins, where they are ressed and eventually cemented into hard rock, which is later uplifted to form younger nountain chains, and the cycle starts all over again. Each "rock cycle" takes tens to undreds of millions of years to complete. We can tell that the clasts that make up the onglomerate were not deposited very far from their erosional source, because: (1) they re large, which means deposited by a steep-gradient streams such as found near nountains; (2) they weren't transported far enough to become rounded; (3) even the soft ocks types had not been ground up in transport, another indicator of short travel distance. rom the composition of the clasts we know that the source area was mainly composed of ld (Precambrian) granites and metamorphic rocks, which are most commonly exposed in nountain ranges. What this tells us is that 230 million years ago, the present Sangres vere the site of a belt of coarse-grained alluvial fans lying next to steep mountain range omposed of old granites and gneisses. That mountain range has long since eroded away, ut left the evidence for its existence in the Crestone Conglomerate.

The Crestone Conglomerate comprises the core of the High Sangres, so you will e hiking over it in the upper valleys of North Crestone, South Crestone, Willow, panish, and Cottonwood Creeks. In many places the trails wind through or cross over eautiful outcrops of the conglomerate, some of which were scoured and polished by ice n past glaciations. In San Isabel Creek, sidewall cliffs on the north valley wall expose onglomerate in which the white granite clasts are up to 30 feet in diameter! For more etails on this fascinating rock, see Smith (2005). You can even buy a rock from The restone Eagle (www.crestoneeagle.com) and they will ship it to you!

HOW GLACIERS SHAPED THE MOUNTAIN VALLEYS

Like all of Colorado's mountain ranges, the Sangres were glaciated in the last period of lobal cooling 35,000 to 15,000 years ago. Glacier ice filled up the valleys with rivers of e (Fig. 2-27), which scoured the valleys like a bulldozer. Beneath the glacier, the owing ice plucked and ripped up blocks of bedrock along preexisting fractures. The ice arried eroded debris and rock rubble toward the glacier terminus, where it dumped them to great piles called moraines.

Each of the major valleys near Crestone (San Isabel, North Crestone, South restone, Willow, Spanish, Cottonwood, and Deadman) was occupied by a valley glacier Refsnider et al., 2009). In five of the seven valleys the glacier terminus did not reach the outh of the canyon, so the deposits of the glaciers are subtle. However, in South restone and Willow creeks the glacier snout advanced out onto the heads of the alluvial ans, bulldozing up huge piles of debris called moraines (Fig. 2-28). The terminal oraine of Willow Creek is an enormous hill of boulders and dirt, rising 800 feet high at ie head of the alluvial fans east of the Baca subdivision.

39

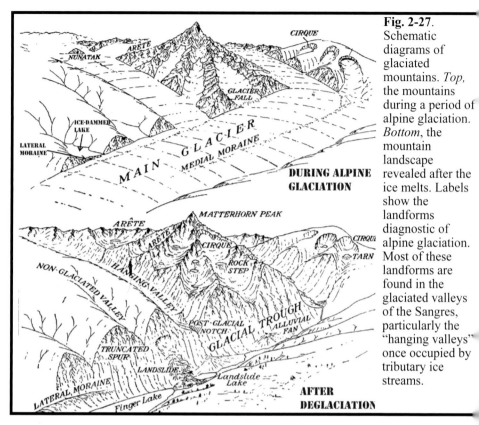

Fig. 2-27. Schematic diagrams of glaciated mountains. *Top,* the mountains during a period of alpine glaciation. *Bottom,* the mountain landscape revealed after the ice melts. Labels show the landforms diagnostic of alpine glaciation. Most of these landforms are found in the glaciated valleys of the Sangres, particularly the "hanging valleys" once occupied by tributary ice streams.

Fig. 2-28. Dotted lines outline the terminal moraines of South Crestone Creek and Willow Creek (lighter dots), as seen from the top of Panorama Way in the Baca subdivision. Each dirt pile is 800 feet high. Note the enormous white boulders perched high on the face of the Willow Creek moraine. A small part of the terminal moraine of an older glaciation pokes out from beneath the Willow Creek moraine (darker dots). The South Crestone Creek Trail and Willow Creek Trail follow numerous switchbacks to reach the crest of these moraines.

40

GLACIAL LAKES

The most popular trails in the Sangres end at lakes (e.g., North Crestone, South Crestone, and Willow Creeks). Each lake lies in the head of the valley, in a rock-bound basin gouged out by the last glacial advance from 35,000 to 15,000 years ago.

Fig. 2-29. The frigid waters of Cotton Lake mirror early summer snowfields at the head of Cotton Creek, a glacial valley 11 miles north of Crestone.

But what is it about these glacial lakes that attracts visitors? It is not the fishing (only perhaps 1 in 10 visitors casts a line into the lake), nor the swimming (the lakes may contain ice until the end of June). And water to boil an evening meal and to wash dishes could just as well be collected from any stream. John Muir felt the appeal was ethereal (see below), but somehow also practical. A lake gives the hiker a goal. You can say to yourself "Only 1 more mile to the lake…", and it keeps you going, knowing you can rest once you get there, drop your pack and collapse into the thick needles beneath the lake-rimming trees.

> "*Among the many unlooked-for treasures that are bound up and hidden away in the depths of Sierra solitudes, none more surely charm and surprise all kinds of travelers than the glacier lakes. The forests and glaciers and the snowy fountains of the streams advertize their wealth in a more or less telling manner even in the distance, but nothing is seen of the lakes until we have climbed above them…. They lie embosomed in the deep woods, down in the grovy bottoms of canyons, high on bald table-lands, and around the feet of the icy peaks, mirroring back their wild beauty over and over again*"
> John Muir, *The Mountains of California*, 1894

For More Information On Natural Science:
Contact the Crestone Science Center; P.O. Box 837, 600 E. Galena Ave., Crestone, CO 81131; 719-256-5228; www.crestonescience.org

3. THE SANGRE DE CRISTO WILDERNESS AREA and Rio Grande National Forest

The **Sangre de Cristo Wilderness Area,** designated in 1993, encompasses 226,455 acres (354 square miles) straddling the divide of the Northern Sangre de Cristo Mountains of Colorado (Fig. 3-2). The Wilderness includes much (but not all) of the National Forest lands in the Northern Sangre de Cristo Mountains.

THIS GUIDEBOOK describes in considerable detail trails, campgrounds, and climbing on the western side of the Sangres accessible from Crestone (all in the Rio Grande National Forest). For broader and less detailed descriptions of hiking in the entire Wilderness Area (both sides of the range), the reader is referred to guidebooks such as O'Hanlon (1999) and Moore (2003).

The Northern Sangres are Colorado's narrowest mountain range, measuring only 8-10 miles across. From the western and eastern bases, the mountains rise abruptly 5000-6000 ft in only 4 horizontal miles, making the Sangres the steepest range in Colorado. The Range contains nine of Colorado's 54 peaks over 14,000 feet high (The "Fourteeners") and over 50 peaks exceeding 13,000 ft. The Wilderness Area also contains over 60 alpine lakes, 400 miles of streams, and nearly 400 miles of trails.

Fig. 3-1. A hiker stands on a glacially-smoothed outcrop on the upper Lake Fork Trail of North Crestone Creek, near timberline. Above her, sharply folded strata rise to unnamed peak 13,153 (called by some *Pico Guante*). At left is the east shoulder of Mount Adams.

Trails in the northern Sangres tend to be short and steep, compared to trails elsewhere in Colorado. You will rapidly ascend from the high desert scrub through the montane forests and up to the tundra. All the trails near Crestone end at glacial lakes in the heads of major valleys, which lie only 3-5 trail miles from the trailhead (but 3000 feet higher). The short distance to the lakes makes round-trip day hikes possible but strenuous (6000 feet elevation gain+loss). Trail runners and speed climbers can ascend a trail to the

42

valley head, even climb a 13,000 or 14,000-ft peak, and be back to their car at the railhead before sundown.

But for the rest of us, a hike to the high lakes is best enjoyed by camping overnight at the lake. By taking some time to explore the valleys on your way to the lake, and the cirque once you get there, you can enjoy the hidden wonders of the Sangre de Cristo Wilderness. As local resident Dogmann used to say, "Slow Down, You're in Crestone. There's No Need to Hurry"!

But what a pleasure it is to know that there is a back country… to retreat to, that nobody is going to push roads through that wilderness, that no RVs or trail bikes or tote goats will roar through those forests and stink up that clean air. The best thing we have learned from nearly five hundred years of contact with the American wilderness is restraint, the willingness to hold our hand: to visit such places for our soul's good, but leave no tracks.
Wallace Stegner, 2002, *Crossing Into Eden*

Hikers and campers should note that the Wilderness Area boundary does not correspond with the National Forest Boundary, but generally lies upslope of it (Fig. 3-2). Accordingly, the first 1 to 4 miles of Forest Trails (depending on location) are in the National Forest but are outside the Wilderness Area, so are not subject to Wilderness Area restrictions. Signs mark the Wilderness Boundary on most major trails. At present no permits are required for recreational (non-commercial) hiking or camping, either in the National Forests or in the Wilderness Area. Not shown on Fig. 3-2 are small private property "inholdings" within the National Forest. In the Crestone area these inholdings are mainly mining claims that predate the establishment of the National Forest, and they remain private property today. Consult the official map of the Rio Grande National Forest for the location of these inholdings (available at the Saguache Public Lands Office, Saguache, CO; 719-655-2547). Restrictions and guidelines for backpacking in the National Forest (outside of Wilderness Areas) are contained in many Forest Service publications; go to: www.fs.fed.us/r2/recreation/camping/backpacking.pdf

If you need additional information about the Wilderness, the Rio Grande National Forest, or lands administered by the BLM (Bureau of Land Management), visit or call the Saguache Public Lands Office, Saguache, CO (46525 Highway 114, Saguache, CO 81149; (719-655-2547; Fax 719-655-2502). General information on camping and hiking in National Forests of the Rocky Mountain Region is available in English, Spanish, Korean, German, Vietnamese, French, and Chinese at: www.fs.fed.us/r2/recreation/camping.

Special Wilderness Area Restrictions:
—Groups are limited to 25, *including pack and saddle animals*, with no more than 15 people in any party.
—Camping and restraining/grazing of recreational livestock is not permitted within 300 feet of lakes and 100 feet of streams and trails. No campfires within 300 feet of lakes, streams, or trails.
—Do not wash dishes or bury human waste within 300 feet of any water.
—Cutting switchbacks in the trail is prohibited.

43

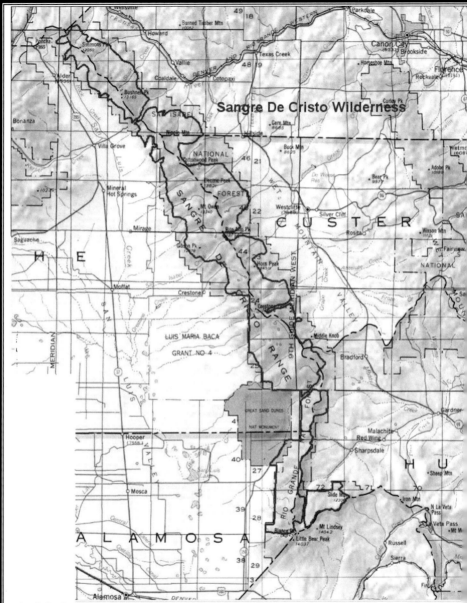

Fig. 3-2. Comparison of the Sangre de Cristo Wilderness Area (thick black outline) with the larger extent of the Rio Grande and San Isabel National Forests (shaded area of mountains). This map predates the 2004 Federal acquisition of Luis Maria Baca Grant No. 4, the expansion of Great Sand Dunes National Park, and the creation of the Baca National Wildlife Refuge out of the Baca Grant. (www.fs.fed.us/r2/psicc/recreation/wilderness/sangre_de_cristo_wilderness_boundary.jpg)

CAMPGROUNDS

There are only two developed campgrounds in the Crestone area, with a total of about 25 sites. The larger one is the North Crestone Campground (US Forest Service), located in the mouth of North Crestone Creek 1 mile north of Crestone. The campground stretches from the canyon mouth, up the narrow valley bottom for 0.7 miles. All its 13 campsites are heavily-treed next to North Crestone Creek, shaded by tall cottonwoods, aspens, pines, Douglas firs, and blue spruces. The Campground received a major "makeover" in June 2009, when the water systems and toilets were upgraded. Cost as of 2010 was $9 per site per night, with a 14-consecutive-day limit.

Although there are 38 campgrounds in the Rio Grande National Forest, only 8 take reservations through the USFS online reservation system, and North Crestone is unfortunately NOT one of them. As a result, North Crestone campsites are taken on a first-come, first served basis. All 13 campsites are often occupied on summer weekends, so grabbing one on a weekday is a good idea.

Due to its high elevation (8800 ft), the campground cools off rapidly once the sun sets and the cold-air drainage begins flowing down the narrow canyon from the mountains. This makes an evening campfire and a jacket definitely welcome, even on summer nights, and mornings may be chilly.

At the end of the campground road is a large parking lot and the North Crestone Trailhead. Forest Trail 744 (North Crestone Trail) begins here and extends 5 miles to North Crestone Lake, and is one of the most popular trails in the Wilderness Area (see Trails section). This trailhead is also a good jumping-off spot for various loop hikes or a hike over the range crest to the Wet Mountain Valley (described later).

RV Camping at Camper Village (3 miles west of Crestone on County Road T)
Approximately 10 RV sites are available at Camper Village, operated by the Baca Grande Property Owners Association. $45+tax the first night, $13+tax each additional night. First come, first served. Call (719) 256-4171 for information.

Undeveloped Camping in Forest Service/BLM Lands
Dry camping is also possible east of Crestone on jeep roads that branch off of Forest Road 949 (East Galena Avenue), between the McAlpine Ranch and the South Crestone/Willow Trailhead (see map in Chapter 8). Fire danger may be high in the summer, so please be careful with campfires.

PLANNING FOR A SAFE HIKE

When it comes to being comfortable and safe while hiking or camping, there are some aspects you can control (like remembering your foam pad or flashlight and some you can't control (like an unseasonal snowstorm). To make sure you don't forget anything important, refer to the Checklist in Appendix 1. You can't prevent bad weather, but you can take items along that will keep you comfortable and safe if it happens.

Things You Have Control Over: For a safe day hike or multi-day camping trip, prepare for the weather, take one flashlight per person, have a map in the party, and file a *Flight Plan* with a friend. A Flight Plan describes where you are going, where you will camp,

Fig. 3-3. A carpet of aspen leaves beckons the hiker on the Willow Creek Trail in October. Hiking step-by-step up a trail is an ancient set of gestures, a mind-body activity of walking meditation. The gold aspen leaves soften your footsteps like a carpet laid down for royalty, welcoming you to the halls of the mountain king.

and when you plan to return. In the summer months days are long (over 15 hours of light per day), but plan to be back before twilight ends. Otherwise you will be stumbling down the trail in the dark, tripping over stones and roots, and losing the trail.

If your party becomes overdue for return (according to the Flight Plan) and a friend has to call Saguache Search and Rescue on your behalf, you'd better have a Colorado Outdoor Recreation Search and Rescue (CORSAR) Card. Otherwise, you may be billed for your search! These cards cost $3 and can be purchased online at **dola.colorado.gov/corsar_order/order_instructions.jsf,** or at these merchants:
Alamosa: Sheriff's Office; Wal-Mart; Kristi Mtn. Sports; Mark's Outdoor Sports
Salida: Wal-Mart, Absolute Bikes, Arkansas Headwaters Park, Salida Mtn. Sports
NOTE: CORSAR cards do not pay for medical evacuation or transport costs, but will pay for aircraft costs if part of the search.

The simple geometry of local valleys makes it difficult to get lost. Valleys described hereon are deep and relatively narrow in their lower parts, and open up into one or more glaciated amphitheaters in their upper part (see trail maps later in this chapter). So, if you hike downslope from any valley head, you will inevitably end up in the narrow lower canyon, where the main trail parallels the creek on one side or the other. All routes leading downhill will eventually bring you to the range front.

46

WARNING: old mine tunnels and shafts are dangerous, due to their unmaintained condition. Approach with caution! Many were permanently closed by the Colorado Division of Reclamation, Mining and Safety between 2000 and 2002. But not all…..

Things You Have No Control Over: "Objective dangers" include altitude sickness, pulmonary edema, lightning, bear or mountain lion encounters, etc. They can be reduced by being cautious, but not eliminated entirely.

Cell Phone Coverage: In the lower sections of valleys near Crestone, cell reception is fair. Verizon Wireless seems to have the best reception around Crestone, but this may change with the construction of a new cell tower in 2011.

For the ultimate in communications when out of cell phone range, consider satellite-based systems such as the SPOT Satellite Personal Tracker (SPOT-1) or Satellite GPS Messenger (http://findmeSPOT.com). Standard satellite phones are also available for purchase or rent from Iridium, Inmarsat, and Globalstar (for a comparison, see www.globalcomsatphone.com).

Fig. 3-4. Sunset light creates a sawtooth silhouette of the jagged Crestone Group across the valley floor of the Wet Mountain Valley.

Fig. 3-5 (next page). Panoramas of the peaks near Crestone.. TOP, peaks from Gibson Peak (left) south to South Crestone Creek. BOTTOM, peaks from South Crestone Creek to Broken Hand Peak at the head of Cottonwood Creek. Unnamed peaks are labeled with spot elevations from USGS 7.5' topographic maps. Because this photo was taken in the Baca Grande subdivision 4 miles south of Crestone, most of the crestline peaks between Mount Adams and Hermit Peak are not visible (includes Fluted, Comanche, Venable, and Eureka). Instead, they are hidden by unnamed 12,000 and 13,000-ft high points on subsidiary ridges.

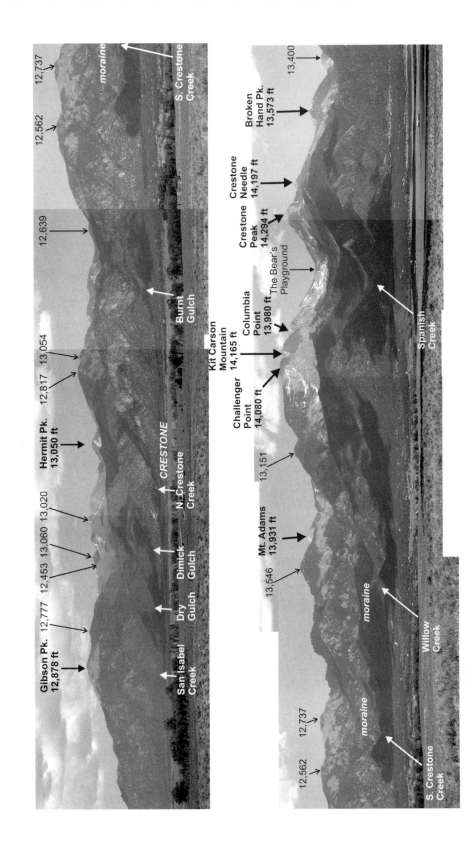

TRAILHEADS AND TRAILS

n the west-side valleys accessible from Crestone, up-and-back hikes are relatively short 4 to 5 miles one-way) and can be done in a single day by fit hikers. For example, from ne South Crestone/Willow Trailhead to Willow Lake on Forest Trail 865 is 4.2 miles ne-way with an elevation gain of 2684 ft (818 m), and 8.4 miles round-trip.

But just because you CAN do this doesn't mean it's the best way to experience ne Sangres. This Guidebook is meant to lure you away from the trails and the speed-ikers, to smell the flowers, hug the trees, see some elk, lie down on a moraine, and isualize the ghostly glaciers passing over you. You won't make it up-and-back in one ay, but maybe that is a good thing.

I felt like lying down by the side of the trail and remembering it all. The woods do that to you, they always look familiar, long lost, like the face of a long-dead relative, like an old dream, like a piece of forgotten song drifting across the water, most of all like golden eternities of past childhood or past manhood and all the living and the dying and the heartbreak that went on a million years ago and the clouds as they pass overhead seem to testify (by their own lonesome familiarity) to this feeling.
Jack Kerouac, *The Dharma Bums*, 1958

or the ambitious hiker, two trail passes at the head of the North Crestone drainage cross e crest of the Sangres and connect to "east side" trails (Venable Pass Trail, Forest Trail 59; Comanche Lake Trail, Forest Trail 746). Between these two trails lies the Venable-omanche Trail, Forest Trail 1345, with the spectacular Phantom Terrace section. The isses make a west-to-east, 9 mile-long traverse possible. There are also loop trails that) up one west side valley and come down another, connecting North Crestone, San abel, Rito Alto, and Cotton Creeks (described later); these are multi-day adventures in a istine wilderness visited by few.

49

COLOR TRAIL MAPS (Plates)

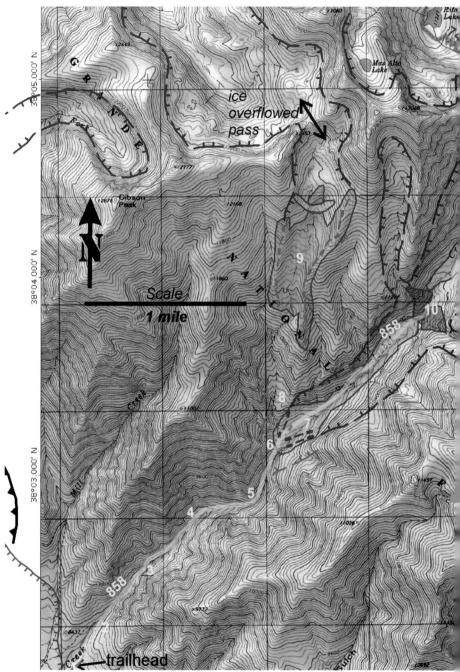

Plate 1. Map of San Isabel Trail and High Loop Trail in the North Fork. *LEGEND for both pag* *Solid yellow line and numbers*, San Isabel Trail (FT 858) and mileage points; *Solid blue line and*

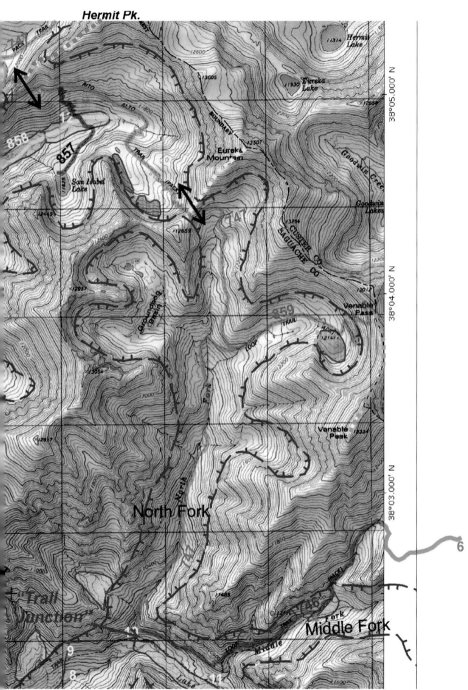

Hermit Pk.

s, North Fork Crestone Trail (FT 747) and mileage points; *Solid green line*, Venable Pass Trail); *Dotted lines*, climbing routes to summits (see Chapter 5). For Geology legend, see Plate 2.

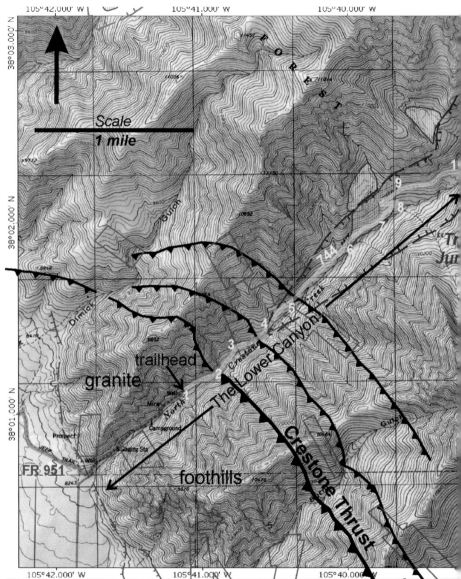

Plate 2. Map of trails from the North Crestone Creek Trailhead; for northern part of the Fork Crestone Trail (FT 747), see the San Isabel Map trail map (Plate 1). *LEGEND for* **on both pages:**
yellow line and numbers, N. Crestone Trail (FT 744) and mileage points;
orange line and numbers, Middle Fork Trail (FT 746) and mileage points;
blue line and numbers, North Fork Crestone Trail (FT 747) and mileage points;
thick dotted lines; climbing routes to peaks.

*...d of Geologic Features on All Color Maps: **thick black lines with triangles**,* thrust
blue dashed line with hachures, limit of latest glacial ice; double-headed arrows, where
...wed over ridges between valleys; *green shading*, younger glacial moraines; brown
...g, older moraines; yellow shading, glacial deposits in hidden valleys; *blue shading*,
... glacial lakes; *purple shading*, landslides; *red dashed line with hachures*, Sangre de
...fault; *purple rectangles*, patented mining claims. See Fig. 10-4 for names of claims in
...estone Mining District.

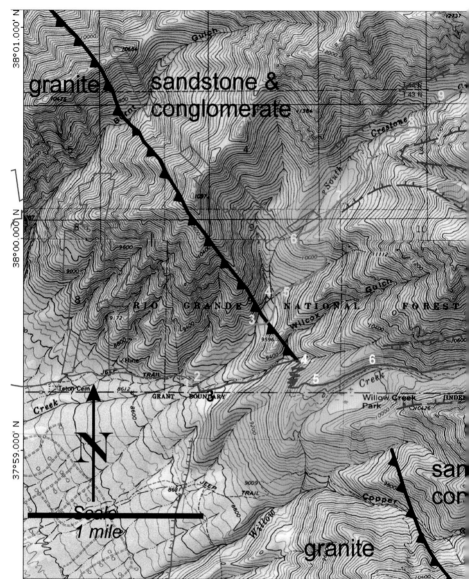

Plate 3. Map of trails from the South Crestone/Willow Creek Trailhead. *LEGEND for on Both Pages:*
red line and white numbers, Willow Creek Trail (FT 865) and mileage points;
orange line and yellow numbers, South Crestone Trail (FT 860) and mileage points;
thick dotted lines; climbing routes to peaks.

54

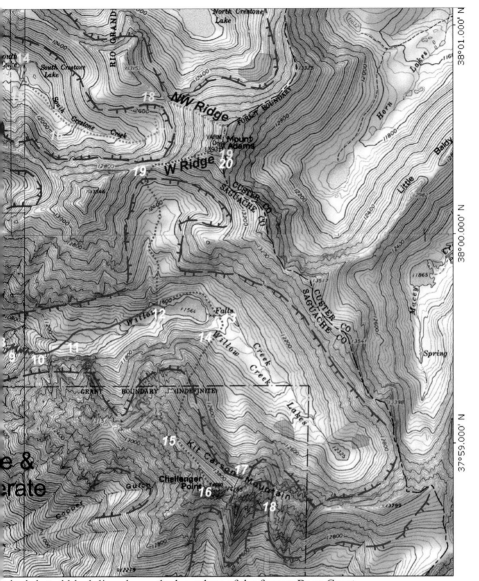

:shed-dotted black line shows the boundary of the former Baca Grant.

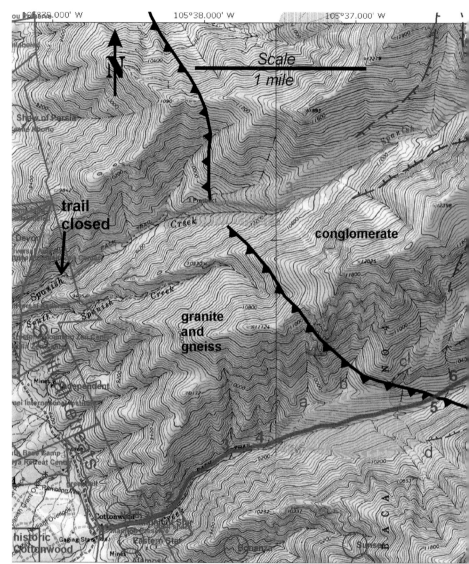

Plate 4. Map of trails in Spanish Creek and Cottonwood Creek. *LEGEND for Trails on Pages*: *Thick blue line and numbers*, Spanish Creek Trail (better trail) and mileage points;
Thick green dashed line, Spanish Creek Trail (very poor trail);
Thick red line and numbers, Cottonwood Creek Trail and mileage points;
Thick light blue line, Sand Creek Trail (FT 743) coming over from Upper Sand Creek
Thick yellow line and yellow numbers, Cottonwood Lake Trail (FT 861) and mileage poi
Thick purple line; informal trail from Cottonwood Lake, over "Eye of the Needle Pass",
down to South Colony Lake; the eastern part of this trail is the standard approach to the
Crestones from the east
thick dotted lines; bushwhacking routes and climbing routes to peaks (see text).

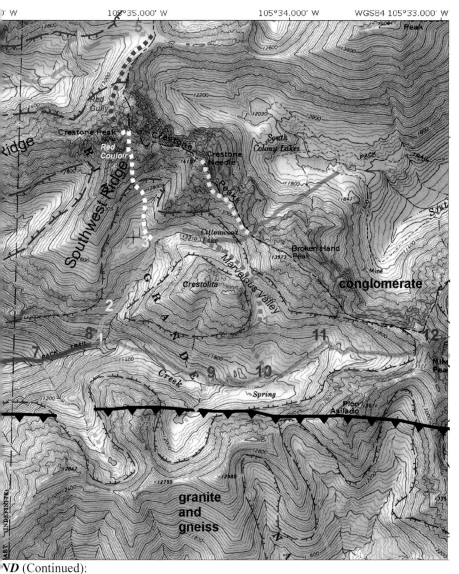

ND (Continued):

rectangles, various spiritual retreat lands (private); red circles, historic mines of the El
Mining District (unpatented).

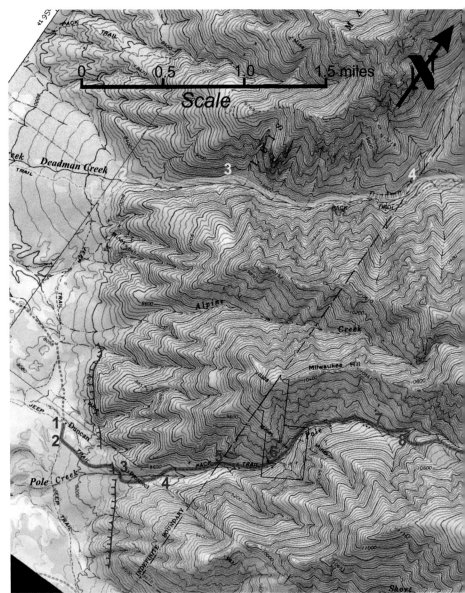

Plate 5. Map of trails in Deadman Creek (upper) and Pole Creek (lower).
LEGEND for Trails on Both Pages:
Thick yellow line and numbers, Deadman Creek Trail and mileage points;
Thick light red line and numbers, Pole Creek Trail (FT 878) and mileage points;
thick dotted lines; bushwhacking routes and climbing routes to peaks (see text).

58

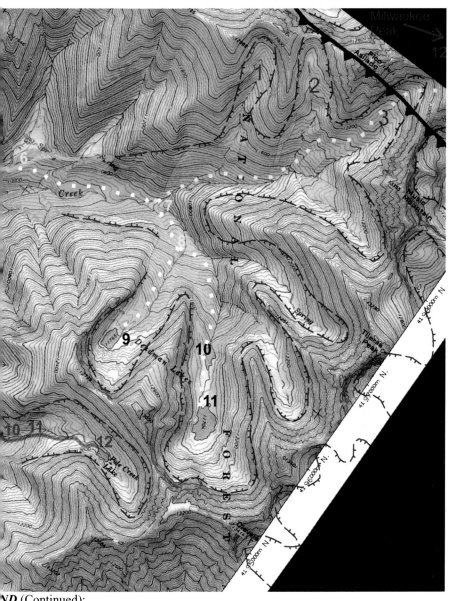

ND (Continued):

:ctangles, patented mining claims of the El Dorado Mining District.

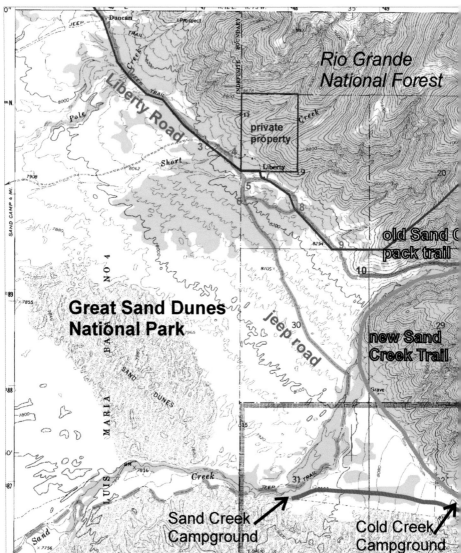

Plate 6. Trails between Duncan and the Great Sand Dunes. Thin purple line shows the boundary between the National Park, Preserve, and National Forest. The Liberty Road (I in the National Forest from Duncan to near Liberty, where it briefly jogs south into the National Park to avoid private land. South of Liberty the road becomes a pack trail (oran finally turning into the old Sand Creek pack trail (yellow) at the mouth of the canyon. Th newly-built NPS Sand Creek Trail (pink) is on the south side of Sand Creek, and branch the Sand Ramp Trail (green).

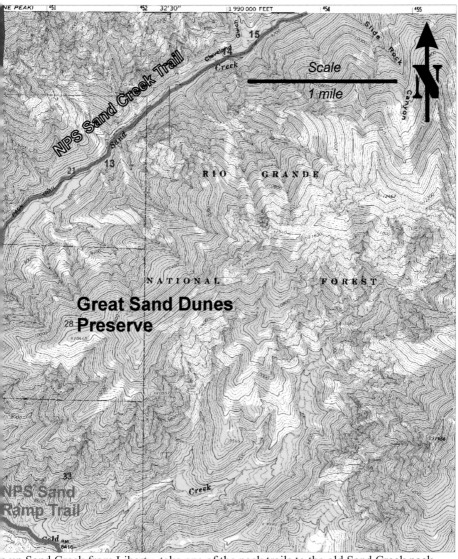

 up Sand Creek from Liberty, take one of the pack trails to the old Sand Creek pack
 reach the Sand Creek Campground from Liberty, continue south on the jeep road for
es, cross Sand Creek at a ford, and walk another 1.0 miles south to the campground.
ere you can take the Sand Ramp Trail south around the east side of the Dunes. A more
oute to the Dunes, and to the Cold Creek Campground, is to cross Sand Creek on the
ad, walk east to the new Sand Creek Trail, and continue SE 1.3 miles to the junction
 Sand Ramp Trail.

TRAILS FROM THE SAN ISABEL TRAILHEAD
San Isabel Trail (Forest Trail 858); San Isabel Lake Trail (Forest Trail 857)

GETTING TO THE SAN ISABEL TRAILHEAD

From Crestone or the Baca Grande subdivision, you have to backtrack west on County Road T 4.5 miles from the entrance to the Baca. Turn right (north) onto County Road 66 Proceed north for 0.5 miles, and the road will bend 45° to the right and begin heading NE (and is now called County Road 66T). After 3.7 miles and a few minor jogs, you will reach the National Forest Boundary. Here the road deteriorates into a sandy jeep road, bu is passable by 2WD vehicles. In ¼ mile the road reaches the giant fault scarp of the Sangre de Cristo fault (Fig. 3-7), and is forced to turn north. It runs along the base of the scarp for the next ¼ mile until it reaches the dense forest along San Isabel Creek, where the road turns east and continues another 0.1 rocky miles to the Trailhead. Low-clearance vehicles may have to park below this rocky section.

Fig. 3-7. The road to the San Isabel Trailhead (foreground), just south of the mouth of San Isabel Creek, runs northward for its last 0. miles along the base of the Sangre de Cristo fault scarp. This 33 ft-high scarp marks where the smooth alluvial surface has been sharply broken and uplifted by geologically-recent surface faulting. The scarp was produced by at least three Magnitude 7+ earthquakes that recur about every 10,000-15,000 years on the Sangre de Cristo fault.

SAN ISABEL TRAIL (FOREST TRAIL 858):

The San Isabel Trail is a 5.2 mile-long, lightly used trail that provides access to San Isabel Lake, and to the North Fork Crestone Trail (FT 747). If you are an experienced hiker and route-finder, and can ford streams that may be running high, this trail will get you through a valley not visited by many. If you are looking for a more manicured trail with more company, try the North Crestone, South Crestone, or Willow Creek trails.

San Isabel Trail (Forest Trail 858)
Beginning:..San Isabel Trailhead
Elev. 8250 ft (2515 *m*)
End:..*junction with San Isabel lake Tra*
Elev. 11,440 ft (3488 m)
Trail length:..5.2 miles (8.3 *km*)
Elevation gain:..3190 ft (973 *m*)

MILEAGE LOG (see Plate 1 for the map)

Point	Mileage	Feature

0.0 San Isabel Trailhead (8250 ft)

0.3 trail enters bedrock canyon; valley walls steepen; trail remains on S side of creek

0.75 1st creek crossing; in the next 0.45 miles there are 4 more creek crossings (#2 to #5), ending with trail on the North side of the creek; this is a deep V-shaped, unglaciated valley

1.2 trail bends to East-West trend and valley opens up a bit; this continues for 0.35 mi

1.55 trail bends to NNE and valley narrows; this continues for another 0.35 mi; in middle of this stretch there are 2 more creek crossings (#6, #7); trail ends of North side of creek

1.9 trail reaches the terminal moraine of the San Isabel paleoglacier; the moraine is an aspen-covered area on the north side of the Creek, composed of low ridges of bouldery moraine that trend N-S toward valley axis; trail ascends ridges

2.15 good camping spots near the crest of the moraine; upvalley from here the valley is a more open, U-shaped glacial valley

off trail a "hidden valley" lies 300 yards NW of Point 7, reached by ascending a steep forested slope; this would be a good campsite that is away from the main trail; elk and deer frequent such hidden valleys

off trail the western glaciated tributary above the hidden valley is a great example of "ice-stagnation topography" (Fig. 3-8). It is a chaotic hummocky topography (knob-and-kettle) produced by debris-laden ice stagnating in place, rather than retreating upvalley in an orderly fashion. The ice in this valley was being fed by an overflow from a cirque of the Rito Alto system to the north. When the ice level in that cirque downwasted below the spillover point, the ice supply to this valley was suddenly cut off, like turning off a faucet, resulting in immediate ice stagnation. Local deer and elk love this hidden valley!

Fig. 3-8. View south from the head of the western glaciated tributary, looking south toward San Isabel Valley (center). Blanca Peak is visible at top center in the far distance. Not only is this off-trail valley a great place to camp, but you can continue north over the pass at the head, and drop down into the valley of Blind Lake. Bushwhacking to Blind Lake is a great adventure.

3.1 after another mile of trail on the North side of the creek, the valley floor is "pinched" at Point 9 by alluvial fans coming in from the north and south; these fans were derived from post-glacial outwash from retreating tributary glaciers; at the narrowest constriction (Pt 9), the trail crosses to the South side of the creek, then ascends 200 ft up the south valley side, before descending back to valley floor level; from the high point, there are good views up the glacial valley

| 11 | 3.85 | trail crosses to North side of creek; there are 2 more creek crossing in the next 0.2 miles; trail ends up on North side of creek |
| 12 | 4.8 | trail intersects the San Isabel Lake Trail (FT 857; Fig. 3-9), which descends the steep valley wall to the north in a series of switchbacks; to continue up the valley to the North Fork Crestone Trail (FT 747), walk on informal trails for another 0.4 miles |

Fig. 3-9. Looking down San Isabel valley from the north valley wall, at the top of the switchback section on FT 857 (San Isabel Lake Trail).

San Isabel Lake Trail (Forest Trail 857)

The San Isabel Lake Trail is a short (0.8 mile) cutoff trail that crosses the San Isabel Valley from north to south. The north half of the trail plunges straight down the north valley wall of San Isabel in a series of switchbacks. The trail then crosses the creek and diagonals SW up a forested bedrock step to the Lake, which lies hidden at 11,625 feet elevation in a hanging valley-cirque (Fig. 3-10). This odd trail alignment is understandable, if you consider that most trail traffic in upper San Isabel is pack trains on the North Fork Crestone Trail (FT 747), rather than hikers coming up from the San Luis Valley. FT 857 provides a more direct route to the Lake for pack trains on the Loop Trail

Fig. 3-10. Looking down on San Isabel Lake from the northern section of the San Isabel Lake Trail, high on the opposite valley wall. The 5.7-acre Lake at 11,625 feet is not in the main valley of San Isabel Creek, but rather perched up in a tributary cirque excavated into the south valley wall.

North Fork Crestone Trail (also called Loop Trail; Forest Trail 747) to Rito Alto Valley and Hermit Pass

The North Fork Crestone Trail connecting the Rito Alto, San Isabel, and North Crestone cirques runs north-south across the head of San Isabel valley. This well-maintained trail is mainly traveled by pack trips from the eastern side of the range, which come up to Hermit Pass via a 4WD road. From there they descend to the Rito Alto cirque, cross over into San Isabel, traverse its cirque, and cross another pass into the head of the North Fork of North Crestone Creek.

Hikers coming up San Isabel from the Crestone side can use the Trail 747 to achieve a west-to-east traverse of the Sangres. From the San Isabel Trail, turn north onto the northern part of the San Isabel Lake Trail and climb it to the pass (elev. 12,240 ft) between San Isabel and Rito Alto cirques. Descend from the pass to the T-intersection with the Rito Alto Trail. Turn right (this is the continuation of the Loop Trail, FT 747) and slowly ascend the Rito Alto cirque on an old mining road to Hermit Pass, passing beneath the summit of Rito Alto Peak (Fig. 3-11). From Hermit Pass it is a 3.3 mile long descent along the road, and an elevation drop of 1680 feet to Hermit Lake, at the head of Middle Taylor Creek. It would be nice if there were a counterpart loop trail on the eastern side of the range crest, that would allow hiking between multiple east-side cirques. But unfortunately, the cirques on the east side are so deep that no ice-passes developed between them in the glacial ages, so it's not possible to hop from one cirque to another.

Rito Alto Peak 13,794'

Hermit Pass 13,010'

Pass between San Isabel and Rito Alto valleys

Fig. 3-11. View north from the North Fork Crestone Trail (FT 747) at the pass from the San Isabel drainage to the Rito Alto drainage. Trail 747 descends to the snowy bench at lower center via switchbacks, and splits into right and left forks. The right fork connects with the old Hermit Pass Road (white dots). Jeeps can reach Hermit Pass from the east side. The left fork descends Rito Alto valley.

TRAILS FROM THE NORTH CRESTONE TRAILHEAD
(Forest Trails 744, 745, 746, 747)

GETTING TO THE NORTH CRESTONE TRAILHEAD

From downtown Crestone drive north on Alder Street to the northern City limits, and continue north on this paved road (now County Road 71) for 1.3 mi. The road bends 45° to the right (NE) and soon passes over a cattleguard into the National Forest. *NOTE: lane to the south of the road is private.* Cross the bridge and enter the Campground.

THE MOUTH OF THE CANYON AREA, INCLUDING THE CAMPGROUND

The mouth of North Crestone Canyon has an interesting human and natural history, easily accessible from the roads.

Forest Road 951

Directly north of the cattle guard is an unmarked dirt road heading west; this is Forest Road 951, open to the public (but land west of the road is private). Much of FR 951 is 4WD only (due to deep sand), but the first 200 yards are usually passable. FR 951 gives quick access to several features of geological and cultural interest.

The Sangre de Cristo Fault and the Quartz Mine

A trace of the Sangre de Cristo fault crosses the mouth of North Crestone Creek and has uplifted the head of the alluvial fan of North Crestone Creek (Fig. 3-12). Park about 150 yards after starting down the road. Directly east, across the road, is a steep hillslope about 25 feet high that faces the road. Ascend the slope by walking due east up its face. At the top of this slope is a large flat area into which the Spillway channel has been excavated (described later); the bridge to North Crestone Creek lies 100 yards east.

Fig. 3-12. *Left*: Fault scarp of the Sangre de Cristo fault across the mouth of North Crestone canyon, on the east side of FR 951; view is to the east. FR 951 travels north-south along the base of the scarp here for about 200 yards, in a linear sandy depression that is probably a fault-created mini-graben; *Right*: The "Quartz Mine" on the Reed Claim, 330 yards north of the fault scarp location at the mouth of North Crestone Creek. To reach it, continue walking north on old mining roads. This large outcrop lies on the northern edge of the Reed Claim, and was worked by a tunnel (now collapsed) behind the juniper trees at lower center.

The Spillway

At the mouth of North Crestone Creek the road to the campground goes over a short bridge. However, this bridge does not span North Crestone Creek, as you might expect. Instead, the bridge spans an overflow channel built to protect the town of Crestone from flooding (Fig. 3-13). The Spillway complex originally had wooden gates that could be lowered to block floods (such as the Great Flood of 1911) from heading downstream to Crestone. The blocked water then flowed west beneath the bridge, and straight out onto the unpopulated valley floor, far north of Town. The last time this happened was June 10, 1973 when the creek flowed at 212 cubic feet per second. The Spillway concept was a cheap, but elegant engineering solution to a problem, and only needs replacement gates to again protect the residents of Crestone.

Fig. 3-13a. The Spillway structure at the entrance to North Crestone Campground. The stream is forced to the north side of its valley by a low dam. At the end of the dam a low stone wall (at center) diverts low flows southward to Crestone. Higher flood flows spill over the wall and pass beneath the bridge.

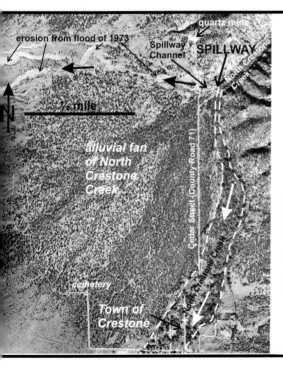

Fig. 3-13b. 1973 Aerial photo showing how the Spillway diverts flood flows. Low flows (white arrows) are diverted south to Crestone along the southern margin of the alluvial fan. Higher flows (black arrows) spill over and flow west out onto the valley floor, along the northern margin of the fan. Light-toned channels at upper left were eroded into wind-blown sand on the edge of the fan, probably during the big flood of June 1973.

67

NORTH CRESTONE TRAIL (FOREST TRAIL 744) TO NORTH CRESTONE LAKE

The North Crestone Campground, the trailhead, and the first 2 miles (*3.2 km*) of the North Crestone Trail lie in the narrow, linear, and deep Lower Canyon section. At the trailhead the canyon is 1600 ft deep, but over the next 2 miles slowly deepens to 2500-3000 ft by its head. We define the head of the Lower Canyon section arbitrarily, as a forested bench at elevation 9900 ft (*3024 m*) where trails branch off to the North Fork (FT 747) and Middle Fork (FT 746). We call this branching spot "Trail Junction" (Plate 2); it is about 40% (2 miles) of the way from the Trailhead to North Crestone Lake.

The Lower Canyon Section of Forest Trail 744

Beginning:..N. Crestone Trailhead
　　　　　　　　　　　　　　　　　　　　　　　Elev. 8760 ft (*2670 m*)
End:..."*Trail Junction*"
　　　　　　　　　　　　　　　　　　　　　　　Elev. 9920 ft (*3024 m*)
Trail length:..2.0 miles (3.2 km)
Elevation gain:.......................................1160 ft (*354 m*)

MILEAGE LOG (see Plate 2 for map)

Point	Mileage	Feature
1	0.0	North Crestone Trailhead (8600 ft)
2	0.3	Crestone Thrust; old mine on left (N)
3	0.45	enter patented mining claims (Spar, then Log Cabin, then Trout)
4	0.7	downvalley limit of glaciation; ahead, road turns to a trail and starts to ascend the north valley wall
5	0.9	leave patented mining claims (Iowa No. 2)
6	1.4	valley floor is covered with glacial moraine boulders
7	1.7	cross tributary stream that flows out of hanging valley to north; crest c moraine is 400 ft higher up the slope; to the north is a "hidden valley"
8	1.8	begin switchbacks up the lateral moraine
9	2.0	leave moraine; trail soon leaves the forest and traverses an open slope good views for the next 0.2 miles

Fig. 3-14. The Lake Fork of North Crestone Creek displays the classic U-shape of a glaciated valley. This view is looking NW down the lower Lake Fork valley from the 600 ft-high bedrock step below North Crestone Lake. The abundance of aspens on the valley floor and walls indicates the local soil is composed of glacial moraine deposits, rather than bedrock.

68

From Trail Junction Forest Trail 744 turns south to ascend the Lake Fork of North Crestone Creek (see Fig. 3-14).

The Lake Fork Section of Forest Trail 744 (see Plate 2, right panel, for map)

Beginning:.."Trail Junction"
Elev. 9920 ft (*3024 m*)
End:..*North Crestone Lake*
Elev. *11,780 ft (3129 m)*
Trail length:..3.0 miles (*4.8 km*)
Elevation gain:.......................................1860 ft (567 *m*)

Point	Mileage	Feature
0	**2.45**	cross the North Fork and reach "Trail Junction"; junction of Forest Trails 744 (to N. Crestone Lake) and 747 (up North Fork); shortly after is the turnoff to Forest Trail 746 which ascends to Comanche Pass
1	**3.0**	cross Middle Fork coming in from NE
2	**3.4**	switchback to NE
3	**3.6**	trail enters a clearing and ascends up bedrock step 160 ft high
4	**3.7**	trail bends to NE
5	**4.0**	trail emerges from forest and valley opens up and flatten
6	**4.8**	trail turns NE and begins to ascend a 600 ft-high bedrock step below N. Crestone Lake; at the base of the step, off the trail, North Crestone Creek goes over a waterfall (Fig. 3-15)
7	**5.3**	trail reaches top of bedrock step
8	**5.5**	trail reaches North Crestone Lake (11,780 ft) and ends (Fig. 3-15).

Fig. 3-15. *Left:* The falls of North Crestone Creek, as it descends the lower part of the 600 ft-high bedrock step below North Crestone Lake. The lake was simply called "Lake Crestone" in 1909. From Baca Grant Development Company, Inc., 1909. *Right:* Looking down on an icy North Crestone Lake (on July 4, 1979) from the head of the Lake Fork. With an area of 28 acres, this is the largest lake on the western side of the Sangres. The valley floor beyond the lake apparently disappears as it drops over the 600 ft-high bedrock step. In the distance are the forested slopes of the Lower Canyon section of North Crestone Creek.

LOOP TRAILS

The Forest Service Loop trails in the High Sangres were built for the convenience of pack trips from the Wet Mountain Valley. Riders and hikers would ride (horse or 4WD) up the jeep road to Hermit Pass on the north end of the Loop, drop down into the head of Rito Alto Creek, cross over the pass into the head of San Isabel Creek, then over the next pass to the head of the North Fork of North Crestone Creek. From here they would descend the North Fork and return to the east side of the Sangres via either Venable Pass (Forest Trail 859, opposite Groundhog Basin), or continue south to the Middle Fork of North Crestone Creek and east up over Comanche Pass (Forest Trail 746).

For us west-siders, however, the same trails make it possible to hike the San Isabel and North Crestone trails in combination with trails in the two west-side glaciated valleys farther the north (Rito Alto and Cotton Creeks), to form a hiking loop. These loop hikes are possible because all four valleys are joined by Forest Trails between their valley heads (cirques) above treeline. Each connecting trail goes through a pass formed when Pleistocene glacier ice from one cirque overflowed and conveniently scoured out the narrow ridge into the adjacent cirque (see Figs. 3-8, 3-14). The other valleys described in this guidebook did not experience ice spillovers, so they are separated by ridges too steep for trails. All the loop hikes are multi-day affairs, at least for the average hiker.

The longest loop accessible from Crestone (The Grand Loop; **A**) would involve hiking up North Crestone Trail, across the heads of San Isabel and Rito Alto Creeks, and down Cotton Creek Trail (or in the reverse order). This loop contains 21 miles of Forest Trails, of which more than half are above treeline in the high cirques. The Grand Loop also provides climbing access to seven Thirteeners, making it a great multi-day hike for bagging multiple high peaks.

Hiking the Grand Loop (as well as other loops in Table 3-1) requires that you either: (1) drop off a vehicle at the ending trailhead, or (2) hike from the ending trailhead to the beginning trailhead (where you left your car) along the foot of the Sangres (mainly in BLM lands, but some may be private). For example, the starting and ending trailheads for the Grand Loop are 20 miles apart by unpaved County roads.

Table 3-1. Loop hikes using the four valleys north of Crestone, on the western side of the Sangre de Cristo Wilderness, listed from longest to shortest.

Valleys in Loop (can be hiked in either direction)	Total Trail Miles	Named Peaks that can be Climbed from the Loop Trail
A, North Crestone & Cotton Creeks (The Grand Loop)	21.5	DeAnza Pk., 13,362; Mt. Owen, 13,340; Mt. Marcy, 13,490; Rito Alto Pk., 13,374; Hermit Pk., 13,350; Eureka Mtn., 13,507; Venable Pk., 13,334 (7)
B, San Isabel & Cotton Creeks	18.5	DeAnza Pk., 13,362; Mt. Owen, 13,340; Mt. Marcy, 13,490; Rito Alto Pk., 13,374 ;Hermit Pk., 13,350 (5)
C, Rito Alto & Cotton Creeks	17.0	DeAnza Pk., 13,362; Mt. Owen, 13,340; Mt. Marcy, 13,490; Rito Alto Pk., 13,374 (4)
D, North Crestone & Rito Alto Creeks	14.0	Rito Alto Pk., 13,374; Hermit Pk., 13,350; Eureka Mtn., 13,507; Venable Pk., 13,334 (4)
E, San Isabel & Rito Alto Creeks	13.0	Rito Alto Pk., 13,374; Hermit Pk., 13,350 (2)
F, North Crestone & San Isabel Creeks	11.5	Eureka Mtn., 13,507; Venable Pk., 13,334 (2)

70

TRAILS FROM THE SOUTH CRESTONE/WILLOW TRAILHEAD
South Crestone Trail (FT 860) to South Crestone Lake
Willow Creek Trail (FT 865) to Willow Lake and Kit Carson Mountain

Getting to the Trailhead
Drive east on Galena Avenue to the eastern City limits of Crestone, where the road bends 45° to the SE. Continue on the good graded road (now County Road T.5) for 1/3 mi through the McAlpine Ranch (private). Public land begins at the BLM sign and the road officially becomes Forest Road 949, but the surface is still graded by the County.

Two-thirds of a mile past the City limits, you arrive at the Rio Grande National Forest boundary and a parking lot for low-clearance vehicles (Fig. 3-16). Beyond this point the road is more like a jeep road, but many 2WD vehicles can make it to the trailhead 1.3 miles farther up, if they have enough ground clearance. The "crux" of the road is a short, steep section only 250 yards short of the parking lot, which sometimes has ruts in it too deep for low-clearance vehicles. In that case, park at the base of the crux and walk to the parking lot from there.

Fig. 3-16. Boundary of the Rio Grande National Forest on Forest Road 949, 1 mile east of the Crestone city limits. From this sign it is another 1.3 miles to the Trailhead. Having good clearance and front-wheel drive also helps.

WHAT TO SEE: On the way to the Trailhead you will pass several jeep roads and the Teton Cemetery. The jeep roads are shown on Fig. 8-1 and can be navigated by mountain bike, ATV, or jeep. There are several informal campsites along the roads which, although in the National forest, have no facilities and thus no fees or time limits. 0.3 miles east of the Forest Boundary sign, the site of the mining camp of Teton and its historic cemetery are about 50 yards south of the road.

The Mining Camp of Teton
On the south side of Forest Road 949, near its junction with Jeep Road B (See Fig. 8-1), lies the Teton Cemetery. This cemetery is all that remains of the mining camp of Teton founded in 1877. Teton was the first mining camp of what later became the Crestone Mining District, predating the town of Crestone by three years. It was established by prospectors who discovered gold in Burnt Gulch in the mid-1870s, probably as placer gold in the bed of Burnt Gulch. Like prospectors everywhere, they then followed Burnt Gulch upstream, looking for the bedrock (lode) outcrops from which that alluvial gold had been eroded. They found their first good lode deposit (the Pelican Lode) in 1877, in Garfield Gulch, and it became the mainstay of Teton.

71

According to Sisemore (1983, p. 39), the last burial in the Teton cemetery occurred in 1950, and is represented by the largest and best-preserved headstone. Most of the burials evidently date from about 1880 to 1902; see Sisemore (1983, p. 39-40) for a list.

SOUTH CRESTONE TRAIL (FT 860) TO SOUTH CRESTONE LAKE

The South Crestone Trail is probably the third most-used trail on the west side of the Sangre de Cristo Wilderness, after the North Crestone and Willow Creek Trails. Like most popular trails, the South Crestone Trail ascends to an alpine lake (South Crestone Lake, area 10 acres), which lies in a rock-scoured basin above treeline at 11,790 ft elevation. The trail is only 3.3 miles (5.3 km) long, but gains 2910 ft (887 m) from the trailhead (8880 ft) to the lake (see Plate 3).

South Crestone Creek and Willow Creeks are the only ones in the western Sangre where the Pleistocene valley glaciers advanced beyond the canyon mouths and deposited large terminal moraines on the head of the piedmont. Because of this, the lowest part of the trail is not in a deep, V-shaped canyon like the lower San Isabel and North Crestone Trails. Instead, the lower valley has a more open feel, as it winds ¾ of a mile toward the face of the tree-covered terminal moraine hill. Three-quarters of a mile from the trailhead, a faint spur trail leads off to the north and crosses South Crestone Creek at the toe of the moraine. This trail continues for a few hundred yards and ends at the site of a large sawmill from the mining days. Trees were cut farther upvalley and the logs were then floated down South Crestone Creek to the sawmill. The sawmill also used water power to turn the saws.

South Crestone Trail (Forest Trail 860); for map, see Plate 3
Beginning:..Trailhead parking lot
Elev. 8880 ft (2707 *m*)
End:..*South Crestone Lake*
Elev. 11,790 ft (3595 m)
Trail length:..**3.3 miles (5.3 *km*)**
Elevation gain:..**2910 ft (887 *m*)**

The main South Crestone Trail continues to the NE and switchbacks up the conifer-covered frontal slope of the terminal moraine, finally attaining the moraine crest after ½ mile and 700 feet of elevation gain (to 10,200 ft). From the top you get an appreciation of how thick the moraine is, and how much material was eroded by the glaciers and dumped here.

The next ¾ of a mile are a gentle, meandering walk through an aspen forest, which has grown up on the fine soils left by the filled in moraine-dammed lake. The only obvious trace of this lake is the open grassy meadow called Logjam Park, so-named because logs on their way to the old sawmill tended to get stuck in this low-gradient section of the stream.

MILEAGE LOG (see Plate 3 for map)

Point	Mileage	Feature
	0.0	South Crestone/Willow Trailhead (8880 ft)
	0.05	trail splits; right fork goes to Willow Lake; continue straight for South Crestone Lake
	0.47	first creek crossing
	0.75	faint trail to left goes to site of historic sawmill
	0.8	begin ascending the toe of terminal moraine
	1.25	reach crest of terminal moraine
	1.6	to left is filled-in basin of moraine-dammed lake (Logjam Park; Fig. 3-17); trail begins ascending hillslope to get above a bedrock step at the head of the old lake; cross the mouth of the (hanging) south glaciated tributary
	2.25	trail reaches the base of another 300 ft-high bedrock step in the valley floor
	2.5	second creek crossing
0	**2.8**	third creek crossing
1	**2.9**	trail reaches base of another 350 ft-high bedrock step in valley floor; lots of switchbacks ahead.
2	**3.1**	reach top of bedrock step
3	**3.2**	fourth creek crossing
4	**3.3**	west end of South Crestone Lake (11,790 ft); see Fig. 3-18.

Fig. 3-17. Looking down S. Crestone Creek toward Logjam Park (meadow at left center) and its enclosing terminal moraine ridges. Photo was taken from the top of the bedrock step above waypoint 8.

Optional Hike to Head of Valley and Mt. Adams (see more details in Chapter 4)

Point	Mileage	Feature
5	**0.0**	outlet of S. Crestone Lake; easiest hiking is on the south side of the lake
6	**0.4**	base of 200 ft-high bedrock step in valley floor
7	**1.0**	reach head of gentle part of valley floor; above you rises the West Face of Mt. Adams; the standard West Ridge route begins at the saddle in the ridge directly north of you (elev. 12,800 ft)
8	**1.2**	saddle at 12,800 ft; from here ascend the West Ridge of Mt. Adams
9	**1.65**	summit of Mt. Adams (13,931 ft)

Fig. 3-18. Looking west to South Crestone Lake (lower center) and South Crestone valley from high on the cirque headwall. The jagged ridge at center separates South Crestone from North Crestone Creek, culminating in the unclimbed pinnacle Pt. 12,737. Photo by Clyde Lovett, crestonecreations.com.

Loop Trail with the Summit of Mount Adams:
Any hike that ends by summiting Mt. Adams can be turned into a loop traverse, because Mt. Adams lies at the heads of three valleys: North Crestone, South Crestone, and Willow Creek.

1—The Most Convenient Loop: the most convenient loop would start at the S. Crestone/Willow Trailhead, ascend Willow Creek, climb up to the saddle west of Mt. Adams and ascend the West Ridge, then descend the Northwest Ridge and return down South Crestone Creek to the trailhead. This loop could also be reversed. The advantage of this loop is that you can hike two of the best-maintained trails in the western Sangres, and you return to the same trailhead you left from. The disadvantage: you gain 5071 ft of elevation (8860 ft to 13,931 ft) and have to descend an equal amount, and if you camped overnight at Willow Lake, you have to lug all your camping equipment with you on the climb. This traverse would be quite strenuous.

2—A Longer Loop: you could also make a loop by ascending (or descending) North Crestone Creek in combination with either South Crestone Creek (and using Adam's NW Ridge for both ascent and descent), or in combination with Willow Creek (using both the Northwest and West Ridges). The drawback to these loops is that you will not return to the same trailhead you started from, and the two trailheads (North Crestone, versus South Crestone/Willow) are 4 miles apart by road. You could leave an extra car or bicycle at one trailhead, or hitchhike (works well around Crestone).

WILLOW CREEK TRAIL (FT 865) TO WILLOW LAKE AND KIT CARSON MOUNTAIN

Beginning:...	Trailhead parking lot Elev. **8880 ft (2707 m)**
End:..	*Willow Lake* Elev. *11,564 ft (3526 m)*
Trail length:..	**4.2 miles (6.7 km)**
Elevation gain:..	**2684 ft (818 m)**

The Willow Creek Trail (FT 865) rivals the North Crestone Trail as the most popular on the west side of the Sangres. There are several reasons. First, the trailhead is easy to drive to from Crestone. Second, the trail rises steeply into a rugged, severely-glaciated terrain of sculpted bedrock and soaring cliffs. Third, Willow Lake is one of the most scenic lakes in the Sangres and a favorite camping spot. Fourth, the easiest ascent route up Challenger Point and Kit Carson Mountain is from Willow Creek. But there are some drawbacks. Although the trail is wide and well-maintained, it is steep. The trails gains 2684 feet of elevation in just 4.2 miles. The elevation gain is so rapid that switchbacks are a necessity. The total number of switchbacks on this trail has been variously reported as 58, 59, 60, or 65. But you get the point.

MILEAGE LOG (see Plate 3 for map)

Point	Mileage	Feature
	0.0	South Crestone/Willow Trailhead (8880 ft)
	0.05	trail splits; take right fork for Willow Lake; cross Willow Creek
	0.15	Trail Register; meadow to right (south) is the site of the old mining camp of Wilcox, named after Mike and Billy Wilcox, early prospectors.
	0.7	beginning of switchbacks (Fig. 3-19) up the north flank of the terminal moraine
	1.2	crest of terminal moraine at elevation 9880 feet. For beginner hikers, hikers wanting to try out a new pair of boots, or parties with small children or older folks, this is a good place to turn around to make a short morning or afternoon hike.
	1.55	junction with trail on right, which descends to the aspen grove at the head of Willow Creek Park; good camping spots there (Fig. 3-20, -21)
	2.3	beginning of short section of switchbacks
	2.7	crossing of Willow Creek (Fig. 3-22)
	2.8	beginning of switchbacks up the "Icefall section"
0	**3.4**	top of the Icefall section; look for nice slabs of glacially-polished conglomerate near the trail in the next half mile
1	**3.6**	second crossing of Willow Creek
2	**4.2**	west end of Willow Lake (11,580 ft; see Fig. 3-23); YOU MADE IT!! Note: The lake covers 12.5 acres and is *very* cold; its depth has never been measured.

Fig. 3-19. Hikers ascend the series of steep switchbacks (14 of them!) of the Willow Creek Trail on the north slope of the terminal moraine. This trail is also used by pack horses as far up as Willow Lake.

NOTE: as the trail nears the top of the terminal moraine, it reaches the old boundary fence of the Baca Grant at one of the last switchbacks. The land south of the fence is private, part of the Preserve owned by the Manitou Foundation.

You will have already ascended 1000 vertical feet from the Trailhead (which you now have to descend), for a 2.4 mile-long round-trip hike. So take a break here, wander down to Willow Creek Park, have a snack, snap some photos, and go exploring the giant boulders left by the vanished Willow Creek Glacier.

Willow Creek Park, a "Tape Recorder" of Climate Changes
Willow Creek Park (Figs. 3-20, -21) is a 20-acre meadow encircled by the terminal moraine ridges of the latest glaciation. When the Willow Creek glacier began retreating upvalley about 20,000 years ago, it left behind a large topographic depression behind the moraines. Meltwater from the retreating glacier quickly filled the depression with water and created a "moraine-dammed lake" or "proglacial lake." The water eventually rose to a low spillover point in the SW corner of the terminal moraine at about 9800 ft elevation. This spillover acted as a stable threshold for the lake's water level. The meadow we see today is the filled-in remains of this proglacial lake.

> When a mountain lake is born… it is an irregular expressionless crescent, enclosed in banks of rock and ice…. Meanwhile, the glacier recedes, and numerous rills, still younger than the lake itself, bring down glacier-mud, sand-grains, and pebbles, giving rise to margin-rings and plats of soil. To these fresh soil-beds come many a waiting plant….. then as the seasons grow warmer, and the soil-beds deeper and wider, other sedges take their appointed places, and these are joined by blue gentians, daisies, dodecatheons, violets, honeyworts, and many a lowly moss. Shrubs also hasten in time to the new gardens…. So the young lake grows in beauty, becoming more and more humanly lovable from century to century…. But while its shores are being enriched, the soil-beds creep out with incessant growth, contracting its area, while the lighter mud particles deposited on the bottom cause it to grow constantly shallower, until at length the last remnant of the lake vanishes " (Muir, 1894).

Over the past 20,000 years Willow Creek flowed into the lake and slowly filled it with sediment, starting at the upvalley end. As the upvalley end of the lake became "dry land", plants slowly colonized the land surface. This process is known as "ecological succession." Today we can see the succession of vegetation types down the length of the meadow, with the wettest plants (marsh sedges) at the western end of the Park where the ground is still swampy, and the driest plants at the eastern end (conifer trees and aspens).

Fig. 3-20. Looking east up the Willow Creek Trail from Willow Creek Park. This 20-acre montane meadow is the remnant of an Ice Age lake. The country beyond displays the best glaciated topography in the Sangres and resembles some of the classic scenery of the Sierra Nevada described by John Muir.

Fig. 3-21. *Left*; Willow Creek Park, as seen from the trail, looking SW. The meadow is 500 yards long and 250 yards wide, roughly the area of 23 football fields. *Right*; The aspen grove at the head of Willow Creek Park, with autumn foliage. The fall is the best time of year to camp in this grove, because the Willow Creek Park meadow has dried out a bit, and the mosquitoes are long gone.

Fig. 3-22. *Left:* A hiker contemplates the creek crossing at the base of the Icefall section. This is the most significant crossing of Willow Creek on the trail, but has no bridge and must be crossed on driftwood logs. At high flows in late Spring/early Summer it would be dangerous to fall into the water, so hiking poles might come in handy. *Right:* Hikers cool their feet in Willow Lake, at the end of a 4.2 mile-long hike. From Willow Lake parties can ascend Challenger Point or Kit Carson Mountain via the standard ascent route, or Mount Adams via the West Ridge; see details in Chapter 5 and on Plate 3. Upper Willow Lake lies another 1.0 mile to the SE at the head of Willow Creek valley (elevation 12,325 ft). It is ice-bound as late as the end of July.

TRAILS FROM THE BACA GRANDE SUBDIVISION
Spanish Creek, Cottonwood Creek, and the "Baca Mountain Tract" of the Rio Grande National Forest

Looking at a map (e.g., Fig. 3-2), it appears that the shortest and easiest routes to the high peaks of the Crestone group would be Spanish and Cottonwood Creek. However, the mouths of both canyons were within the privately-owned Baca Ranch (1864-1971), which restricted access. From 1971 to the mid-1980s the canyon mouths were in the Baca Grande subdivision and could be accessed by the public. But in the mid-1980s the lands were granted to various spiritual groups or placed under conservation easement by the Manitou Foundation. So at present there is a strip of privately-owned land, 850 to 1400 yards wide and 5 miles long, that separates the Baca Grande subdivision from the Rio Grande National Forest (Fig. 3-23). These private lands lie across the courses of Willow Creek, Spanish Creek, and Cottonwood Creek, and block hikers from legally ascending the latter two trails along those drainages to reach the National Forest.

Spanish Creek trail and the pack trail up Cottonwood Creek were mainly in the privately-owned Baca Grant, and thus off-limits to public use, prior to 2004. When the Federal government purchased the Baca Ranch in 2004 it gained title to the upper parts of the two trails, but the lower parts are still privately owned by several spiritual groups, and traverse their retreat lands.

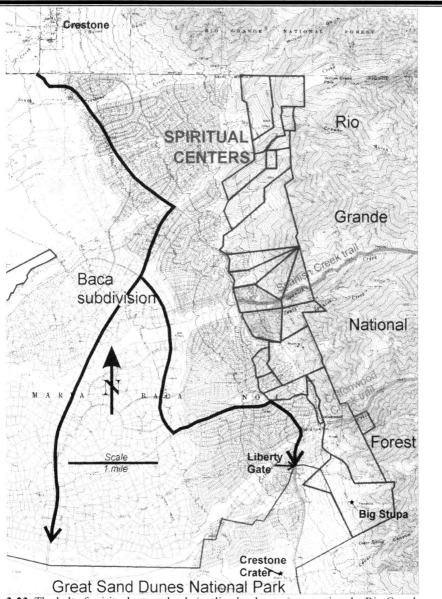

Fig. 3-23. The belt of spiritual retreat lands (outlined polygons) separating the Rio Grande National Forest from the Baca subdivision. The Spanish Creek trail across spiritual lands is currently closed to the public; the Cottonwood Creek trail is open with restrictions. The thick black line shows the major paved roads within the subdivision. The eastern branch leads to the northern Access to the National Park at Liberty Gate. The first 1.1 miles of the Liberty Road south of the gate (thick gray line at lower right, leads to Crestone Crater) are in the National Park, the remainder is in the Rio Grande National Forest. The western paved road goes to the BLA Cottonwood Creek greenbelt.

Since August 2007 the spiritual groups have closed the lower parts of the trails to public access, but some hikers and climbers continue to use them, which has created a conflict. Some Crestone locals assert that the trails were used prior to withdrawal of the land from the public domain (which occurred in 1864), and thus qualified for a permanent right-of-way under the 1866 Federal law named "RS2477." However, the Saguache County Commissioners disagreed, pointing out (in January, 2009) that the 186<sup> withdrawal occurred two years prior to passage of RS2477, which in their view was not retroactive. Thus, they concluded that the land owners were within their rights to close the trails. In early 2011 the Colorado Mountain Club (CMC) was still negotiating with the spiritual centers to permit public access.

The upper parts of the two trails lie in land added to the Rio Grande National Forest as part of the "Baca Mountain Tract." This late addition to the National Forest is not part of the Sangre de Cristo Wilderness, partly because it contains historic mines, camps, and the mining ghost town of Duncan.

Willow Creek; You can also access the Willow Creek trail from the top of Pine Cone Way, in case the Forest Trailhead parking lot is totally full. However, there is not much parking at this informal trailhead, so use it only as a last resort. To reach Pine Cone Way drive south from the entrance to the Baca 0.8 miles on Camino Baca Grande; after the fire station, turn left (east) on Moonlight Way; drive 1.15 miles east and then southeast on Moonlight to Ridgeview Way, and turn left; proceed 0.4 miles until Ridgeview dead-ends into Brookview Way; jog right (south) on Brookview for only 130 yards, and then turn left onto Pine Cone Way; follow it up a steep hill 0.3 miles to its end. This is the highest road in the Baca, ending at 8800 feet. Park in cul-du-sac; a foot trail goes east fo 270 yards through greenbelt land (owned by the Baca Grande Property Owners Association) to the Willow Creek Trail. At that intersection the trail also touches the extreme northwest corner of land owned by the Manitou Hermitage Project, so don't wander south of the old Baca fenceline.

SPANISH CREEK—CLOSED!!

The foot trail up Spanish Creek was almost entirely within the Baca Grant prior to 2004. and this legacy has created a problem for public access (see Plate 4). The lower 0.9 mile of the approach east of Dream Way and beginning of the trail pass directly through the heart of two spiritual retreats. In order to preserve the peace of the retreatants, the owner have closed the lower part of the trail to public access. 0.6 miles above the canyon mout the old pack trail enters the Rio Grande National Forest and is open to public use from that point eastward. However, at present there is no way for hikers to reach the trail in th National Forest without trespassing on spiritual retreat lands. This situation may change in the future, so inquire locally about the status of this trail.

COTTONWOOD CREEK TRAIL- *UNDER NEGOTIATION*

Only the lowest 1/2 mile of the Cottonwood Creek Trail crosses privately-owned land (Manitou Institute; www.manitou.org), after which it enters the Rio Grande National Forest (see Plate 4). Most of the trouble between hikers and the landowners has arisen from: (1) hikers parking on private land at the mouth of Cottonwood Creek, because the

80

s no Forest Service-owned trailhead with parking, and (2) hikers camping along the first
.5 mile of the trail in the canyon, while they are still on private land. Assuming that the
ccess issue will someday be resolved in the public's favor, here is how to get to the
Cottonwood Creek "trailhead."

Beginning:...**Road crossing Cottonwood Creek**
Elev. 8420 ft (2567 *m*)
End:...*Milwaukee Pass*
Elev. 13,300 ft (4055 m)
Trail length:...**5.8 miles (9.3 *km*)**
Elevation gain:...**4880 ft (1488 *m*)**

      Enter the Baca Grande subdivision and drive 2.2 miles south on Camino Baca
Grande (the main paved road; formerly the grade of the Sangre de Cristo Railroad). After
you cross Willow Creek turn right (west) onto Camino Real (locally called "Two Trees
Road"). Continue 3.4 miles on Camino Real to the intersection with Camino del Rey.
Turn left (east) and drive 2.6 miles toward the range front. At this point you intersect
Camino Baca Grande again. Turn right onto Camino Baca Grande and drive 0.4 miles
SE; turn left (east) before you cross Cottonwood Creek and drive 0.3 miles to the large
water tank. Continue past the water tank and park in an informal area on the north side of
the creek. From here, walk east on the north side of Cottonwood Creek on an old road
bed. For the next 0.5 miles the trail crosses private retreat land owned by spiritual groups.
Please respect their privacy and move along quietly. Half a mile from the trailhead is a
sign showing that you are now entering the Rio Grande National Forest.

      There is also some confusion about the correct name and number of the old Baca
Grant pack trail that ascends Cottonwood Creek, arising from its legacy in private
ownership. Prior to the 2004 Federal acquisition of the Baca Grant, this pack trail was on
private land for the first 3.7 miles. East of that, the trail entered National Forest lands and
merged with a Forest Trail that came over the range crest from the east, from the Sand
Creek cirque via the pass north of Milwaukee Peak. This pass has no formal USGS name
but several informal ones ("Milwaukee Pass" of Moore, 2003; "Beer Pass" or
Cottonwood Pass" of Winger & Winger, 2003). Prior to 2004 that trail was the only one
that could access upper Cottonwood Creek and yet avoid the Baca Grant, and was named
the Sand Creek Trail (Forest Trail 743) because most of it was in Sand Creek. So
perversely, the uppermost 2.3 miles of the trail in Cottonwood Creek (between
Milwaukee Pass and the Cottonwood Lakes Trail) are part of the Sand Creek Trail.
Presumably the Forest Service will eventually recognize this trail as the Cottonwood
Creek Trail described in numerous hiking guides (e.g. Moore, 2003).

MILEAGE LOG (see Plate 4 for map)

Point	Mileage	Feature
	0.0	Water tank at mouth of Cottonwood Creek (8410 ft); beginning of Cottonwood Creek Trail, an old jeep road on the N side of the creek; first 0.45 mi of trail is in private land
	0.45	trail enters Rio Grande National Forest
	0.9	trail crosses alluvial fan from steep northern gully; valley floor widens out on glacial outwash from moraines ahead

4	1.1	downvalley limit of glacial moraine; next 150 yards is in low ridges of older moraine (150,000 years old); then next 0.7 miles is in younger moraine (25,000 years old; Fig. 3-24); the lateral moraines form ridges 300 feet above the stream, and have dammed small hidden valleys (a, b, c, d)
5	2.2	trail crosses the Crestone-Sand Creek Thrust, here mainly buried by moraine; to the west all rocks are granite; to the east, Crestone Conglomerate
6	2.3	trail crosses stream coming down north valley wall from a large glaciated tributary;
7	3.0	trail reaches the base of a much steeper valley section, which rises 700 feet in the next 0.3 miles; the trail becomes poorly defined because it winds its way through glacially-polished outcrops of Crestone Conglomerate (Fig. 3-25); generally it is north of the creek within 50 yards; to the south of trail is a large hanging valley, formed by a glaciated tributary; the lip of the hanging valley is 700 feet above the valley floor, which is the minimum thickness of late glacial ice here; a small lake lies at the head of the hanging valley;

Fig. 3-24. *Left,* looking down towards the mouth of Cottonwood Creek, from the inner side of the latest glacial lateral moraine. Note moraine boulders embedded in the slope. This shot was taken near the crest of the north lateral moraine, about 300 vertical feet above the Trail. *Right,* view sou across the valley from the north lateral moraine. The south lateral moraine (center) is covered by lighter aspens, with the unglaciated slopes above covered by the darker spruce-fir forest.

Fig. 3-25. Looking downvalley from the steeper valley section, from one of the many glacially-polished outcrops of Crestone Conglomerate (foreground). Elevation about 11,000 feet, surrounded by a dense spruce-fir forest.

3.3 junction of Cottonwood Creek Trail with Cottonwood Lake Trail (FT 861) to left (see Fig. 3-26); continue straight (east) to reach the head of Cottonwood Creek; the trail from this point on (shown in gray) is currently [2011] named the Sand Creek Trail (FT 743), although this may change. Historically, all hikers reached this trail from Upper Sand Creek, by coming over "Milwaukee Pass" at the head of Cottonwood Creek, just north of the summit of Milwaukee Peak.

4.1 after traversing a very flat section of valley for 0.8 miles, trail reaches the base of a bedrock step 300 feet high; to the south is another hanging valley, the lip of which is only 400 feet above the valley floor; this small secluded valley contains a small lake (1.6 acres).

ig. 3-26. View of the Crestone Group from the lip of the large hanging valley south of ɔint 7 on Plate 4. At far left, the high grassy slope is part of the Southwest Ridge of ʳestone Peak. At center is the route of the Cottonwood Lake Trail; note small waterfall dead center. Cottonwood Lake lies in a small valley we call "Marvelous Valley", ndwiched between Crestone Needle and Crestolita.

4.6 after half a mile of switchbacks through scattered trees, the Trail reaches treeline at 11,800 feet; the valley floor here was heavily scoured by glacial ice, creating classic streamlined, white bedrock knobs called "*roches moutonees*" (sheep's backs; Fig. 3-27); to the north is the southern lip of "Marvelous Valley" (Fig. 3-28), the glaciated valley that separates the peak "Crestolita" (13,270 ft high) from Broken Hand Peak and Crestone Needle; the lip is 600 vertical feet above the trail, the thickness of ice here in the last glacial phase.

5.1 trail reaches 12,200 ft elevation by diagonaling NE across the valley

| | | floor in glaciated outcrops, to bypass a 300 ft-high bedrock step in the |
| 12 | **5.8** | south half of the valley floor; from this point, trail straightens and goes due east to the cirque headwall summit of Milwaukee Pass at about 13,300 ft; ascending the cirque headwall does not look possible from Point 11 (see Fig. 3-29), but previous Forest workers (CCC, 1930s?) created a workable pack trail with many small rock retaining walls; the view from the Pass is staggering. |

Fig. 3-27. Glacially-smoothed bedrock outcrop dot the floor of Cottonwood Creek at an elevation of 11,800 feet, near treeline. The ice flowed over the Crestone Conglomerate from left to right, grinding and polishing it into streamlined knobs.

"The map-like distinctiveness and freshness of this glacial landscape cannot fail to excite the attention of every beholder, no matter how little of its scientific significance may be recognized. These bald, westward-leaning rocks, with their rounded backs and shoulders toward the glacier fountains of the summit-mountains, and their split, angular fronts looking in the opposite direction, explain the tremendous grinding force with which the ice-flood passed over them, and also the direction of its flow."
John Muir, *The Yosemite*, 1912

Fig. 3-28. Looking up to th southern lip of Marvelous Valley from the Cottonwoo Creek Trail at Point 10. In the last ice age, glacier i came pouring out of this valley to join the main Cottonwood Creek glacier. The upper ice limit is show by the dotted lines, and the ice flow directions by the arrows. Note how the bedrock has been smoothe and polished by the ice.

Fig. 3-29. The headwall of Cottonwood Creek valley, with the pack trail shown as a dotted line. The trail here (officially called the Sand Creek Trail) comes into the valley over Milwaukee Pass, from the Upper Sand Creek valley. This pass makes it possible to hike a loop trail up Cottonwood and down Sand Creek (or vice versa).

COTTONWOOD LAKE TRAIL (FOREST TRAIL 861) TO CRESTONE PEAK AND CRESTONE NEEDLE

The Cottonwood Lake Trail is a short (1.3 mile) spur trail that connects the Cottonwood Creek Trail to Cottonwood Lake (Plate 4). Prior to 2004, the trail was used mainly by climbing parties originating at Music Pass and Upper Sand Creek. The parties would climb over "Milwaukee Pass", descend Cottonwood Creek to 11,100 feet on the so-called "Sand Creek Trail", and then ascend Cottonwood Lake Trail to the approach to Crestone Peak. In addition, about 25% of the parties climbing Crestone Peak and Needle between 2000 and 2010 ascended from the west side via Crestone and the Cottonwood Creek Trail. The other 75% came from South Colony Lakes on the east side, over "Eye of the Needle Pass" between Crestone Needle and Broken Hand Peak, and down into Marvelous Valley."

Fig. 3-30. Looking north from the high point in Marvelous Valley (elevation 12,750 ft) toward Cottonwood Lake and the Crestones. The slope at far left rises to the summit of Crestolita (Point 13,270). The Cottonwood Lake Trail is not visible here, because it ends at the west end of Cottonwood Lake, just out of sight in this view.

MILEAGE LOG (See Plate 4 for map)

Point	Mileage	Feature
1	0.0	Start of trail; junction with Cottonwood Creek Trail; for first 0.3 miles trail ascends the steep slope leading up to the lip of the hanging valley containing Cottonwood Lake
2	0.3	lip of hanging valley, 500 vertical feet above Point 1; from here on the valley gradient is much gentler
3	0.8	trail crosses small creek coming from a small valley that drains the south face of Crestone Peak, between the Peak's Southwest Ridge and Crestone Needle. This small valley is the approach to the standard ascent route up Crestone Peak.
4	1.3	trail reaches the west end of Cottonwood Lake; this area is full of blooming columbines (the Colorado State Flower) in mid-summer.

TRAILS ACCESSED FROM LIBERTY GATE (GREAT SAND DUNES NATIONAL PARK)

Three valleys lie south of the Baca subdivision and are accessed from the Northern Entrance to Great Sand Dunes National Park. In early 2011 that entrance was the Liberty Gate, at the SE corner of the subdivision, and the northern terminus of the historic Liberty postal road. To reach the mouths of Deadman, Pole, and Sand Creeks you have t⚫ walk (or perhaps drive after summer 2011) south on Liberty Road (described in more detail in Chapter 4). Below we describe the Deadman and Pole Creek trails, which lie entirely within the Rio Grande National Forest; for Sand Creek Trail, see Chapter 4.

DEADMAN CREEK TRAIL

The head of Deadman Creek contains 8 cirques, the northernmost 3 of which are numbered on Plate 5 to correspond to the photograph in Fig. 3-31.

Beginning:...mouth of canyon, creek crossing
Elev. 8300 ft (2530 *m*)
End:...*Upper Deadman Lake*
Elev. 11,704 ft (3568 *m*)
Trail length:..6.9 miles (11.0 *km*)
Elevation gain:...3404 ft (1038 *m*)

The trail up Deadman Creek (see Plate 5) is different from those in the other valleys described previously, in several ways. First, this trail was never part of the Forest Servic⚫ system, because the lower half of the trail was within the privately-owned Baca Grant, s⚫ there was no public access. The trail was built and maintained (barely) by the owners of the Baca Grant for their personal use, mainly for hunting, and fishing at Deadman Lakes. Second, the part of the trail between the canyon mouth and the terminal moraine, where the valley is narrow and winding, is 3.7 miles long, much longer than in other valleys (f⚫ example Cottonwood Creek, where that section is only 1.1 miles long).

Third, there is no easy way out of the head of Deadman Creek, no trails leading⚫ over the cirque headwalls. This is because the head of Deadman is composed of 8 deepl⚫

86

eroded cirques, unlike most of the other valleys that only have one or two cirques. These cirques lie at the head of 8 glaciated tributary valleys that fan out in a half-circle.

Why are there so many cirques in this one valley? Maybe because Deadman Creek is entirely underlain by granitic basement rocks, and has no areas of the harder Crestone Conglomerate. The granite is very susceptible to frost wedging and shattering, much more so than the massive conglomerate. As a result the slopes in Deadman, especially above treeline, are covered with frost-shattered granite rubble (Fig. 3-31), and bedrock cliffs are virtually absent. This abundance of rubble must have also existed in the last glacial age, because Deadman Creek contains much more extensive moraine deposits than any other valley. The moraines have nicely blocked off two hanging valleys on the northern valley wall (mileage point 6 and next valley to the east).

MILEAGE LOG (see Plate 5 for map)

Point	Mileage	Feature
0	**0.0**	(off map); Liberty Road just after it crosses Deadman Creek; turn left (east) onto jeep road that ascends the alluvial fan and stays within 50-100 yards south of the creek for the next 1.2 miles
	1.2	trail splits; take left fork and continue uphill; after 200 yards trail turns north and heads toward mouth of canyon
2	**1.5**	trail crosses Deadman Creek at canyon mouth
3	**2.2**	trail rises on north side of valley and enters a clearing; from here the valleys narrows and the sidewalls become very steep and cliffy
4	**3.4**	trail reaches the eastern boundary of the former Baca Grant, now the Baca Mountain Tract of the Rio Grande National Forest; ahead lies the Sangre de Cristo Wilderness
	3.7	trail begins climbing a low bouldery ridge; this is the older glacial moraine of Deadman Creek; trail steepens and ascends the inner slope of the younger terminal moraine; you gain 500 feet of elevation in the next 0.5 mile
	4.4	fork in trail; old hunting trail to left, continues rising to access the two "hidden valleys" to the north, blocked off by the lateral moraine; these would be a good places to camp, or to watch wildlife; continue on right fork, which begins contouring slightly downslope to reach the valley bottom

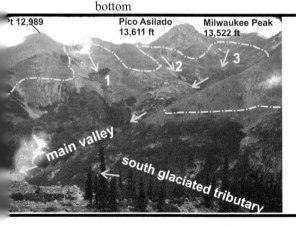

Pt 12,989

Pico Asilado 13,611 ft

Milwaukee Peak 13,522 ft

main valley

south glaciated tributary

Fig. 3-31. View of the 3 northern cirques of Deadman Creek, looking north from the south glaciated tributary. The upper limit of late glacial ice is shown by the dash-and-dot line; arrows show direction of ice flow. Note the absence of cliffy outcrops and the abundance of frost-shattered rubble on slopes.

Point	Mileage	Feature
7	**5.4**	trail crosses tributary stream coming out of a group of four cirques to the south of the main valley
8	**5.65**	good trail ends in open area of ground moraine, after switchbacking up to base of steep hanging mouth of south glaciated tributary; from here to any of the four southern cirques, you have to bushwhack
9	**6.3**	Alternate Route: the westernmost lake in the Deadman Lakes group (area of 5.5 acres) lies at 11,765 ft elevation in the southwestern-most cirque
10	**6.5**	Alternate Route: the lower (and at 4.2 acres, smaller) of the two eastern Deadman Lakes in the large southern cirque
11	**6.9**	Alternate Route: upper of the two eastern Deadman Lakes (elevation 11,704 ft; area 13.6 acres) in the large southern cirque. Although this is the largest Deadman Lake, with an area 1 acre larger than the more famous Willow Lake, it is seldom visited.
12	**7.9**	summit of Milwaukee Peak (summit is just off map), via the southwest face; this long bushwhacking route ascends the third numbered cirque to the southwest face

POLE CREEK TRAIL (FOREST TRAIL 878)

Although the lower 1/5 of the Pole Creek Trail was in the Baca Grant, the remaining 4/5 is Forest Service Trail 878 (see Plate 5). According to the website of the Rio Grande National Forest, trail length is 3.4 mi, starting elevation is 8800 ft (the old Forest Boundary), and ending elevation is 12,000 ft at Pole Creek Lake. The Forest Service says the trail is "not maintained because there is no public access, and may be difficult to follow", but that statement was made before the Forest Service acquired this part of the Baca Ranch in 2004. The trail can now be accessed from the Liberty Road and the Town of Duncan.

The main attraction of the Pole Creek Trail was historically Pole Creek Lake at the head (area of 2 acres), even though the Forest Service maintains there are no fish in the lake. But for visitors interested in history, Pole Creek has another attraction. The mining claims and cabins in Pole Creek were used until the 1930s, and were subsequently protected from vandalism by the closed nature of the Baca Ranch. Since 2004 the public has had access to this time capsule of the old mining days, where cabins and mine workings have scarcely been disturbed. While walking along the trail for 0.8 miles between Points 6 and 7, you will see many relics of the mining era. The structures within the patented mining claims are still privately owned; please respect private property in these areas.

Beginning:..Town of Duncan
Elev. 8120 ft (2476 *m*)
End:...*Pole Creek Lake*
Elev. 11,980 ft (3655 m)
Trail length:...*4.25 miles (6.8 km)*
Elevation gain:...*3860 ft (1176 m)*

MILEAGE LOG (see Plate 5 for map)

Point	Mileage	Feature
1	0.0	Town of Duncan and Liberty Road; proceed south
2	0.1	turn left (east) off the Liberty Road onto the old wagon road to the mouth of Pole Creek
3	0.6	old wagon road crosses Pole Creek to the south side
4	0.9	road crosses Pole Creek to north side
5	1.3	road reaches the eastern boundary of the former Baca Grant
6	1.6	trail enters an area of patented mining claims, which it stays in for the next 1/3 mile. After that there are clusters of historic cabins along the trail for an additional 0.5 mile; Sisemore (1983) interviewed several people who lived in these cabins, which are remarkably well preserved.
7	2.4	trail leaves area of historic mining cabins
8	2.6	trail crosses to south side of creek and begins to ascend a bedrock step; in the next 0.3 miles you will ascend 500 feet; at top of step, trail is on the terminal moraine ridges of the older glaciation
9	3.3	after 0.7 miles on the south side of the creek, amidst older subdued moraine ridges, the trail crosses the creek to the north and enters younger, stonier moraines
10	3.6	trail crosses to south side of creek
11	3.75	base of 300 ft-high bedrock step in valley floor
12	4.25	Pole Creek Lake, elevation 11,980 ft; the Colo. Division of Wildlife says "the lake is not known to support any fish."

Origin of the Word "Crestone"

The spelling may be unique to our town, but has the name Creston been given to towns in California, Illinois, Iowa, New Mexico, South Dakota (ghost town), Washington, Wyoming, and British Columbia. [The California Creston is noted for containing the ranch and deathplace of L. Ron Hubbard (in 1985), founder of Scientology]. In the New Mexican dialect of Spanish, "crestón" can mean "hillock" or "summit", but it can also mean "cockscomb" or "large crest" (Julyan, 1996)." Several conspicuous rocky ridge crests are named Creston in New Mexico, including the Ortiz Mountains and a ridge southwest of Las Vegas, New Mexico, site of the original Luis Maria Baca Grant.

There are several possible explanations for the name Crestone. The first is that it was imported by an immigrant from a town named Creston in another state. Colorado newspapers of the late 1800s mention many immigrants from Creston, Iowa. A second possibility is that the Baca heirs, after they moved from Las Vegas, NM to Baca Grant No. 4 in the San Luis Valley in 1864, described the jagged crest of the Sangres lying within their Ranch (including Kit Carson Mountain) as El Crestón. A variant of the name was applied to the Crestonie Post Office in the Baca Grant in 1872.

Another possibility is raised by the spelling of the Christonie Mining District and Christonie Creek, suggesting a derivation from the name of Christ, as in the Sangre de Cristo Mountains. This spelling was the dominant one in newspapers, and was used for the area's voting precinct in official County documents, until the founding of Crestone in 1880. Finally, some erudite miner may have named the area for Crestonia, the ancient region of classical Greece directly north of Mygdonia, later annexed to the Kingdom of Macedonia in the 5th Century BC. Its capitol city was named Crestone.

89

4. GREAT SAND DUNES NATIONAL PARK AND PRESERVE

"The better and stronger nation of the future will be a park-using nation. Many wrecked nations have tried to get along without outdoor parks and recreation places. It is but little less than folly to spend millions on forts and warships, on prisons and hospitals, instead of giving people the opportunity to develop and rest in the sane outdoors."
Enos Mills

On Sept. 13, 2004, Great Sand Dunes National Monument (established in 1932) became Great Sand Dunes National Park & Preserve. This "upgrade" within the National Park System was accompanied by: (1) adding 64,000 acres of the former Baca Grant to the National Park, more than doubling its original size of 43,000 acres, and (2) transferring 42,000 acres of the Rio Grande National Forest to a newly-created Great Sand Dunes National Preserve. The Preserve consists of the entire Sand Creek watershed, which is the largest watershed in the Sangre de Cristos. The expansion brought the National Park boundary up to the southern boundary of the Baca Grande subdivision. From Crestone, a drive to the Park now became a 7-mile journey through the Baca subdivision to the Northern Entrance, instead of a 58-mile drive via Moffat and Mosca to the Southern Entrance. In addition, the acquisition opened up Deadman, Pole, and Sand Creeks to hiking access from Crestone.

LIBERTY ROAD (NORTH ENTRANCE TO GREAT SAND DUNES NATIONAL PARK & PRESERVE)

Public access to the northern part of the National Park and to the Rio Grande National Forest is currently at Liberty Gate. Liberty Gate lies directly south of the southeast corner of the Baca Grande subdivision, and can be reached as follows: 1- from the entrance to the subdivision, drive south on Camino Baca Grande for 2.1 miles. After you cross Willow Creek, turn right on the first paved road (Camino Real; aka Two Trees Road). You will know you are on the correct road, if in about ¼ mile you pass two Ponderosa Pines growing in the middle of the road; 2- continue SW for 0.8 miles and turn left (south) onto Wagon Wheel Road (paved); 3- drive south for 1.8 miles to Camino de Rey (also paved) and turn left (east); 4- drive 1.1 miles east on Camino del Rey, to the T-intersection with Camino Baca Grande; turn right (south); 5- drive 0.8 miles south until you reach Liberty Gate. Liberty Road south of the gate is for federal administrative use only, so the Gate is locked to prevent public motor vehicle use. The road is currently (2011) open to foot and horse traffic south of the gate. There is limited parking at Liberty Gate, not enough room for more than a few horse trailers. Inside the gate about 100 feet is a portable toilet serviced by the Park Service. There are no other facilities at Liberty Gate, and no camping is allowed there.

However, in 2011 the Park Service and Forest Service plan to upgrade the Liberty Road for 1.7 miles south of the Liberty Gate. The upgraded road section will extend to a new public parking lot just south of the Crestone Crater, on the north side of Cedar Creek. Once that parking lot is built (2011?), Liberty Gate will be left unlocked and the road will be open to public motor vehicle access to the new parking lot. This

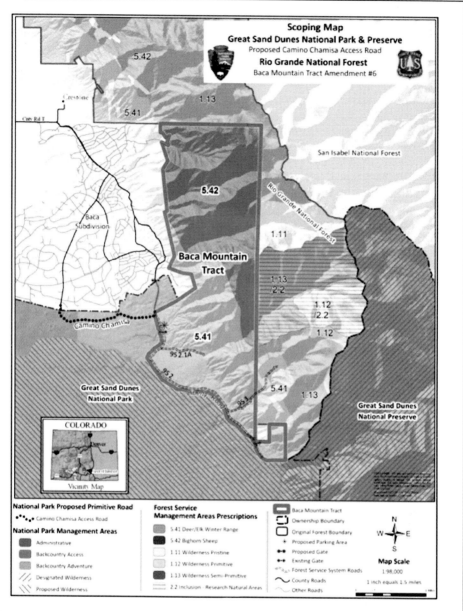

Scoping Map
Great Sand Dunes National Park & Preserve
Proposed Camino Chamisa Access Road
Rio Grande National Forest
Baca Mountain Tract Amendment #6

San Isabel National Forest

Crestone

5.42

1.13

5.41

5.42

Baca
Subdivision

1.11

**Baca Mountain
Tract**

1.13
2.2

1.12
/2.2

Camino Chamisa

5.41

1.12

95 2.1A

95.2

**Great Sand Dunes
National Park**

5.41

1.13

**Great Sand Dunes
National Preserve**

COLORADO

Denver

Vicinity Map

National Park Proposed Primitive Road	Forest Service Management Areas Prescriptions	
•••••• Camino Chamisa Access Road	5.41 Deer/Elk Winter Range	Baca Mountain Tract
National Park Management Areas	5.42 Bighorn Sheep	Ownership Boundary
Administrative	1.11 Wilderness Pristine	Original Forest Boundary
Backcountry Access	1.12 Wilderness Primitive	+ Proposed Parking Area
Backcountry Adventure	1.13 Wilderness Semi-Primitive	•• Proposed Gate
/// Designated Wilderness	2.2 Inclusion - Research Natural Areas	++ Existing Gate
Proposed Wilderness		Forest Service System Roads
		County Roads
		Other Roads

N
W—E
S

Map Scale
1:98,000

1 inch equals 1.5 miles

Fig. 4-1. Management categories of Federal lands south of Crestone. At center is the Baca Mountain Tract (BMT), that part of the former Baca Grant recently added to the Rio Grande National Forest. The Spanish Creek and Cottonwood Creek Trails traverse the BMT, and eventually reach the Sangre de Cristo Wilderness. South of the Baca Grande subdivision lies the Great Sand Dunes National Park, most of which is also designated as wilderness. A small area directly south of the subdivision is designated as Backcountry Access or Backcountry Adventure, rather than wilderness. Camino Chamisa was proposed by the Forest Service in 2009, but withdrawn in 2011.

Cedar Creek parking lot will then become the main trailhead to access the northern part of the Park, the canyons of Cedar, Deadman, Pole, Alpine, and Short Creeks in the Rio Grande National Forest, and Sand Creek in the Great Sand Dunes Preserve.

THE LIBERTY ROAD

Liberty Road is the mining-era road from Crestone to Duncan and the mines of the El Dorado mining district. It served as the official postal wagon road to Duncan (1892-1900 and Liberty (1900-1921). After the 1920s and the gradual abandonment of Liberty, the road was used as a ranch road within the Baca Ranch. Even after the development of the Baca subdivision in 1971, the Liberty gate was locked and only guests of the Baca Ranch (mainly hunters) and owners of private inholdings such as Liberty were permitted to use the road. Despite eight decades of light use, Liberty Road was still a decent two-track road in 2004, when the Baca Ranch was purchased by the Federal government. The northernmost 1.2 miles of the Liberty Road are now in Great Sand Dunes National Park (see Fig. 3-23); the remaining 6.8 miles is in the Rio Grande National Forest.

Mileage Log for Liberty Road (see Plate 6 for map of road south of Duncan).
Mileage Feature
0.0 Liberty Gate (northern end of Liberty Road); Northern entrance to Great Sand Dunes National Park
1.2 Liberty Road leaves the National Park and enters Rio Grande National Forest
1.3 Crestone Crater lies 250 yards west of Liberty Road

THE CRESTONE CRATER
An odd feature along the Liberty Road is the "Crestone Crater" (Fig. 4-2), a suspected meteor crater (Marvin and Marvin, 1966). According to eyewitnesses in Crestone, a spectacular fireball fell somewhere in this general vicinity in the middle 1930s. The crater was first noticed in the late 1930s by rancher V.M. King, who believed it might be the crater formed by that meteorite impact. It is an elliptical bowl 350 feet long by 250 feet wide, oriented NE-SW, with a maximum depth of 23 feet (Fig. 4-3).

Fig. 4-2. The "Crestone Crater", a suspected meteor crater; view is toward Crestone Peak (in center background). The Crater lies only about 200 yards west of the Liberty road (note truck on road, white arrow). Park rangers in the center and at rim of the crater (circled) provide the scale. GPS coordinates 37.65244°N, 105.91110°V

The Crater has been studied twice by scientists. In 1941 the famous meteorite expert H.H. Nininger came down from the Denver Museum of Natural History. He searched the ground for meteorite fragments, and then drilled in the crater and sunk a shaft. Although he found no meteoric material, he speculated that the crater could have been formed by the impact of an icy comet fragment (Nininger, 1963). Twenty-four years later, two scientists from the Smithsonian Institution of Washington, D.C. spent two weeks in the summer of 1965 studying the crater (Marvin and Marvin, 1966).

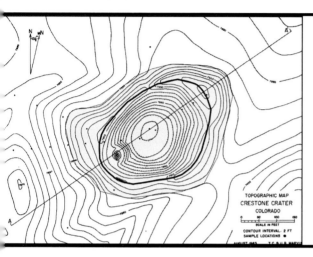

Fig. 4-3. A topographic map of the Crestone Crater, with a contour interval of 2 feet (from Marvin and Marvin, 1966). The Crater and its raised rim are shaded; thick line shows the crest of the crater rim.

The Smithsonian party sifted through 600 pounds of sand and dug numerous boreholes looking for meteorite fragments, but likewise was unable to find any trace of meteoric debris. They concluded that the crater was probably a windblown landform called a "blowout", and had nothing to do with meteor or comet impact. In 2011, however, the National Park staff and Colorado School of Mines Geophysics Department began testing new geophysical survey techniques in the crater, developed after 1965, to detect magnetic meteorite particles. So the story is not over yet………..

Mileage Feature
.4   jeep road intersects Liberty Road; to east, jeep road ascends 1.1 miles to Cedar
        Spring, gaining 700 feet in elevation
.8   road crosses Cedar Creek; future site of the public parking area
.2   Liberty Road begins to swing west, away from the range front
.6   Liberty Road crosses Deadman Creek [see Deadman Creek trail]
.0   Liberty Road crosses Alpine Creek
6   Town of Duncan; jeep road comes into Liberty Road from west

THE TOWN OF DUNCAN (adapted from Slaughter, 2007 and Harlan, 2010):
The mining town of Duncan sprang up near the mouth of Pole Creek (Fig. 4-4), about 2 mi SE of the mouth of Cottonwood Creek and the camp of Sangre de Cristo (later Cottonwood),. The town was founded by and named after John Duncan. Duncan was born in Indiana in 1851, but emigrated to Colorado and arrived in the Sangre de Cristo area in 1874. Although he was not the first prospector in this area (Wm. Steele and

Edward Pratt had established a base camp on Pole Creek in 1870, and prospected until 1872), Duncan discovered lode gold on the slope of Milwaukee Hill, the high ridge that separates Alpine Creek from Pole Creek. By 1890 gold had also been discovered up Pole Creek, leading Duncan to establish a permanent settlement between there and his claim on Milwaukee Hill, thus founding the town of Duncan. The major mines were the Honest Abe; the Golden Treasure (Bryon Rolson), and the Sultan (Frasier brothers).

The Monte Cristo Tunnel, which is caved in but still visible today, is located jus above the base of Milwaukee Hill. The mine tunnel was a community endeavor of Duncan townspeople, and unsuccessfully attempted to intersect Duncan's Denver Belle vein at a depth of about 1000 feet below the surface. The town flourished and it is rumored that approximately 4000 people lived in or near Duncan by 1892, the year the Duncan Post Office opened. Businesses in Duncan included three grocery stores, a drugstore, dry goods & hardware, mining supplies, two general merchandise stores, a lumber supplier, a stage line (which also carried the mail), two saloons, a barber, a shoemaker, boarding house, doctor, attorney, assay office, the *Duncan Eagle* newspaper, and one school. But no churches.

From 1879 to 1900 independent miners and prospectors operated on the Baca Grant, erroneously assuming that the Grant owners owned only the surface and grazing rights, but not the mineral rights. When the US Supreme Court ruled that the Grant owned all minerals rights, most of the miners moved away, but a few around Duncan continued to work mines under lease to the Grant owners. John Duncan was the last resident to leave his namesake town, and died in Saguache in November, 1918.

Subsequent to 1918 the town of Duncan was slowly reclaimed by the pinyon-juniper forest. Being within the Baca Grant, the townsite was protected from vandalism and lay undisturbed for 90 years. But in 2004 the National Forest acquired Duncan and performed an archeologic assessment (Slaughter, 2007). The archeologists were amazed at the preservation of the town's building foundations and streets, which were preserved as in a time capsule, a Colorado version of Macchu Pichu.

Point	**Mileage**	Feature
2	**6.0**	Liberty Road crosses Pole Creek [see Pole Creek trail]
3	**6.7**	intersection with the Hooper Postal Road from the west
4	**6.9**	road forks; left fork is the original Liberty Road that goes to private property around old Town of Liberty (No Trespassing); right fork is new Liberty Road that bypasses private land to access Sand Creek and the Great Sand Dunes. NOTE: visitors wanting to hike up Short Creek have to avoid the private land in doing so.

THE TOWN OF LIBERTY (summarized from Harlan, 2002)
When the Baca Grant owners evicted the gold miners in 1900, many of them moved just outside of the eastern grant boundary and founded the town of Liberty (Fig. 4-4). They founded the Liberty Mining & Milling Co., which owned the April Lode, Mountain Dee Elk, Yellow Bird, and Yellow Metal claims, together known as the Liberty Lodes. In 1902 a 5-stamp mill (see Chapter 10) was built at the mouth of Short Creek, by the Mutual Mining & Milling Company. Much of the ore treated came from Sand Creek, because the mines up Short Creek were rapidly giving out. Later a 10-stamp mill was built at the Liberty Lodes by the Liberty Mining & Milling Co., which later sold out to

he Cripple Creek-Chicago Mining & Milling Company (CCM). However, in 1910 CCM
:eased mining operations, and performed only maintenance and assessment for the next 4
vears. When the Company finally closed in 1914, those who remained in Liberty worked
it mines in Pole Creek, Sand Creek, or prospected.

The exact population of Liberty is unknown, but it boasted a US Post Office for
'2 years (1900-1921), a school for 14 years (1906-1919), a newspaper *The New
Distributor* (1902-1905). Businesses included the Norviel General Merchandise Store;
he Liberty Hotel; Mrs. Ott's Boarding House; a barber shop; a Fine Bread and Pastries
'hop; a shoe repair shop; an emporium; and a livery and feed.

Point	Mileage	Feature
	7.1	trail goes east from new Liberty Road, down the center of a large clearing just south of the private land; the west half of this clearing is in the National Park, the east half in the National Forest; their boundary is the old Liberty Road coming south out of the private land
	7.2	a second trail goes off Liberty Road to the east
	7.3	good camping spot in a clearing south of private land; in National Forest (camping not allowed in the National Park part of the meadow)
	7.6	on trail leading to mouth of Sand Creek; a second trail comes in from the west
	8.0	trail passes from National Forest into National Park
0	8.2	arbitrary "mouth" of Sand Creek, and beginning of old Sand Creek pack trail
1	9.2	old pack trail crosses Sand Creek to south side, and joins the newly-built section of the Sand Creek Trail
2	9.55	old pack trail crosses Sand Creek to north side; collapsed mine shaft and headframe, plus a well-preserved stamp mill
3	11.1	old pack trail crosses Sand Creek to south side
4, 15	12.1	pack trail crosses Sand Creek twice, west and east of the mouth of Cleveland Gulch

SAND CREEK TRAIL (FOREST TRAIL 743)

he Sand Creek Trail is the longest trail in the Sangres, extending for 12.5 miles from its
>uthern terminus at the Sand Ramp Trail in the old Great Sand Dunes National
1onument (see Plate 6), to Upper Sand Creek Lake in the cirque. This is the new Sand
reek Trail of the National Park Service since 2010. However, guidebooks and maps
1ade before 2004 show the trail as quite different, so a brief explanation is in order.

The terminology and extent of the "Sand Creek Trail" is a bit confusing, due to
1e past presence of private land at the canyon mouth. Before the Baca Ranch was
urchased in 2004, the lower part of the Forest Service Sand Creek Trail was blocked
om reaching the valley floor by a closed gate at the Baca Ranch boundary 1.5 miles
ovalley from the canyon mouth. From that point up to the valley's head, the trail was
pen to the public because it was in the Sangre de Cristo Wilderness. However, the lower
5 miles of the trail (everything downvalley from Little Sand Creek) saw little use
ecause hikers using the Forest Trail were "dead-ended" by the closed private gate before
ey could reach the floor of the San Luis Valley. The only way to reach Great Sand

Dunes National Monument from the Sand Creek Trail in those days, without trespassing on the Baca Ranch, was a difficult bushwhack southward over a steep forested ridge that few chose to take.

This problem disappeared in 2004 with the Federal acquisition of the Baca Ranch. The 1.5 miles of formerly-private lands at the canyon mouth were added to the National Park, as was the valley floor all the way north to the Baca subdivision. The remainder of the Sand Creek watershed was transferred from the Rio Grande National Forest to the Great Sand Dunes National Preserve. As a result, the public can now access the mouth of Sand Creek from either the National Park's Southern Entrance (via the Sand Ramp Trail and a newly-built section of the Sand Creek Trail), or via the new Northern Entrance (Liberty Road). Hikers can also ascend the entire length of Sand Creek to its cirque and to the Music Pass Trail (9.2 miles) (see Fig. 4-4).

The Sand Creek Trailhead at the canyon mouth can be reached from the south or the north. From the south (in the old National Monument), hike the Sand Ramp Trail in the "old" part of the Great Sand Dunes National Monument, to the Cold Creek Campground. From the CG take the newly-built section of the Sand Creek Trail on the south side of Sand Creek for 2.8 miles, as it curves to the right to hug the foot of the mountains, eventually intersecting the old Sand Creek pack trail which comes in from the north side of the creek.

Coming in from the North Entrance, take the Liberty Road south to Liberty, then work your way south on old mining roads (now pack trails) to the mouth of the canyon (Figs. 3-11, 4-4). 0.8 miles south of Liberty this trail will pass from the National Forest into the National Park. In another 1.3 miles the trail will reach Sand Creek and an old ford to the south side of the Creek, where it will join the newly-built section of the Trail. From this point upstream, the trail follows the alignment of the old privately-built pack trail, but has been rebuilt and upgraded by the Park Service since 2004.

The Trail continues another 6.5 miles up the valley bottom beyond the limits of the map in Plate 6, to Upper Sand Creek Lake (Fig. 4-4), following the old alignment shown on all topo maps.

OVER THE DUNES

To reach the Dunes without going to the mouth of Sand Creek, continue south from Liberty for 1.5 miles on the old jeep road (Figs. 3-11, 4-5). There you will find a ford across Sand Creek. The old jeep road continues another 1.0 miles south and west to the Sand Creek Campground, which lies at the base of the dunes. If you want to skirt the Dunes on their eastern side, walk east from the ford a few hundred yards to the newly-built section of the Sand Creek Trail, and walk south on it 1.3 miles to the Cold Creek Campground and junction with the Sand Ramp Trail. On the Sand Ramp Trail it is a 5.5 mile-long hike southeast along the edge of the dunes to reach the Medano Primitive Road. From the Medano Primitive Road, you can head south to the developed part of Great Sand Dunes National Park (campground, Visitor Center), or ascend the road to Medano Pass and cross over into the Wet Mountain Valley.

LOOP HIKE; COTTONWOOD CREEK-SAND CREEK LOOP (27 MILES)

Federal acquisition of the Baca Grant makes it possible, for the first time, to hike a spectacular but challenging loop combining the Cottonwood Creek Trail with the Sand Creek Trail (Forest Trail 743). This loop trail is 26.8 miles long, goes over Milwaukee

Pass at 13,300 feet, and follows many miles of barely-maintained trail. The one advantage; you won't be plagued by crowds. The trail segments below assume hiking up Cottonwood and down Sand Creek, but he loop can be hiked in either direction. The most difficult trail segment to follow is the unmaintained lower Cottonwood Creek section.

Segment 1; Informal trailhead parking area at the mouth of Cottonwood Creek, to Milwaukee Pass", on the Cottonwood Creek Trail (6.0 mi of difficult-to-follow trail)
Segment 2; Over Milwaukee Pass to Upper Sand Creek Trail and its junction with the Music Pass Trail (2.0 mi)
Segment 3; Continue downvalley on the Sand Creek Trail (FT 743) from the junction with Music Pass Trail, to mouth of Sand Creek (10.0 mi)
Segment 4; At the mouth of Sand Creek, cross Sand Creek to the North and walk on old jeep roads to Liberty (1 mi)
Segment 5; North on Liberty Road from Liberty to the future NPS/USFS Liberty Road parking lot (5.5 mi)
Segment 6; North on Liberty Road from the future NPS parking lot to Liberty Gate at National Park-Baca subdivision boundary(1.5 mi)
Segment 7; on subdivision roads from Liberty Gate to the Cottonwood Creek parking area (0.8 mi); TOTAL LOOP MILEAGE: 26.8 miles

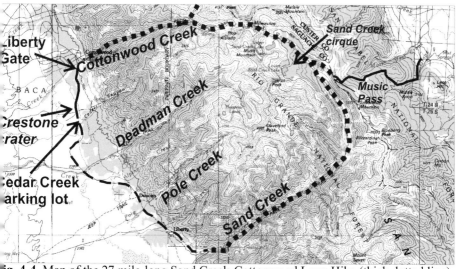

Fig. 4-4. Map of the 27 mile-long Sand Creek-Cottonwood Loop Hike (thick dotted line). Solid black lines show roads that can be driven; dashed lines, old roads that can be walked or biked (motor vehicles prohibited); dotted lines, trails. After 2011 and the opening of the Cedar Creek parking lot, the loop could be facilitated by leaving a 2nd car (or a bicycle) at that parking lot, and driving (or biking) back to the first car at the Cottonwood Creek trailhead. This would eliminate 2.3 miles of hiking (Segments 6 and above).

5. MOUNTAIN CLIMBING

The Sangre de Cristos rise up out of the earth like the spine of a giant dragon, each vertebra forming a separate peak on the range crest (Fig. 5-1). When you climb the peaks of the range and straddle this crest, the experience is like being in an airplane, yet your feet are solidly connected to the roots of Mother Earth. It is a dizzying feeling, an unexpected juxtaposition of heaven and earth.

Many climbers come to the area just to "bag" one of the Fourteeners, and then scurry back to the Front Range. However, there are 39 peaks above 13,000 feet accessible from the Crestone area, 22 of which are unnamed and many of which are unclimbed. Some of these are considerably safer, and all are less crowded, than our Fourteeners.

Fig. 5-1. Named peaks and creeks covered in the Guidebook. Image from Google Earth.

SUMMITS IN THE AREA COVERED BY THIS BOOK
(FROM HERMIT PEAK, SOUTH TO CLEVELAND PEAK)

There are 39 summits in the Sangres more than 13,000 feet high, in the 16 mile-long stretch of the Sangres covered by this book, which are either named (17) or have spot elevations shown on USGS topographic maps (22). The total includes four Fourteeners, with a 5th Fourteener lying 1.5 miles east of the range crest (Humboldt Peak, 14,064 ft; rank 37), but difficult to access from the Crestone side. In Table 5.1, I omitted Humboldt

98

Peak but added one summit *almost* 13,000 ft high. Peaks that are not named on USGS topos are generally referred to as "Unknown", abbreviated as "UN [elevation]", or as Point [elevation]. Some peaks not named on USGS maps are named on the privately-printed "Sky Terrain" map of the Sangre de Cristos (Schulte, 2010); these names are shown in quotation marks in the Table.

In general, the routes up the higher peaks are the more difficult ones (see ratings below in the Yosemite Decimal System). The Standard Routes (aka easiest routes) up most peaks higher than 13,500 are Class 3, whereas most of those less than 13,500 are Class 2, but there are many exceptions (see Garratt and Martin, 1992).

Satori On the Mountain

Then suddenly everything was just like jazz: it happened in one insane second or so: I looked up and saw Japhy running down the mountain in huge twenty-foot leaps, running, leaping, landing with a great drive of his booted heels, bouncing five feet or so, running, then taking another long crazy yelling yodelaying sail down the sides of the world and in that flash I realized it's impossible to fall off mountains you fool and with a yodel of my own I suddenly got up and began running down the mountain after him doing exactly the same huge leaps, the same fantastic runs and jumps, and in the space of about five minutes I'd guess Japhy Ryder and I (in my sneakers, driving the heels of my sneakers right into sand, rock, boulders, I didn't care any more I was so anxious to get down out of there) came leaping and yelling like mountain goats or I'd say like Chinese lunatics of a thousand years ago, enough to raise the hair on the head of the meditating Morley by the lake, who said he looked up and saw us flying down and couldn't believe it. In fact with one of my greatest leaps and loudest screams of joy I came flying right down to the edge of the lake and dug my sneakered heels into the mud and just fell sitting there, glad. Japhy was already taking his shoes off and pouring sand and pebbles out. It was great. I took off my sneakers and poured out a couple of buckets of lava dust and said "Ah Japhy you taught me the final lesson of them all, you can't fall off a mountain."

"And that's what they mean by the saying, 'When you get to the top of a mountain, keep climbing', Smith."

"Dammit that yodel of triumph of yours was the most beautiful thing I ever heard in my life. I wish I'd a had a tape recorder to take it down."

"Those things aren't made to be heard by the people below," says Japhy dead serious.

Jack Kerouac, *The Dharma Bums*, 1958.

CLASSES OF CLIMBS USED IN THIS BOOK (YOSEMITE DECIMAL SYSTEM)

Class 1; hiking on a trail or bike path; walking uphill; walking along a clear, well-establish trail

Class 2; hiking across-country (no trail), requiring route-finding skills; occasionally using hands for balance, but not pulling yourself up with them; dogs can climb this

Class 3; scrambling on rocks using hands as well as feet; must use hands for progress but don't need to search for holds; hands pull straight up, not complicated counterforce holds (laybacks, stemming, etc.); rope may be used to provide comfort; might survive a fall

Class 4; exposed climbing such as a ladder going up the side of a water tank; climbing on steep terrain requiring a roped belay; rope required to prevent serious injury if a fall occurs; unroped falls fatal

99

Table 5-1. Summits higher than 13,000 ft, listed from HIGHEST TO LOWEST. Locations given are general; refer to Maps for exact locations. UN means unnamed summits on USGS 1:24,000-scale topographic maps that have spot elevations.

Name	Elev. Ft	Rank	Location	Class
Crestone Peak	14294	7	Crestone Group	3
Crestone Needle	14197	19	Crestone Group	3
Kit Carson Mtn	14165	23	Crestone Group	3
Challenger Point	14081	34	Crestone Group	2.5
Columbia Point	13980	56	Crestone Group; aka "Kat Carson"	2.5
Mt Adams	13931	66	North of Crestone Group	2.5
UN 13799	13799	107	Crestone Group; "Obstruction Peak"	2
Pico Asilado	13611	188	Head of Cottonwood Creek	3.5
Tijeras Pk	13604	189	Head of Deadman Creek	3
UN 13580	13580	200	South of Mt. Adams	2
Broken Hand Pk	13573	209	Head of Cottonwood Creek	2.5
Fluted Pk	13554	216	Head of Lake Fork, N. Crestone Cr.	2
UN 13546	13546	222	W of Mt Adams; "Montana Mujeres"	2.5
UN 13541	13541	224	btwn Willow and Macey Creeks	2
Milwaukee Pk	13522	242	Head of Cottonwood Creek	3
UN 13517	13517	244	btwn Willow and Macey Creeks	3
Eureka Mtn	13507	252	Btwn San Isabel and N. Crestone Cr.	3
UN 13495	13495	260	S of Tijeras Peak	2
UN 13419	13419	308	btwn Fluted and Comanche Peaks	3
Cleveland Pk	13414	311	Head of Pole Creek	2
UN 13401	13401	321	btwn Pole Cr and L. Sand Cr.	3
UN 13398	13398	322	btwn Willow and Macey Creeks	3
UN 13384	13384	327	aka "Deadman Peak"	3
Music Mtn	13380	333	Head of Deadman Creek	2.5
Hermit Pk	13350	353	Btwn Rito Alto and San Isabel Cr.	3
Venable Pk	13334	367	Head of N. Crestone Creek	2
UN 13325	13325	373	Mt Adams NE Ridge	2
UN 13290	13290	408	Btwn Tijeras Pk and Music Mtn	3
Comanche Pk	13277	418	Head of Middle Fork, N. Crestone Cr.	2
UN 13270	13270	423	aka "Crestolita"	2
UN 13254	13254	438	btwn Venable Peak and Eureka Mtn	3
UN 13244	13244	444	btwn Comanche and Venable Peaks	2
UN 13202	13202	489	btwn Pole Cr and Cleveland Gulch	2
UN 13153	13153	520	aka "Pico Guante"	2
UN 13151	13151	522	on NW Ridge of Kit Carson	3
UN 13054	13054	606	SE corner Groundhog Basin	3
UN 13050	13050	609	between the Deadman Lakes	2
UN 13012	13012	632	just N of Venable Pass	1.5
UN 13005	13005	635	Btwn Eureka Mtn and Hermit Peak	1.5
UN 12957	12957		head of Groundhog Basin	3

1 Climbing Class, per the Yosemite Decimal System, of the easiest route up. A rating of 2.5 indicates a mostly Class 2 climb with some short class 3 sections.

A Warning: Gravity Doesn't Care

Experienced climbers understand that mountains are unforgiving of mistakes. It doesn't matter whether you are an experienced climber or a complete novice. Whether you are a good person or a bad person, have lots of friends or none. If you are in steep terrain, get into difficulty beyond your abilities, and slip or fall unroped, gravity WILL take you down. And it happens very fast. Every year climbers on our local Thirteeners and Fourteeners get into trouble and nearly every year one or more people are injured and sometimes killed. To bring this point home, accident statistics are provided for the higher peaks in Appendix 2.

The solution is to *not get into difficulties beyond your abilities*, and to have your climbing partners assist you in regaining easier terrain before you fall. Most accidents on 2nd- and 3rd-Class, unroped routes result from one or more of three causes: (1) climbing by yourself (see Bairstow, 2006); (2) getting off-route by mistake (usually on the descent), and then trying to "save time" by pioneering a new path back to the intended route, or (3) ascending a route prepared for a climb on dry rock, with no ice axe, crampons or rope, and encountering snow or ice in a particularly critical spot. When people are tired on the descent they often get lazy or make poor decisions due to fatigue. Understandably, nobody likes to climb back up something they just descended, or admit to their party that they made a mistake and that everyone is going to have to re-climb a stretch they just downclimbed. But that solution is infinitely preferable to blundering on into uncharted terrain trying to "save face", and making dangerous moves trying to get back on route (see the trip report under Crestone Needle). And **never** glissade down steep snow without an ice axe.

Search And Rescue; CALL 911 from any phone

In the event of injury in the backcountry, or for a seriously overdue party, call the Saguache County Search and Rescue at 911. Call are received at the Saguache County Sheriff's Office, but local S&R teams will be dispatched, usually with help from the Baca Volunteer Fire Department.

The Confusing Terminology of the Crestone Group Peaks

Since the early 1900s, there have been four named Fourteeners in the Crestone Group; Crestone Peak (the highest at 14,294 ft, with twin summits 500 ft apart), Crestone Needle 14,197 ft, a sharp pinnacle on the divide, 0.6 mi ESE of Crestone Peak; named in 1923), Kit Carson Mountain (a flat summit 1 mile long with two deep declivities, which flank the central spire of the true summit, at 14,165 ft), and Humboldt Peak (14,064 ft, lying 1.8 mi ENE of Crestone Peak, off the divide). However, the terminology of the 1800s is more confusing. The group of jagged high peaks was called the Trois Tetons by French fur trappers in the early 1800s, but called the Spanish Craggs by other early Anglo map makers. Hayden (1877) named two of the peaks Crestone and Kit Carson, but later cartographers ignored his names and continued to refer to the group as the Trois (or Tres) Tetons (e.g. Wheeler, 1877). Wheeler named the flat-summit mountain Frustrum Peak, a name not used by anyone else before or after. To make matters worse, some miners in Crestone called the flat-summit mountain Mount Crestone or Crestone Peak, although that latter name was the name of another mountain, the summit of which was barely visible from Crestone. To understand the confusing history of usage, read Hart (1931).

101

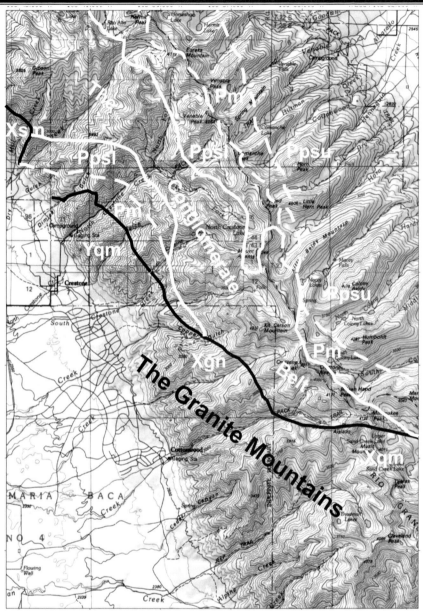

Fig. 5-2. Geology of the Crestone high peaks, from Hermit Peak in the north to Cleveland Peak in the south. West of the black line (the Crestone Thrust fault) the mountains are composed of Precambrian igneous/metamorphic basement rocks (granites Xqm, Yqm /gneisses Xgn). To the north and east of the Crestone Thrust, the four "Fourteeners" lie at the southern end of "The Conglomerate Belt", underlain by the Crestone Conglomerate. Flanking the conglomerate belt are peaks of sandstone, labeled Pm, Ppsl, and Ppsu.; all high peaks from Mt. Adams north are composed of sandstone. Contours and elevations are in meters.

THE SANDSTONE PEAKS (Hermit Peak, south through Fluted Peak; see Fig. 5.2)

Attitude is Everything

The northern peaks described in this Guide (Hermit, Eureka, Venable, Comanche, and Fluted Peaks) are similar in elevation and rock type, so likewise in climbing style. All five are composed of well-stratified beds of sandstone (Minturn and Sangre de Cristo Formations), tilted 25° to 50° to the west or southwest. Geologists call the tilt (and its direction) the "attitude of the strata". In all five peaks, this "attitude" strongly determines the nature of the climb. The obvious stratification and tilt controls the shape of these mountains, which generally have smooth, planar, grassy slopes on the west side of the divide, and much steeper and cliffier slopes (cirque headwalls) on the eastern side of the divide.

As climbers know, the easiest climbing on well-stratified ("boilerplate") rock slabs is on ridges, or up faces where the beds tilt into the slope. There the breaks along bedding-planes make nice sharp bucket-holds for upward climbing, and tend to catch loose debris from above, leaving the ridge relatively clean. In contrast, where slabs tilt out of the slope, you end up climbing up a series of outward-sloping ramps littered with loose rocks. The outward tilt of the ledges and slabs constantly keeps you a little off balance (ever tried pulling yourself up onto an outward-sloping ledge?), and loose rocks lying on the slabs act like ball bearings under your feet. It's also easy to dislodge such rocks onto your climbing partner. On steeper ridges, outward-sloping slabs become a real pain.

Edward Whymper discovered this principle on the Matterhorn, where after 7 attempts on the south ridges (where fractures tilted out of the slope), he finally found success on the (even steeper) Hornli Ridge on the opposite (north) side, because there the fractures dipped into the slope. When he finally attained the summit, he looked down on the competing Italian party, still struggling far below on the outward-sloping ledges.

The climbing routes described below start at the northernmost peak in this Guidebook (Hermit Peak, at the head of San Isabel Creek) and proceed southwards.

HERMIT PEAK (13,350 FT; RANK 353)

Hermit Peak is the easiest Thirteener to climb in the entire Sangres, because you can drive a 4WD vehicle to within 0.3 miles of the summit at Hermit Pass! (from the east side only). To reach Hermit Pass from the west side, you have to hike to the head of North Crestone, San Isabel, or Rito Alto Creeks and take the Loop Trail (Forest Trail 747) to Hermit Pass. From the pass it is an easy 0.3 mile walk south to the summit, with an elevation gain of only 350 feet.

Hermit Peak can also be climbed by its long Southwest Ridge from the Loop Trail where it passes from the San Isabel to the Rito Alto valleys. From this high pass (elevation 12,450 ft) it is a 0.85-mile scramble to the summit, gaining 900 ft in elevation (Plate 1). The crux is a steep cliffy section 100 feet high about 0.3 miles from the pass, at 12,800 feet. Unfortunately, the ridge is composed of lower Sangre de Cristo Formation (Psl, red sandstone), in which all beds tilt SW at 38°-47°, that is, out of the slope. The summit is formed by a resistant conglomeratic sandstone bed, 40-70 m thick, in the uppermost Minturn Formation (Pmu on Fig. 5-2).

EUREKA MOUNTAIN (13,507 FT; RANK 252)

Like Hermit Peak, Eureka Mountain can be climbed by either following the crest of the Sangres (Fig. 5-3), or by climbing its Southwest Ridge from a high pass on the Loop Trail (see Plate 1). The pass connects the San Isabel and North Crestone valleys and lies at 12,460 feet elevation. It is a 0.5 mile walk and scramble up the SW Ridge, but at a steeper average angle (elevation gain of 1047 feet in 0.4 miles) than on the SW Ridge of Hermit Peak. As at Hermit Peak, the strata on the SW Ridge unfortunately dip directly out of the slope on this ridge at 40-45°. For trip reports, see www.summitpost.org/mountain/rock/151851/eureka-mountain.html

Fig. 5-3. A view of Eureka Mountain, looking south from the summit of Hermit Peak 1.2 miles away. The broad pass in the foreground lies directly upslope of Horseshoe Lake or the east side of the divide; below the pass to the right (west) is the cirque of San Isabel Creek. To reach Eureka's summit you have to climb over UN 13,005 on the divide, and continue 0.5 mile south on the North Ridge of Eureka Mountain. Photo by Jon Bradford.

VENABLE PK (13,334 FT; RANK 367)

Venable Peak lies at the head of North Crestone Creek, between the North Fork and the Middle Fork. The easiest route is from Venable Pass (elev. 12,800 ft; Plate 1), which is accessed via the Venable Pass Trail (FT 859); from the Pass walk south along the range crest (Venable's North Ridge) for 0.6 miles, gaining about 400 ft (Fig. 5-4). To reach the summit, leave the range crest and continue SW for 0.2 miles to the summit, an additional gain of 134 ft. Because the summit lies west of the divide, it has a great view westward between the North and Middle Forks. Some of the ridges leading up to the summit from the North Fork Trail would also make good ascent routes. For trip reports, see www.summitpost.org/mountain/rock/415256/venable-peak.html.

Fig. 5-4. Venable Peak is illuminated by evening light, looking east from Groundhog Basin. The long, gentle North Ridge of Venable provides an easy ¾-mile ascent from Venable Pass and Trail 859. A more direct route ascends the Northwest Ridge (dotted line in center). In the foreground *krumholz* hunkers down in the lee of a ridge at treeline. Photo by Kane Engelbert

COMANCHE PEAK (13,277 FT; RANK 418)

Comanche Peak is probably the second-easiest Thirteener in the Sangres to climb, because it lies conveniently only 0.3 miles south of where the Venable-Comanche Trail (FT 1345) and Middle Fork Trail (FT 746) cross the divide at 12,700 feet elevation (Comanche Pass) (see map, Fig. 3-14). Walk and scramble 0.3 miles south from the pass along Comanche's North Ridge, for an elevation gain of only 577 ft (175 m). As at Venable Peak and northward, the North Ridge and summit are underlain by sandstone beds dipping 50° to the SW. For trip reports, see www.summitpost.org/mountain/rock/421023/comanche-peak.html.

Left photo by Charles Baxter; right photo by David Jilk.

Fig. 5-5. *Left*: the North Ridge of Comanche Peak, looking south from Comanche Pass. The ascent route is up the grassy slopes, which lie on a very planar bedding-plane surface. In the cliffs at left you can see the strata dipping to the right. *Right*: Looking down the North Ridge from near the summit, toward Comanche Pass (just to left of timber). In the distance, the upper trail is the Venable-Comanche (connector) Trail leading north to Phantom Terrace. The lower trail is the Middle Fork Trail of North Crestone Creek, Forest Trail 746.

FLUTED PEAK (13,554 FT; RANK 216)

Fluted Peak lies directly upslope of and NE of North Crestone Lake, but the easiest route from the Lake is not directly up that slope (the Southwest Face). Instead, from the north side of the lake, about in the middle, ascend a "hanging" tributary stream due north (see map, Fig. 3-14). The first 400 ft gain is steep, but then you reach the lip of the hanging valley and the slope eases. Continue north on the floor of this glaciated hollow for about 0.4 miles, then start turning east to aim for the prominent saddle on the crest of the range north of Fluted Peak; ascend due east up to the saddle at about elevation 13,180 ft. From there, follow the North Ridge of Fluted Peak southward for 0.3 miles to the summit, a gain of only 375 ft. As at all the peaks to the north, beds of the Sangre de Cristo sandstone dip 35°-40°SW, but don't cause a hindrance on this North Ridge route. For trip reports see www.summitpost.org/mountain/rock/153135/fluted-peak.html.

Fluted Peak, 13,554'

North Crestone Lake

Fig. 5-6. View of the Southwest Face of Fluted Peak, looking northeast from the Northwest Ridge of Mount Adams. The gray dotted line shows the easy route to the summit starting on the north shore of North Crestone Lake. Photo by Ryan Schilling.

NOTE: Because Venable, Comanche, and Fluted Peaks comprise the range crest at the head of the North Crestone drainage, all three can be climbed in an 11.3 mile-long loop from a camp at the "Trail Junction" in North Crestone Creek (elevation 9800 ft). To ascend to the range crest on a good trail, ascend the North Fork to the Venable Pass Trail and then up to Venable Pass (3.35 miles). From the Pass walk south 0.75 miles on the ridge crest to Venable Peak; backtrack to the divide and walk SE on the divide 0.3 miles until you intersect the Venable-Comanche Trail; walk 0.87 miles south on the trail (whic is west of the range crest here) to Comanche Pass; continue south 0.3 miles to Comanche Peak; walk SSE along the range crest to a saddle and then up to UN 13,419, a total of 0.85 miles; [this unnamed point is not ranked as a separate peak, but if so would rank about 308th in the state, being higher than either Venable Peak or Comanche Peak!]; continue SE along the range crest 0.77 miles to Fluted Peak; from Fluted Peak return to the saddle north of the peak, and descend west then south via a tributary valley to North Crestone Lake, 1.08 miles; walk downvalley on the North Crestone Trail (FT 744) 3.0 miles back to your base camp. Total elevation gain over the 11.3 mile loop is 5105 ft, including gains made summiting four Thirteeners along the range crest. Although the climbing on this loop is easy, and 7.2 miles of the route is on good trails, it will take a fit party to complete the loop in a single summer day (15 hours of daylight).

MT. ADAMS (13,931 FT; RANK 66); First Ascent July 23, 1916 (?) by the Ellingwood party (see Bueler, 2000, p. 122)

Mt. Adams has been climbed by three ridges (West, Northwest, and Northeast; see Fig. 19). Climbers often favor the route with the shortest approach and best trail (up Willow Creek to Willow Lake, then up the West Ridge), although the approach up South Crestone Creek to South Crestone Lake and the NW Ridge is only slightly longer. The longest approach is up N. Crestone Creek to N. Crestone Lake, and thence up the Northwest or Northeast Ridges. Mount Adams is a harder and more dangerous mountain than the peaks farther north. On July 10, 2002 Michael O'Hanlon, author of a 1999

Guidebook to the Sangres and an experienced climber, fell to his death. Treat Adams with respect, and avoid snowbanks high on the peak unless you have an ice axe and experience. See www.summitpost.org/mountain/rock/150608/adams-mount.html

Approach to West Ridge of Mount Adams from Willow Lake (see Plate 3)

Point	Mileage	Feature
9	0.9	from the west end of the lake, ascend the hanging valley directly to the north, to the saddle at 12,900 ft, directly west of Mt. Adams. This saddle was formed by erosion where a fault crosses the ridge
20	1.3	scramble from saddle to summit of Mt. Adams

West Ridge: The easy route stays on the grassy slopes on the south side of the West Ridge, which is 3rd class to about 13,400 ft. At that point you have two choices. To continue on 3rd class, traverse around below the cliffs on the south side of the mountain and ascend the south ridge ledges to the summit. A more direct route (West Ridge Direct) stays on the ridge crest all the way to the summit block. From 13,400 ft you continue straight up the ridge nose, which turns 4th class on some slabs (which unfortunately all dip out of the slope at 25-35°). Then, from the small notch below the summit block, you will have to ascend a low 5th-class headwall 40 feet high, before reaching the summit. The entire West Ridge is underlain by well-bedded sandstone of the lower Sangre de Cristo formation.

Fig. 5-7. *Left*: The saddle between Mt. Adams (peak at right) and UN 13,564 (peak at left) can be reached from Willow Lake (upper part of approach shown by black lines). From there Adam's summit is attained via the West Ridge route (white line); *Right*: view east up the West Ridge route (white line) from the saddle (foreground).Photos by Clyde Lovett, estonecreations.com.

Northwest Ridge: is said to be the easiest route up Adams by Roach and Roach (2001). There are two approaches, from the head of South Crestone Creek, or from North Crestone Lake (see Plate 2). Both approaches lead to a prominent saddle at 12,780 feet on Adam's Northwest Ridge. From this saddle the Ridge is a 3rd class ascent in dry conditions, but a step at 13,400 feet might require rope if ridge is icy or wet. From a bench on the ridge just north of the summit block, you once again have two choices. In dry conditions, traverse (3rd class) east across the upper East Face and some small gullies, then pick a gully and ascend to the summit. Early in the season the East Face and its gullies may be snow covered, which makes this exposed traverse a bit dicey. An alternative route continues upward on the Northwest Ridge, but on this route you will have to surmount a class 5.3 step about 15 ft-high. The bedrock is all sandstone of the lower Sangre de Cristo Formation, and lamentably, dips 25-35°SW, out of slope, creating the ball bearing effect.

Northeast Ridge: this is the long ridge on the crest of the Range that connects to Fluted Peak. It is a sustained 3rd Class climb and is usually tackled by more experienced parties as part of a longer traverse, descending Adams by another ridge.

THE CONGLOMERATE PEAKS (Challenger Point, Kit Carson Peak, Crestone Peak, Crestone Needle, Broken Hand Peak, Milwaukee Peak)

The conglomerate peaks are those underlain at the summit, and/or on the approaches, by the Crestone Conglomerate. Peaks made of conglomerate comprise the highest part of the range, including the four prominent Fourteeners of the Crestone Group. This is no coincidence. First, the Crestone Conglomerate is so hard it is more resistant to erosion than the other rock types, even the granite (which is typically the hardest rock in Colorado Mountain ranges). Second, the uplift of the range along the Sangre de Cristo fault has been greatest in the northern part of the Conglomerate Belt, based on the height of recent fault scarps that displace the alluvial fans (McCalpin, 1982). The combination of most rapid uplift and most resistance to erosion ensures that the peaks above Crestone will be continue to be the highest ones for the foreseeable geologic future.

Peaks underlain by the Crestone Conglomerate offer a unique style of climbing which often takes advantage of "knobs" (actually, gravel- or cobble-size clasts embedded in the conglomerate) and sometimes pits (voids left where clasts have weathered out). In places the fracture spacing in the conglomerate is so wide (greater than 30 feet) that crack climbing is not feasible, and is replaced by friction climbing using the knobs. On a grand scale, weak beds occur in the conglomerate hundreds of vertical feet apart, and in places these offer the only easy avenues for ascent (e.g., Fig. 5-14). One famous such avenue is "Kit Carson Avenue", which provides the standard ascent route to Kit Carson Mountain from the Challenger Point-Kit Carson saddle.

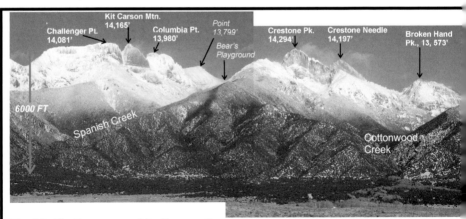

Fig. 5-8. The Fourteeners of the Crestone Group. Photo taken 25-January-2010.

CHALLENGER POINT (14,081 FT; RANK 35); First recorded ascent on June 24, 1881 by Wm. Edward White and party (White, 1881)

Challenger Point is the highest point on the large summit of the Kit Carson Mountain massif, which forms the prominent flat-topped peak seen from the floor of the San Luis Valley. This entire flat-topped summit ridge lies northwest of Kit Carson's true summit elevation 14,165 ft), formed by a rather sharp pinnacle flanked by two deep gashes. Prior to 1986 the point-now-known-as-Challenger was not named on USGS topo maps and was not considered a separate named peak, much less one of Colorado's 54 "Fourteeners." However, when White (1881) ascended the mountain in 1881 from Willow Lake, he called the mountain "Crestone Peak," a name later given by USGS to another peak!

Fig. 5-9. View of the Kit Carson Massif, looking south from the saddle between Mt, Adams and Pt. 13,546. Dotted lines in center show some of many possible 3rd-class scrambling routes up to Challenger Point (see Plate 3). The right line ascends the "dirty gully", which contains ice and loose rocks at many times of year. Additional ascent lines exist to the right of the dirty gully, along the edge of Kit Carson's impressive triangular North Buttress (unclimbed, as far as I know).

FROM WILLOW LAKE: Challenger Point is the most-climbed mountain on the western side of the Sangres, because it has a relatively easy standard route from Willow Lake, and because the approach to Willow Lake and camping there is popular and pleasant.

Standard (North Ridge) Route up Challenger Peak, Kit Carson Mountain (Plate 3)

Point	Mileage	Feature
3	0.4	from west end of lake, hike around north side of lake and cross Willow Creek above the waterfall
4	0.6	begin ascending the northern slopes of the Kit Carson massif, on the standard route to Challenger Point. There are many possible routes that avoid the steep boilerplate slabs to the south; two are shown above. The most common route ascends between the slabs and the 'dirty gully", but you can also use the gully, or ascend to the right of it.
5	1.1	reach crest of ridge at about 13,900 ft elevation; from here walk southeast along the crest of the summit ridge
6	1.35	summit of Challenger Peak, 14,081 ft (35th highest peak in Colorado)
7	1.5	descend to the notch between Challenger and Kit Carson Mountain
8	1.8	the point on Kit Carson Avenue where you turn left and begin ascending a broad gully toward the summit of Kit Carson

Fig. 5-10. Memorial plague at the summit of Challenger Point. It was officially named Challenger Point as a memorial after the Challenger Space Shuttle explosion of Jan. 28, 1986. Photo by Jared Workman.

Fig. 5-11. Routes on the "back side" (east side) of the Kit Carson massif, south of the summit of Challenger Point. The tw most popular routes are snow gullies that lead to the saddles on either side of Kit Carson's summit. Kirk Couloir leads to the Challenger-Kit Carson saddle, and the Outward Bound couloir to the Kit Carson-Columbia Point saddle. Both couloirs have steep snow at the to and require an ice axe, rope, and crampons in season. Photo by Jeff Valliere.

For many visitors to Crestone, Challenger is the first (and only) Fourteener they ever climb. Casual or inexperienced climbers may simply reverse their ascent route back to Willow Lake without continuing on to the true summit of Kit Carson Mountain, which involves more difficult and exposed climbing. Most of the difficulties parties have had o Challenger have resulted from descending, not using the standard ascent route, but wandering off farther east (to the right) where the slopes steepen downward. The result i they either become cliffed and have to backtrack northwest, or they try to downclimb steep slabs or snow chutes off-route, and slip. Kirk Couloir, which leads up to the notch between Challenger and Kit Carson, stays snow-filled until late in the season, and is a tempting quick descent route. However, it has a slope of 45 degrees at its steepest and cannot be glissaded safely until lower down where the gradient lessens, and then only by an experienced person with an ice axe.

Routes up Challenger Point From the West

Challenger Point can also be ascended via its Southwest Ridge, although the approach is more problematic now that the lower part of Spanish Creek trail is closed. From Willow Creek Park, hike south over the south lateral moraine and down into Copper Gulch. From Copper Gulch ascend through the trees to the crest of the Southwest Ridge, reaching it anywhere below about 13,200 feet. From that point the ridge steepens to 3rd class, and the last 400 vertical feet is very exposed 4th class which definitely requires a rope and protection. Parties can ascend either the linear gullies to their left, which rise to the summit ridge (and may be snow filled early in the season), or try the even more exposed ridges between. This is a sustained climb with no easy escape routes. Once you reach the 4th class section, you are committed.

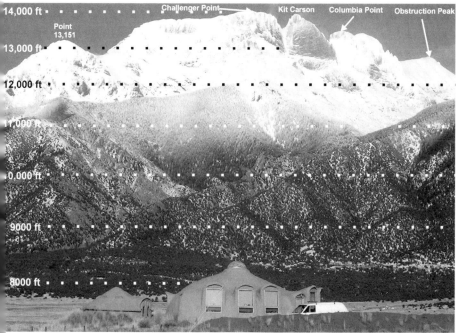

Fig. 5-12. Winter photo of Kit Carson Mountain from the Grants unit of the Baca Grande Subdivision. Directly below Challenger Point, the ridge trending directly toward the viewer above treeline, which then turns to the left below treeline, is the Southwest Ridge. The West Ridge forms the skyline at extreme left, punctuated by Point 13,151.

The only ridge that contains no known climbing routes is the West Ridge. This is the ridge that descends from the north end of the summit ridge of Kit Carson Mountain, and rounds the south side of Willow Creek valley. This ridge is less appealing than the Southwest Ridge, because the climbing parties either have to: (1) attain the ridge where crested, in which case they have to climb over UN 13,151 and descend it 250 ft to the saddle at 12,900 ft, before beginning to ascend the summit slabs, or (2) ascend directly to the saddle from Copper Gulch, a route guarded by cliffs they will have to work through. The only advantage of the second route is it allows you a close look at the so-called glacier perched at the head of Copper Gulch.

111

KIT CARSON MOUNTAIN (14,165 FT; RANK 23); First Ascent July 22, 1916 by a mixed party of seven (see Robertson, 2003)

On USGS topo maps, the label "Kit Carson Mountain" is splashed across the entire 1 mile-long top of the mountain mass, including three named summits (from north to south Challenger Point, Kit Carson, and Columbia Point). Only the sharp middle summit at 14,165 feet is the true summit of Kit Carson Mountain. This summit is a difficult Fourteener, guarded by deep cols to the north and south.

ROUTES FROM WILLOW CREEK: Class 3 via Challenger Point (standard route)
The standard rock route to Kit Carson's summit begins at the Challenger Point. Descend the ridgeline south for 300 vertical feet to the Challenger-Kit Carson notch. From the notch, follow a large ledge (Kit Carson Avenue) across the west face to a notch at the top of The Prow. Then follow the same ledge angling down across the south face to any of the large gullies that intersect it. In general, the gullies become easier to ascend the farther east you walk on the Avenue, so don't feel you have to ascend the first one. Kit Carson Avenue can snow covered early in the season, turning what would be a walk in the summer, into a nail-biting traverse over a 1400 ft-high cliff. So take a rope, ice axe, and crampons if you can see snow from Crestone. On your descent from the summit, tak care not to descend to soon, or you will be going down a harder gully than you ascended from Kit Carson Avenue. Kit Carson is not a summit to underestimate, and has been the scene of quite a few climbing accidents (see Appendix 2). The class of climbing is only moderate (Class 3), but the exposure is ferocious. Most accidents have happened to people climbing alone, and on the descent.

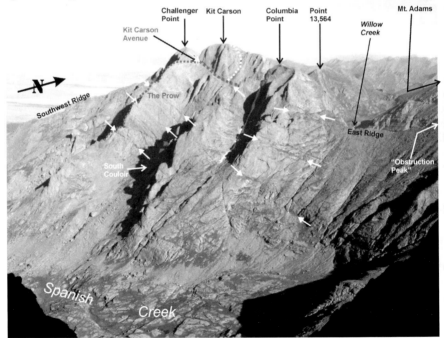

Fig. 5-13. The complex South Face of the Kit Carson massif. White arrows highlight beds ir the Crestone Conglomerate. Dotted lines show climbing routes. Photo by Jared Workman.

(summarized *from Robertson, 2008*)

Kit Carson Mountain (true summit), Crestone Peak, and Crestone Needle were the last three of Colorado's Fourteeners to be climbed. You might think that the final conquerors of these "unclimbable" summits were macho-men fueled by brute muscles and testosterone. But you would be wrong. All three summits were climbed in the space of three days, in July of 1916, by a mixed man-woman team of professors from Colorado College. Sorry, guys.....

Team leader Albert Ellingwood was born in 1888 in Cedar Rapids, Iowa, but attended high school and college in Colorado Springs. After he graduated in 1911, he became the College's first Rhodes Scholar and spent three years in England, where he joined the Oxford University Mountaineering Club. The Club took its holidays in English climbing centers and in the Swiss Alps, using ropes and pitons for technical climbing. In 1914 Albert returned to Colorado College to begin teaching political science, but he also brought with him his pitons (the first introduced to America) and his new technical skills in rock climbing. While playing tennis one day he met a fellow CC faculty member, Eleanor Davis.

Eleanor was born in 1885 in Greenfield, Massachusetts. She graduated from the Boston Normal School of Gymnastics (later absorbed by Wellesley College), and was a natural athlete. When she met Albert in 1914 she was a new instructor in the Department of Physical Education at Colorado College, where she would continue teaching until 1930. Albert and Eleanor began climbing together in 1914, starting around Colorado Springs.

However, by the summer of 1916 Albert was aiming for higher goals. So in July 1916 he organized a party to attempt the last unclimbed Fourteeners in Colorado, the Crestone Group in the Sangre de Cristo Mountains. His group of eight climbers set out from Colorado Springs. Eleanor's sister Sarah took most of the party's gear by train, using a spur railroad that ran three times a week from Villa Grove into the town of Crestone.

In Crestone Sarah met the rest of the party, who had walked for several days to save train fare. They then hired burros to take their gear up Willow Creek, and the next morning made a first ascent of Kit Carson Mountain, via Challenger Point and Kit Carson Avenue. Two days later the "more energetic four of the party" (Albert Ellingwood, Eleanor Davis, Joe Deutschbein, and Bee Rogers) moved their camp to Spanish Creek. On July 24 the four made the first ascent of Crestone Peak, presumably via the Red Couloir on the northwest face. After summiting, Bee Rogers and Joe Deutschbein decided to return to camp. But Eleanor and Albert continued on to Crestone Needle via the Peak-to-Needle Traverse, making its first ascent in the same day. Thus in the space of three days, Albert and Eleanor had climbed the three "unclimbable" Fourteeners, including the Peak-To-Needle traverse, an intimidating route even today.

This was not the end of their association with the Crestone Group. In August of 1924 Albert and Eleanor returned to Crestone Needle, this time to attempt its eastern arête. Climbing as a team they reached the summit about 5 pm. This route, now known as the Ellingwood Arete, established a new standard for its day in Colorado rock climbing.

Albert went on to a distinguished climbing career, being one of three men in the '20s who had climbed all of Colorado's Fourteeners. However, his career was cut short when he died in 1934, at age 46 in Evanston, Indiana. [See an interesting interview from 2006 with Albert's son, Robert Ellingwood (born 1918), at http://boulderlibrary.org/oralhistory/]. In contrast, Eleanor married George Ehrman in 1930 and gave up teaching and rock climbing to become a homemaker. She died in 1993, at the age of 107.

There are two mixed snow-and-rock routes up Kit Carson, leading to the notches on either side of the summit pyramid (Fig. 5-11). These couloirs start out from Willow valley between Willow Lake and the unnamed upper lake.

Fig. 5-14. Descending Kit Carson Avenue from its high point at the top of the Prow, toward the Kit Carson-Challenger saddle. Early-season snow still covers part of the Avenue, requiring a delicate traverse. An unroped fall here would be fatal. Photo by Jared Workman.

The Kirk Couloir: Grade II, Class 3, steep snow and ice; This broad couloir leads to the Challenger-Kit Carson notch (13,780 feet). Most climbing parties are coming from Willow Lake so they ascend rock slabs to the downhill end of th broad snowfield that persists long into the summer, about halfway up the "back side" of the massif (Fig. 5-11). The broad snowfield narrows progressively into a couloir at 13,000 feet, and steepens. The steepest part of the snow is between 13,400 and 13,600 feet, where the slope approaches 45°. The couloir should only be attempted by experienced parties with ice axes, crampons, rope, and protection. Care must also be taken in glissading this route, because the snow surface stays steep until it hits big rocks (lack of runout). Fatalities have occurred here (see Appendix 2).

The Outward Bound Couloir; Grade II, Class 3 steep snow & ice; The Outward Bound Couloir leads up to the Kit Carson-Columbia Point saddle at 13,620 feet. This couloir is narrower than the Kirk and makes for more of an alpine-feeling snow climb. Trip report on Summitpost.org have all had good things to say about this couloir, as being a fun and truly alpine experience. Because you reach the saddle south of Kit Carson's summit, you will avoid all the traffic going to Carson's summit on the standard route from Challenge Point. That includes luckless people trying to glissade down Kirk's Couloir.

ROUTES FROM SPANISH CREEK:
South Couloir; Grade II, Class 3 moderate snow; The only non-technical climb from Spanish Creek is the prominent snow couloir east of The Prow (30-35 degrees). This is the South Couloir and it leads to the same notch as does the Outward Bound Couloir, bu from the opposite side of the mountain. The South Couloir melts out long before the north-side couloirs, so makes a good snow climb only early or very late in the season; in July and August it is a dirty, rock-filled gully. It can also be used as a descent route from the notch.

Southwest Ridge; Grade II, Class 3+; The Southwest Ridge was described under routes to Challenger Point.

COLUMBIA POINT (13,980 FT; RANK 56); First Ascent 1925.

Prior to 2003 this summit had long been referred to as "Kat Carson", and was listed as the 56th highest peak in Colorado (with the highest 53 peaks being the Fourteeners). The summit was officially named by the Board of Geographic Names in June 2003 as a memorial for the Space Shuttle Columbia, which disintegrated upon reentry on Feb. 1, 2003. The easiest route up is its East Ridge from "Obstruction Peak", and is used by parties coming up from South Colony Lakes. However, parties coming up from the Crestone side will be ascending it from Kit Carson Avenue and the Kit Carson-Columbia Point saddle. Roach and Roach (2001) suggest that you climb directly up "exposed, Class 3 blocks" from the saddle to the summit.

CRESTONE PEAK (14,294 FT; RANK 7); First Ascent July 24, 1916 by a 2 man-2 woman party (see Robertson, 2003)

Crestone Peak is the highest peak in the Crestone Group, whose twin summits comprised two of the three Trois Tetons, the name used for Crestone Peak and Needle up through 1892 (Hart, 1931). Crestone Peak was the second-to-last Fourteener to be climbed (1916). It is still proclaimed by many to be the hardest Fourteener to climb, yet that does not discourage dozens of climbers attempting the peak every summer. Most parties (75%) approach the Peak from South Colony Lakes on the eastern side, rather than from the west via Cottonwood Creek. However, now that almost all of the Cottonwood Creek Trail is in the Rio Grande National Forest and open to public access, there will probably be more attempts from the western side.

Below we describe only the two easiest, class 3 routes up the Peak. There are many harder routes of a semi-technical (Class 4) and technical (Class 5) nature, but refer to Roach (1999) for descriptions of those routes.

Fig. 5-15. Climber ascending the South Face (Red Couloir) route up Crestone Peak. Due to the popularity of this route, there may be parties above you, and loose rocks are a constant problem here. Note the helmet on the climber, which we definitely recommend for this route, particularly on summer weekends. Photo by Jared Workman.

ROUTES FROM COTTONWOOD LAKE: The Standard Route is the South Face, which goes right up the Face along a shallowly-indented couloir made by a weak bed of red conglomerate (Fig. 5-15). This is a non-technical route, as long as you stay in the couloir. Most parties ascend up the midline of the swale, which has the easiest climbing, but is also the most exposed to rockfalls from parties higher up. After 700 vertical feet of climbing in the red couloir, you top out in the 14,180-ft saddle between the West and East peaks, called the Red Notch. To reach the higher West Summit of Crestone Peak, scramble 250 feet westward up easy Class 3 to the summit. To attain the slightly lower (14,260 ft) east Summit, return to the Red Notch and scramble up slightly harder Class 3 to the East Summit.

ROUTES FROM THE BEARS PLAYGROUND: The original ascent route of Ellingwood and Davis, and the standard route up Crestone Peak for many years, was the "Northwest Couloir" or "Red Gully" Route on the North Face. From the Bear's Playground at the head of Spanish Creek, work up and west into a large reddish or snow-filled trough (the Red Gully). Parties who have recently ascended this gully have given it mixed reviews. The gully contains more loose rock than the South Face routes, and naturally retains snow later in the year. The route actually makes a better snow climb in early season than a rock climb later in the summer. However, be aware that the head of the Gully slopes at 45°-50° and there is little runout at the lower end of the gully, but instead steeper rock bands. For snow climbs take a rope, crampons, and ice axe. In summer when the snow begins to melt in the Gully, pockets of refrozen water ice persist throughout the summer, hiding under a thin layer of dirt, sand, and loose rocks. This slows parties down as they try to avoid dislodging rocks onto their partners. Overall, the Red Gully is not a frequently used route and should be undertaken only by experienced parties who get an early start from the Bear's Playground.

CRESTONE NEEDLE (14,197 FT; RANK 19); First Ascent July 24, 1916 by a 1 man-1 woman party (see Robertson, 2003)
Crestone Needle was the last of Colorado's Fourteeners to be climbed, by the intrepid party of Ellingwood and Davis (see Albert and Eleanor). Roach (1999) proclaims that the Needle is "slightly easier to climb than Crestone Peak, but still one of the hardest Fourteeners." The standard and easiest route goes up the two prominent couloirs on the eastern edge of the South Face. The most common approach is via a high, traversing trail that leads from the Eye of the Needle Pass to the bottom of the eastern (right) couloir, crossing the grassy slopes and rock ribs just below and on the south side of the Needle-Broken Hand ridge. When the right couloir begins to steepen, look for cairns indicating the crossover to the left (western) couloir. Ascend the western couloir until it merges with the eastern one. When the couloir tops out, scramble west to the summit. The knobby holds on the Crestone Conglomerate have been compared to those on a climbing wall.

Despite its reputation for being easier than Crestone Peak, the Needle sees twice as many accidents (Appendix 2). One-third of those accidents are from the technical Ellingwood Ledges (Ellingwood Arete) route. The remainder, however, involve the more heavily-trafficked, Class 3 South Face route. Many of these accidents are due to being hit by falling rocks dislodged by parties above, or from getting off-route during the descent.

Jared Workman shares a scary, yet typical, account of the dangers of getting off-route during the descent:

"At first I thought I was OK and [down]climbed quickly. I came upon a sketchy 4th class down climb and here I should have known better and turned back. I was a fool and kept going. The next down climb was 5+ and required a good bit of mental concentration. Soon I came to a down climb with a rappel sling set up. For some stupid, asinine reason, I free handed down it.

I have to say that I don't know at what point my wits and common sense left me. I realized my serious error when I finally came upon a rappel point which was not climbable. The walls sloped outward leaving no way to climb. I looked out and saw a huge drop down to Cottonwood Lake. I think it was here that I realized the enormity of my error. I didn't want to climb back up because the prospect of returning over the sections I had come down was very daunting. I spent some time considering my situation. I quickly realized that I may have to wait at a point overlooking some tents on Cottonwood Lake to call for help if I couldn't find another way out. I contemplated the fact that no one would know where I was and a broken leg might mean death. The only positive of this point was that I managed to keep a cool head. It was good to learn that I don't panic.

I climbed back up a 5th class section and headed towards the wall of the couloir. From there I gained a new couloir and headed down into it. The bottom was even worse with no prospect of escape. At this point I really started to worry. I contoured up the side of this couloir and into the next.

God must have been smiling on me because this one let out below the correct route. I sat down and collected my wits, this basically meant shaking for about ten minutes. It was here that I decided I would buy walkie talkies, carry rope, and bring a partner on any real climbs I attempt in the future. " (underlining added).

PEAK-TO-NEEDLE TRAVERSE

This traverse is the ultimate climbing experience in the Crestone Group, and has been called "one of Colorado's great Fourteener traverses." However, it requires good route-finding skills, Class 4 climbing ability, and a tolerance for sustained exposure at high elevations. Because the traverse requires solid Class 4 climbing skills, it is a semi-technical climb and too advanced to cover in this Guidebook. Consult Roach (1999) for a good route description. Note that half of the accidents cited for Crestone Peak in Appendix 2 occurred on the Peak-to-Needle Traverse, even though the Traverse experiences only a tiny fraction of the traffic on the main peak.

BROKEN HAND PEAK (13,573 FT; RANK 209)

Broken Hand Peak is the prominent sentinel at the head of Cottonwood Creek, visible from the floor of the San Luis Valley. Broken Hand is, like Crestone Peak and the Needle, composed of west-dipping beds of Crestone Conglomerate. The west slopes are gentler, broken and grassy, permitting a zig-zag Class 2 scramble (Fig. 5-17, right). The West Face can be climbed from Cottonwood Lake, although it is more often climbed by parties from South Colony lakes that enter Marvelous Valley via Eye of the Needle Pass. From the summit of Broken Hand you get a great view of Crestone Needle, without having to deal with crowds. You can also look down the staggering East Face of Broken Hand, and feel relieved you did not have to come up that way.

Fig. 5-16. A climbing party nears the summit of Crestone Needle, after completing the Peak-to-Needle Traverse. They have just ascended the most difficult part, the 500 ft rise on the north side of the needle. View is to the Northwest. Photo by Jared Workman

Fig. 5-17. *Left*: View of Broken Hand Peak (center) from near the summit of Crestone Needle; view is to the south. Dotted line shows one possible Class 2 route that zig-zags up through grassy ledges. Photo by Ed Fornataro; *Right*: View of a rock pinnacle above the grassy ledge route up Broken Hand. Photo by Ryan Schilling.

MILWAUKEE PEAK (13,522 FT; RANK 242)

The easiest route up Milwaukee Peak is to hike up Deadman Creek and ascend the gentle and grassy Southeast slopes (Class 2). However, the hike up Deadman is no picnic (see Chapter 3). If you find yourself in Cottonwood Creek, you can climb Milwaukee Peak from the Cottonwood Creek Trail, which crosses between the twin summits of Milwaukee Peak (Chapter 3). To attain the higher (South) summit of Milwaukee Peak, the standard route is a Class 3 climb on the East Face, starting at Milwaukee Pass.

Photo by Ryan Schilling.

Fig. 5-18. The beginning of the route utilizes a ramp that is normally 6 feet wide, but which disappears in one short stretch, necessitating a very exposed crux traverse above the ramp. The view here is looking south from Milwaukee Pass at the ramp; note the beds of Crestone Conglomerate dipping into the slope to the right, making good handholds and footholds. Once the ramp ends, work your way upslope via a grassy shelf, and then one of several 3rd- Class gullies to the summit.

PEAKS OF GRANITIC ROCKS

The southernmost four peaks covered by this Guidebook all lie south of the Crestone-Sand Creek Thrust fault, and are composed of Precambrian granites and gneisses. So say goodbye to the knobby handholds and ramplike ledges of the Crestone Conglomerate, and say hello to fractured rock crack climbing.

PICO ASILADO (13,611 FT; RANK 188)

The summit of Pico Asilado lies half a mile southwest of the summit of Milwaukee Peak, separated by a broad saddle created by erosion of the Crestone-Sand Creek Thrust fault. The standard summit route lies on the East Ridge, which connects Pico with Milwaukee Peak (Fig. 5-20), but it is a class 4 climb, making it the hardest "standard route" in the region. Garratt and Martin (1992) suggest that an easier route for parties ascending Cottonwood Creek would be to ascend its easternmost glaciated tributary (from Point 9 in Plate 4) to the ridge crest west of Pico Asilado, and ascend to the summit via UN 3,020 and Pico's West Ridge. This route may become the "new standard", if the Cottonwood Creek Trail becomes open to public access.

Now that Deadman Creek is publicly accessible, an even easier route is available from Deadman's cirque #2 (see Plate 5). This route would ascend to the head of cirque #2 and then wander up the grassy slopes of Pico's West Face, on the way to attaining the West Ridge. From there it is a 0.3 mile hike and a 0.2 mile low Class 3 scramble to the summit. This route may replace the dangerous East Ridge Route, the Class 4 pitches of which have been responsible for at least one fatality (July 2, 2006; 58 yr-old man, who had climbed all of Colorado's Fourteeners, fell to his death).

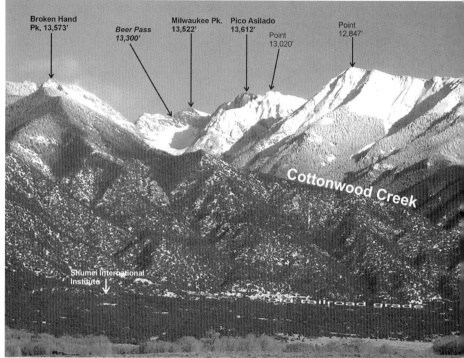

Fig. 5-19. Thirteeners rim the head of Cottonwood Creek, above the Baca Grande subdivision. Broken Hand and Milwaukee Peaks are composed of Crestone Conglomerate, whereas Pico Asilado and its satellites are composed of granite; the Crestone-Sand Creek Thrust runs between them. The three southernmost granite mountains of this Guidebook (Music, Tijeras, Cleveland), which lie south of Milwaukee Peak and rim the head of Deadman Creek , cannot be seen in this view.

Fig. 5-20. View of Pico Asilado's Southeast Face (center) and the East Ridge (right of the Face) that connects to Milwaukee Peak. The standard route for parties originating at Sand Creek Lakes ascends the East Ridge to the notch below the summit, and then wanders left to use Class 4 gullies to reach the summit. Easier routes to the summit exist on the "back side" of the mountain, which faces the San Luis valley (seen in the distance). Photo by Ryan Schilling.

120

MUSIC MOUNTAIN (13,380 FT; RANK 333)

The summit of Music Mountain looms over Upper Sand Creek Lake, 1635 feet below. Like the other summits south of Crestone Needle (Broken Hand, Milwaukee, Tijeras), Music Mountain is asymmetrical, with a very steep East Face and a gentler West Face with many grassy slopes and gullies. Historically, the standard route has been the 3rd Class East Ridge (Fig. 5-21), accessed from Lower Sand Creek Lake, because until recently there was no public access for west-side approaches up Deadman Creek.

However, with Deadman Creek now being public land, the easiest route up Music would ascend its West Ridge south of cirque 3 of upper Deadman Creek (see Plate 5). This West Ridge route is gentler than the East Ridge, particularly its last part.

ig. 5-21. Tijeras Peak and Music Mountain dominate the Upper Sand Creek cirque, as seen om Marble Mountain. This cirque was featured as "The Oldest Church in America" by ature-worshipper Blair Brown in John Belushi's second-to-last movie, *Continental Divide*. ttp://movieclips.com/nWZqB-continental-divide-movie-the-oldest-church-in-america/ heir scene was shot from Music Pass. Photo by Jon Bradford.

IJERAS PEAK (13,604 FT; RANK 189)

he standard route up Tijeras has traditionally been from the east side and Lower Sand reek Lake, because the west side approach (Deadman Creek) was closed to the public ccess prior to 2004. Climbers would work their way through the cliff band above Lower and Lake and up the North face to the Northwest Ridge, and from there to the summit.

The West Ridge of Tijeras can also be ascended all the way from treeline in eadman Creek, via the ridge that separates the four northern cirques of the main valley, om the four southern cirques of the south glaciated tributary (see Fig. 3-34). Most of is 1.15 mile-long ridge from treeline (11,200 ft) to UN 13,290 trends due east-west.

From the crude trail to Deadman Lakes, hike directly east uphill through the trees for ¼ mile at the base of the West Ridge. The ridge is gentle but long, and gains 2090 feet before reaching UN 13,290. At that point the ridge turns SE and continues 1/3 of a mile across a broad saddle, and to the summit of Tijeras.

CLEVELAND PEAK (13,414 FT; RANK 311)

Although Cleveland Peak could be approached from the north from the largest of the Deadman Lakes, Jacobs and Ormes (2000) recommend an approach from Pole Creek Lake (elevation 11,980 ft) at the head of Pole Creek. From the Lake ascend the remainder of the valley floor and then scramble up the cirque headwall to the SE to the ridge at 13,020 feet. This is the West Ridge of Cleveland Peak. Hike NE and then E along this very flat ridge for 2/3 of a mile to Cleveland's summit.

Lito Tejada-Flores; A Philosopher of Mountaineering

Crestone's best-known mountaineer did his signature climbs in other ranges, starting in the 1950s at Taquitz Rock and Yosemite Valley in California, moving on to Chamonix and the French Alps (first ascents of the Aguille du Plan and le Cardinal), the Tetons of Wyoming (first Grand Traverse), a first ascent of a new route on Devil's Thumb, (Alaska), and a filmed ascent of the Nose of El Capitan in Yosemite Valley. His film on the 3rd ascent of Mount Fitzroy in Patagonia is a classic among mountaineering films, and was later incorporated into the DVD *Mountain of Storms* (www.patagonia.com).

But aside from his technical accomplishments, Lito is just as well known for his philosophical writings on climbing, such as the classic "Games Climbers Play" published in Ascent magazine. In a follow-up piece in 1990, Lito gives further perspective on the relationship of climbing to life below the mountains:

> *"The act of climbing was its own definition, its own reason and motivation, a self-justifying feedback loop that never looked outside itself to society for validation.... If the climb was demanding enough, if you'd understood the game and sharpened the rules to that perfect pitch, then you wouldn't have room in your consciousness for anything else. Your universe would both shrink and expand to the next hold, the next few feet of face, the next phase of this empty-in advance safe you were cracking, hidden combination by hidden combination, fo its own sake, empty of everything but the challenge accepted, the problem solved......*
> *But sometimes, of course, it doesn't work out like that. The rest of your life follows you up the crag like an endless haul line clipped to your harness, heavier and heavier each pitch"* (Tejada-Flores, 1990).

Since the 1980s Lito has been teaching skiing, authoring *Backcountry Skiing* for Sierra Club Books, and hitting the slopes with clients from all over the world (www.breakthroughonskis.com). Nowadays, Lito lives in the Baca subdivision with his wife, photographer Linde Waidhofer (www.westerneye.com). Their living-room windows frame Kit Carson and Crestone Peaks in an awe-inspiring view.

6. THE BACA NATIONAL WILDLIFE REFUGE

The Baca National Wildlife Refuge (BNWR) is a 78,697-acre federal Reserve, part of the system of National Wildlife Refuges administered by the US Fish and Wildlife Service (FWS). It was authorized by Congress in 2000 and formally established in 2003, as part of a complex of National Wildlife Refuges in the San Luis Valley, including the Alamosa NWR (established 1962) and Monte Vista NWR (established 1953). However, the BNWR dwarfs the two older Refuges (www.fws.gov/alamosa/BacaNWR.html).

The BNWR was created out of the western half of the former Baca Grant, plus additional land to the west and south. The Congressionally-approved boundaries of BNWR (e.g., Figs. 6-2, -3) are much larger than its current (2011) extent and include BLM, State, and private lands not yet acquired.

Fig. 6-1. Entrance to the headquarters area of the BNWR, which was also the headquarters of the former Baca Ranch. A tiny sign marks it as a National Wildlife Refuge, but warns "Unauthorized Entry Prohibited." The only public access allowed to BNWR is to drive down the road shown above to the office building at headquarters, "when the gate is open."

A PLACE FOR WILDLIFE, NOT FOR PEOPLE

The Alamosa and Monte Vista NWRs, like most NWRs, are open to the public and accessible from hiking trails or roads. The Baca NWR, in contrast, has been closed to the public since its acquisition by the Fish and Wildlife Service (2003) and is still closed as of this writing (early 2011; see www.fws.gov/refuges/profiles/index.cfm?id=65512). Why does FWS not want the public to travel to this piece of Federal land ? Their justification is twofold: (1) BNWR was added to the SLV-NWR complex "without expanding its operating budget or personnel base", and (2) due to 1, BNWR cannot determine where public access should be allowed, without causing injury to the resource. It is hard for some to accept these reasons for an indefinite public closure, because that must surely contradict the stated purpose of the Refuge...... or does it?

123

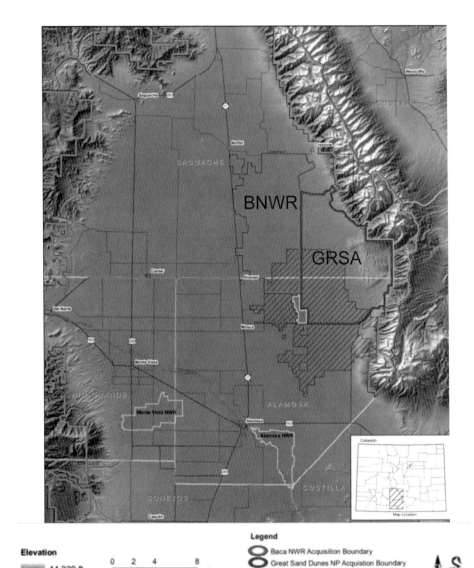

Fig. 6-2. Map of the three National Wildlife Refuges in the San Luis Valley: BNWR (upper right center), Alamosa NWR (white outline, lower center), Monte Vista NWR (white outline, lower left). GRSA is Great Sand Dunes National Park. Diagonal lines show The Nature Conservancy's Medano and Zapata Ranches.

In fact, BNWR was created by the Great Sand Dunes National Park and Preserve Act of 2000, and strangely enough, that bill nowhere explains why the Refuge was created! This omission was brought to light because, between 2000 and 2007, Lexam Exploration proposed to drill for oil and gas in the Refuge. Lexam's proposal sent many

124

opponents of drilling on a search for how such use compared with the stated purpose of the Refuge. Imagine their surprise when they discovered that the enabling legislation forgot to state the purpose of the Refuge!

The omission was brought to the attention of Congressman John Salazar (D-CO). In 2007 Mr. Salazar submitted House Bill 1658, *"To Amend the Great Sand Dunes National Park and Preserve Act to explain the purpose and provide for the administration of the Baca National Wildlife Refuge."* The bill would *"amend the Great Sand Dunes National Park and Preserve Act of 2000 to provide that the purpose of the Baca National Wildlife Refuge shall be to restore, enhance, and maintain wetland, upland, riparian, and other habitats for native wildlife, plant, and fish species in the San Luis Valley"* (note that drilling is not mentioned). The bill was referred to the House Committee on Natural Resources in April 2007, but was allowed to die in committee. Only after the 2008 election was a bill successfully sponsored by Senator Ken Salazar (D-CO) to contain the purpose stated above (the Baca National Wildlife Refuge Management Act, within the Omnibus Public Land Management Act of 2009).

Meanwhile, managers of the San Luis Valley Refuges state that the BNWR cannot be opened to the public until they finish their Comprehensive Conservation Plan (CCP), which will determine the location and sensitivity of plant & animal communities to exposure to the visiting public. The CCP process was begun in February 2011.

WHAT'S IN THE REFUGE?

Because the public cannot wander the Refuge now, nor could they when it was the Baca Ranch (1860-2004), we know very little about what actually lies within this 123 square miles of public lands. Most of what we know comes from the 2005 Conceptual Management Plan of the US Fish and Wildlife Service (see link on the BNWR home page, www.fws.gov/alamosa/bacanwr.html). We know there are wetlands and elk.

The Refuge Wetlands

When William Gilpin rhapsodized about the "saturated savannahs of luxuriant grass", he was talking about the vast wetlands now in the Refuge. As shown on the National Wetlands Inventory (Fig. 6-3), these wetlands are not lakes, but intermittent marshes and wetland meadows seasonally watered by the "losing streams" of North Crestone, South Crestone, Willow, Spanish, Cottonwood, and Deadman Creeks. The meadows have historic significance: (1) they forced the Old Spanish Trail toward the east valley margin, so it passed near Crestone, and (2) they induced the Baca family to choose this Land Grant 150 years ago, out of all the lands they could have chosen in the west, because the meadows made excellent forage for cattle. True, the cattle do love these meadows of lush grasses. But so do the elk, whose numbers have exploded in the past 30 years.

Got Elk?

The Crestone area and Jackson Hole, Wyoming have several similarities: both have a rugged mountain range rising above a sage-filled valley, caused by rapid uplift on an active fault (The Teton and Sangre de Cristo faults, respectively). The valley floor and range front are preserved in a National Park, and in private open space funded by (coincidentally) Laurance S. Rockefeller (1910-2004). The final similarity is the presence of a large elk herd protected by a National Wildlife Refuge.

125

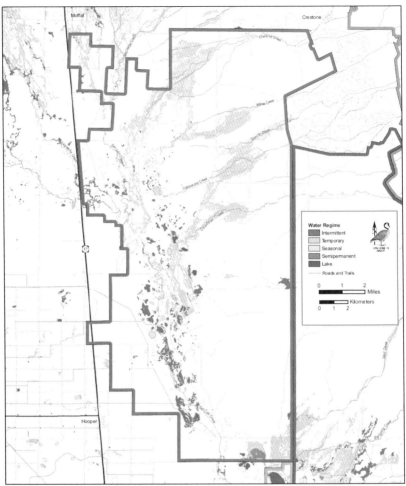

Fig. 6-3. National Wetlands Inventory in the Baca National Wildlife Refuge (center), the Great Sand Dunes National Park (lower right) and vicinity. The town of Crestone is at upper right. From FWS (2005).

The National Elk Refuge (NER) in Jackson Hole was founded in 1912 and encompasses 25,000 acres. Prior to settlement, the southern part of Jackson Hole was winter range for about 20,000 elk. NERs purpose was to resuscitate elk herds, which had faced mass starvation after bitterly cold winters and human encroachment. An artificial winter feeding program was begun (now costing about $550,000/year), inadvertently causing a population explosion. The overcrowded elk then decimated plants that provide natural forage. Further, the crowded herds became at risk for devastating diseases such a chroni wasting disease. (These unintended consequences are a lesson to managers of BNWR).

Today the NER supports about 8,500 wintering elk, a large number in a small area. On the positive side, elk-related tourism generates about $2.5 million in direct revenue for the Jackson economy, and 41 jobs with a total employment income of $662,500 (Halverson, 2000).The benefits include the National Museum of Wildlife Art,

126

(www.wildlifeart.org) located across Highway 89 from the NER. The winter sleigh rides alone generate $275,000 per year (Kahn, 2000), and the annual Antler Auction generates $95,000 per year. NER is visited by 20,000 to 25,000 people per year.

By comparison, the Baca National Wildlife Refuge is over three times as large 78,697 acres) but contains only half as many elk. From a management standpoint that ow density is a good thing. But the miniscule budget of BNWR means that it can offer none of the visitor services and events offered by NER. Not even those that make money!

Table 6-1. Comparison between the Baca National Wildlife Refuge (BNWR) and the National Elk Refuge (NER) in Jackson, Wyoming.

	Date Founded	Area (acres)	Elk	FTEs[1]	Volun-teers	Activities	Events
BNWR	2004	78,697	4,000	3	5	Rare public tours	none
NER	1912	24,700	8,000 to 10,000	10	dozens	Sleigh rides; tour historic ranch buildings; wildlife viewing from roads	Annual Artist-in-Residence; Elkfest and Antler Auction

Full-Time Employees

Fig. 6-4. Fig. "Return of the elk"; photo was taken at the northern edge of Deadman Creek on the Great Sand Dunes National Park, just east of the BNWR. It was estimated that there were between 300-500 elk in the herd. About 200 elk are shown in this photo. Photo by Matthew Crowley.

Unknown to most Crestone residents, there is a difference between the Jackson Hole elk and the Crestone elk; our elk are very recent immigrants, from Wyoming in fact. In the late 1800s all the elk in the Sangre de Cristo Mountains had been killed by hunters, to feed the hungry miners. The Sangre's last native elk vanished in 1878 (Geary, 1997, p. 6). Sixty years later elk were re-introduced to the northern San Luis Valley, brought in from Yellowstone National Park in Wyoming and first located in the Saguache area. So our elk are actually cousins to the Jackson Hole elk.

The elk slowly spread eastward from Saguache toward the Sangres. According to Schoenecker (2006), by 1983 the northern valley herd had built up to about 1300 animals (Fig. 6-5). Bob King, who was born in Crestone in 1927 and worked for the Baca Ranch for many years, says he did not see his first elk in the area until 1987 (Erdman, 2004). Once the elk reached the Baca Ranch they found it very hospitable. There were no predators, hardly any hunters on this huge private parcel, and lots of good things to eat. In the summer, half of the herd drifted up into the cool valleys and meadows of the Sangres, unimpeded by roads or fences. In this protected and idyllic environment, the elk were fruitful and multiplied.

The herd hit 2000 in 1986, 3000 in 1991, 4000 in 1994, and 5000 in 1999. Faced with the exploding population, managers of the Ranch began to offer limited hunting of the herd (cows only) through a guided hunting program run by the Colorado Division of Wildlife (DOW). Between the effects of that program and the effects of the drought that began in 2000, the herd stabilized, and then began to shrink as the devastating drought of 2002 set in. By 2004 the herd was back to 4000, the same size it had been in 1994.The DOW believes that the ideal number of elk for this herd to remain healthy should be around 1500 (Keno, 2004b). Reducing the herd to this number would require several years of large-scale hunting. It is unknown whether that scale of hunting would be allowed in the National Wildlife Refuge.

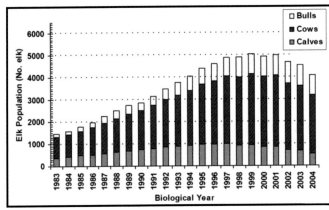

Fig. 6-5. Estimated elk population in the San Luis Valley, Colorado, by age/sex for biological years 1983–2004 (calendar years 1984–2005). The decrease in population from 2002 to 2005 coincides with a severe statewide drought, which broke in 2005. From Schoenecker et al., 2006.

Elk in the BNWR are *Rocky Mountain elk*, one of six subspecies of North American elk *(Cervus elephus)*. There are about 850,000 Rocky Mountain elk in the USA, 300,000 of which are in Colorado. Rocky Mountain elk range from New Mexico north to British Columbia. Bulls weigh an average of 900 pounds and cows 600, with calves weighing 30 pounds. During the early summer, elk graze on various grasses and browse on tender seedlings and twigs. In late summer, when grasses are dried and yellow they browse on saplings, berries, and mushrooms. During the winter elk eat dried grass, pawed from beneath the snow, browse on trees and berry bushes, and eat bark from trees and large shrubs. Elk feed most actively after sunrise and before sunset (Keno, 2004b).

WHERE'S THE HERD?
What are your chances for seeing elk around Crestone? First, you will not see the entire 4000 elk in a single herd. The elk move around in groups of 100-500, over an area that stretches from Villa Grove in the north to Blanca Peak in the south, a distance of 70 miles. They are unimpeded by the 4 foot-high fences built on the San Luis Valley floor t contain cattle. An elk survey of the entire valley was undertaken in 2005 and revealed several interesting patterns (Fig. 6-6).

First, there is a smaller separate elk herd in the high country around Poncha Pas that does not mix with the valley elk. Second, the elk range expands in the summer months (June-August) and contracts in the snowier months. Third, some elk groups mov up into the Sangres in June as the snowline recedes, to browse on the deciduous vegetation through the summer. However, these groups have detached themselves from the majority of the elk groups, which remain on the valley floor through the summer. Fourth, the high-altitude elk are still up high in September; they do not begin moving back down out of the mountains until later.

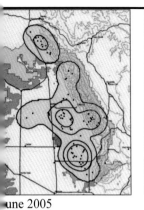
June 2005

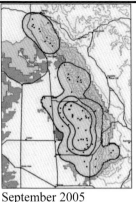
September 2005

Fig. 6-6. Maps showing the location of elk groups (small dots) and contours of population density (lines) from the 2005 elk survey. In May the elk are still on the valley floor. By June part of the herd has split off and wandered up into the National Forest. Another small part has wandered west into agricultural fields near Saguache. In August even more of the herd is grazing in the cool mountains, trying to escape the heat on the valley floor. By September the mountain elk are starting to move back down out of the high country, and the Saguache elk have returned to the fold . All data from Schoenecker et al. (2006).

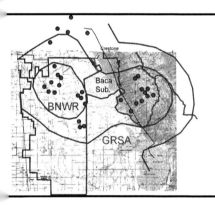

Fig. 6-7. Close-up of the location of elk herds (dots) in June of 2005. Thick lines are contours on elk density/acre. The elk are about evenly divided between those on the plains of the BNWR and those in the mountain canyons of the Rio Grande National Forest. Elk generally avoid the area in-between, containing the Baca Subdivision and the Town of Crestone, because of traffic and loose dogs. Your best viewing in the summer would be in the far southwest corner of the Grants Unit of the Baca Grande subdivision, which is close to the BNWR and far from traffic. From Schoenecker et al. (2006).

Finally, the summer split between the mountain elk and the valley elk means that there is an absence of elk around the Crestone-Baca area in summer (Fig. 6-7). This is not especially good news for summer visitors wishing to see elk. The most likely place to encounter an elk group is along the eastern half of County Road T between Moffat and Crestone.

TOURS OF BNWR

Staff-led "Management Perspective" tours can be requested by the public (normally groups rather than individuals) during the Spring and Summer months, on a first-come, first-served basis, and as time and FWS manpower allow. Call (719) 256-5527. Tours that have already been scheduled will be advertised in the Crestone Eagle newspaper.

7. THE CRESTONE-BACA AREA;
YOUR BASE CAMP FOR ADVENTURE

After a drive across the treeless San Luis Valley and its relentless high-altitude sun, it is always a relief to pull into tree-rich Crestone. In summer the shady cottonwoods and the babbling brooks bring down the temperature; the smell of moisture is in the air. Parties of climbers and hikers descend the mountains after multi-day adventures and head straight for the coffee shops and cafes, basking in the murmur of conversation, caffeine, cell phone reception, and Internet access. In their reacquaintance with civilization, Crestone is like a halfway house.

Fig. 7-1. The Old and the New. *Left*: an unusual 3-story log cabin from the mining days rises above North Crestone Creek in downtown Crestone; *Right*: Entrance to the Baca Grande subdivision, buil in 1971 and now home to more than 90% of the local population. Photos by Peggy Clark.

THE LAYOUT
The Town of Crestone was laid out by George Adams, owner of the Baca Ranch, in 188(as a 120-acre L-shape, later filled in to a square by annexing the "missing" 40-acre SE quadrant (Fig. 7-2). That size remained unchanged until 2007, when a 40-acre parcel NE of Town was annexed. In 2010 another 40-acre agricultural parcel southeast of Town wa annexed. The latest parcel lies in a new zoning district entitled "Community Services and Recreational", allowing for "*education, conferences, training, local government, parks, ball fields, swimming pools, tennis courts, libraries, animal shelters, nursery and day care.*" This list includes several facilities that exist today and service the Crestone-Baca population, but are located inconveniently 4 miles west of Town on County Road T. The long-term plan is to relocate such high-demand services such as the Crestone Charter School closer to the locus of population, and so reduce energy consumption.

People familiar with other Colorado mining towns will note absence of brick buildings in Crestone. The mining booms in Crestone were too short-lived, and yielded too little profit from the mines, to support construction of brick or stone buildings such a exist in the longer-lived or more prosperous mining towns (e.g., Aspen, Central City, Leadville, Telluride). Even the mining-era bank building in Crestone was built of wood (it is now the Town Center Building). The chronology of town development and the mining districts is detailed in Chapter 10.

130

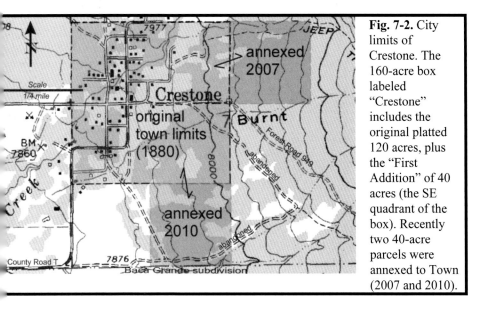

Fig. 7-2. City limits of Crestone. The 160-acre box labeled "Crestone" includes the original platted 120 acres, plus the "First Addition" of 40 acres (the SE quadrant of the box). Recently two 40-acre parcels were annexed to Town (2007 and 2010).

Towns are like people. Old ones often have character, the new ones are interchangeable
    Wallace Stegner, 2000, *Angle of Repose*

Crestone is divided into 64 blocks bounded by 9 streets running north-south and streets running east-west. This ambitious plat assumed that Crestone would develop into another Leadville or Aspen, but that did not happen. Most of the platted streets were ever built and do not exist as driveable roads today (Fig. 7-3). All the north-south streets are called "streets" and named after trees (from west to east, Birch, Willow, Cottonwood, lder, Cedar, Spruce, Hemlock, Pine, and Pinyon Streets), whereas the east-west streets are called "avenues" named after rocks or minerals (from north to south, Mica, Granite, on, Carbonate, Galena, Silver, Golden, Copper, and Lime Avenues). The street address system originates at the intersection of Galena Avenue (the main east-west street) and lder Street (the main north-south street). Locals refer to this intersection as "downtown" restone, a designation even more appropriate today, since the SW corner is occupied by e new Town Center Building. As shown on the 1910 plat (Sisemore, 1983), Crestone's 4 blocks were subdivided into "big lots" (1/6 acre, residential) and "small lots" (1/12 cre, commercial). The commercial lots lie only on the north and south sides of Galena venue, and the east side of Alder Street. Although businesses are no longer clustered ere (Fig.7-3), their legacy remains, since almost all of those "small lots" are still zoned ommercial, while the remainder of Town is zoned Residential.

In this Chapter we give a tour of the Crestone-Baca area, its facilities, services, d buildings as they existed in early 2011. This includes lodging, restaurants, cafes, loons, grocery stores, gas stations, banks, ATMs, auto repair, parks, laundromats, ternet, medical clinics, churches, and anything else a visitor might need. Chapter 9 then scribes local Activities and Events, and Chapter 10 describes the modern community d its historical roots.

131

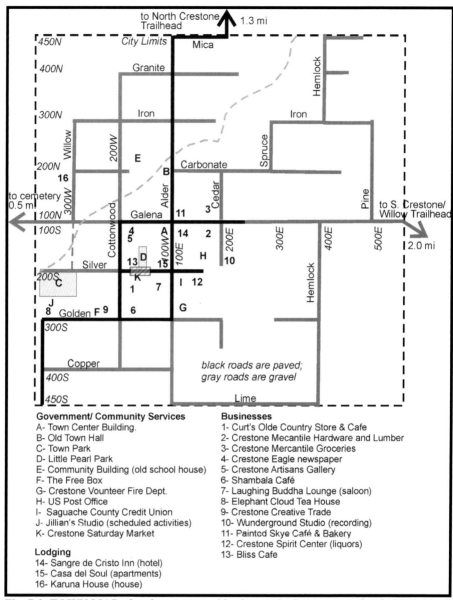

Fig. 7-3. **TOWN MAP**, showing streets and businesses in Crestone, as of early 2011. North Crestone Creek (gray dashed line) meanders through Town. Black roads are paved, gray roads are gravel. The only public access to North Crestone Creek is from Town Park, using the Willow Street right-of-way (dashed gray line, 60 ft wide).

Government/ Community Services
A- Town Center Building.
B- Old Town Hall
C- Town Park
D- Little Pearl Park
E- Community Building (old school house)
F- The Free Box
G- Crestone Vounteer Fire Dept.
H- US Post Office
I- Saguache County Credit Union
J- Jillian's Studio (scheduled activities)
K- Crestone Saturday Market

Lodging
14- Sangre de Cristo Inn (hotel)
15- Casa del Soul (apartments)
16- Karuna House (house)

Businesses
1- Curt's Olde Country Store & Cafe
2- Crestone Mecantile Hardware and Lumber
3- Crestone Mercantile Groceries
4- Crestone Eagle newspaper
5- Crestone Artisans Gallery
6- Shambala Café
7- Laughing Buddha Lounge (saloon)
8- Elephant Cloud Tea House
9- Crestone Creative Trade
10- Wunderground Studio (recording)
11- Painted Skye Café & Bakery
12- Crestone Spirit Center (liquors)
13- Bliss Cafe

SHELTER FROM THE STORM-- *Lodgings in Crestone-Baca*

For a town at the end of a dead-end road, with an in-town population of only 127, Crestone-Baca has a surprising number of beds for travelers. This is partly due to the summer influx of visitors to the area's spiritual retreat centers. But even hardy

132

mountaineers have been known to hear the call of a bed with clean sheets, after a week up in the mountains. The Town Map above shows lodging within the City limits. Most of the Bed & Breakfast Inns are located in the Baca Grande subdivision; see the Crestone Eagle newspaper for listings. The best on-line map of the circuitous roads of the Baca can be found on this National Geographic website: www.fourcornersgeoturism.com/map.php. The largest lodging open to the public is White Eagle Village, located 4 miles west of Crestone on County Road T.

White Eagle Village Conference & Retreat Center, 67485 County Road T, Moffat, CO 81143; (719) 256-4865; (800) 613-2270; (www.whiteeaglevillage.com)

The largest hotel in the area lies 3.8 miles west of Crestone on County Road T, so you will pass it on the way into town. The Village contains 50 hotel rooms, 7 apartments, several meeting rooms, and a large dining room (open only by prior arrangement). The White Eagle regularly hosts events and conferences, such as the annual Metaphysical Fair. Weekly rates are available off season. 100% non-smoking, WiFi, gym and sauna. Call 719-256-4116 or email info@whiteeaglevillage.com.

Fig. 7-4a. Extensive stonework surrounds the White Eagle Village and Conference Center. It is the only non-sectarian conference center in the area, that is, one not on the premises of one of the spiritual centers in the Baca Grande.

Fig. 7-4b. Examples of the Old West architecture of Crestone. Photos by Peggy Clark.

FINE VICTUALS AND DRINK—*Restaurants*

The number of cafes/restaurants open at any given time in the Crestone-Baca area is a fluid and unpredictable number. In 2011 there were three, all shown on the Town Map (Fig. 7-3), plus the Desert Sage inside the entrance to the Baca Grande subdivision. All venues offer casual dining and serve beer and wine. The Laughing Buddha Lounge offers a full-service bar and live music (http://laughingbuddhalounge.com). For package liquor, visit the Crestone Spirits Center, 158 East Silver Avenue (http://crestonespirits.com).

FROM THE VAULT—*Banks and ATMs*

Saguache County Credit Union (110 E. Silver Avenue; letter I on Town map) (www.sccu4u.net). SCCU was founded in April, 1996 in Moffat (12 miles west of Crestone), the result of a grassroots effort by local residents. It is locally owned and operated. The Crestone branch office opened in 2008, bringing a bank back to Crestone after a hiatus of 100 years. SCCU is a full-service banking establishment.

In 2010 Saguache County introduced its own currency, called "Mountain Money", currently available in one "MoMo" bills, which can be purchased for $0.95 each at the Saguache County Credit Union. Participating merchants in Saguache County will accept MoMos for retail purchases, at the rate 1 MoMo=$1.00. So, using MoMos is like getting a 5% discount on purchases at those merchants. For a list of participating merchants, go to: www.scseed.org.

MOSEYIN' AROUND—*Ground Transportation*

Living 50 miles from the nearest city, Crestonians are dependent on long-range, fossil-fueled vehicles whether they like it or not. This enforced dependence has created a love/hate relationship with cars and with the Oil Business, and has encouraged some to search for a better way.

Gas & Diesel Sales: only available at Curt's Olde Country Store, 200 S. Cottonwood Street. Features a slow-but-reliable pump that takes credit cards 24 hours. The closest gas stations once you leave Crestone are:
Heading south, at Hooper (29 miles via Moffat, then south on CO 17)
Heading north, at Poncha Springs (55 miles via Moffat, the CO 17 and US 285)
Heading west, at Saguache (30 miles via Moffat, then County Roads west)

Auto Repair
Terry's Auto Repair is located 4 miles west of Crestone on County Road T, in Casita Park. Terry repairs all makes and models, but specializes in Subarus, the "unofficial car" of Crestone. Call 719-937-3393.

Windhorse Transportation and Tours: will take you or your guests wherever you need to go. It is a helpful service for picking up visitors who end up at the Alamosa Airport or bus station, the bus stop at Moffat, etc. Call (719) 256-4091, browse to http://windhorse.crestonecolorado.com, or email: keithc1320@fairpoint.net.

PICNIC IN THE PARK—*Public Parks*

Town of Crestone Parks—the main Town park is located at the west end of Silver Avenue (Fig. 7-3) and contains a public restroom, covered picnic tables, and playground equipment. Among other uses, it hosts the annual San Luis Valley Energy Fair every September. The smaller Little Pearl Park is pocket park on the north side of Silver Avenue between Cottonwood and Alder Streets, adjacent to the street venue for the Crestone Saturday Market.

Fig. 7-5. Visitors and residents crowd the Town Pocket Park for entertainment after the annual 4th of July Parade. The visitor's T-shirt acknowledges Crestone as the gateway to a particular higher realm. Photo by Peggy Clark.

Baca Grande Subdivision Parks—the Baca's main park is on the south side of South Crestone Creek off of Camino Baca Grande, 0.7 miles south of the entrance to the Baca. This park has restrooms, a sand volleyball court, basketball half-court, baseball diamond, covered pavilion, BBQ grills, and a fenced playground area (Fig. 7-6).

The smaller Willow Creek Park is on the south side of Willow Creek, just west of where Camino Baca Grande crosses the creek. Turn west onto Camino Real (aka "Two Trees Road") and take the first dirt driveway on the right (north) side. This park has a few picnic tables but is otherwise undeveloped.

Fig. 7-6. South Crestone Park in the Baca subdivision in May, when the cottonwoods (center) unfold fresh new leaves. South Crestone Creek flows along the park's north side (at left), carrying the spring snowmelt. The park is owned by the Baca Grande Property Owner's Association and is used by all local residents.

In the background, the two snowy 13,000-ft peaks visible are unnamed, and the one on the left, apparently unclimbed.

Privately-Owned Parks

The Tarboche Memorial Park (Fig. 7-7) is located 0.5 miles down Camino Real from its intersection with Camino Baca Grande. It is a memorial to Tibetan civilians and monks killed in the Chinese invasion of Tibet. The park contains a 30 foot flagpole, a smaller version of the great 80 foot pole at Tarboche in Tibet at the foot of Mt. Kailash, a major pilgrimage destination in south Asia. The pole is re-flagged and re-raised annually during the first full moon of June. The public is invited to participate and to join a pot-luck lunch afterwards. Call (719) 256-5037 or go to www.crestonecreations.com/tarboche/ for more information.

Fig. 7-7. Community members and Buddhist monks from Tibet join in the flag-raising ceremony at Tarboche Memorial Park, Baca subdivision. The park contains plaques explaining the plight of Tibet and destruction of its Buddhist monasteries since the Chinese invasion and takeover in 1959. Photo by Kim Malville.

THE SATURDAY NIGHT BATH—*Laundry & Showers*

The Crestone Mercantile Grocery store (the steel building on the north side of Galena) has a coin-operated Laundromat in back. 183 E. Galena Ave., Crestone; (719) 256-5885. At present there is no facility for campers to take showers in Crestone, outside of renting a room at a local B&B.

SMOKE SIGNALS—*News & Telecommunications*

The Crestone Eagle Newspaper : *The Crestone Eagle* was one of Crestone's two newspapers in the early 1900s (the other was named, predictably, *The Crestone Miner)*, but it lasted only about 5 years. After a hiatus of 83 years, the Crestone Eagle was resurrected in a curious way. In 1986 the Baca Grande Property owners Association (POA) hired Kizzen Laki as the new editor of their POA Newsletter. Over the next 3 years she expanded the scope of the Newsletter to include all local news, not just that emanating from the Baca Grande subdivision. By 1989 the POA wanted to "get out of the newspaper business", so she resurrected the name of the mining-era newspaper *The Crestone Eagle* and in December 1989 published the first issue.

The Eagle celebrated its 20th Anniversary in 2010 and continues to be both a source of local news, and a minable archive for recent history. Go to: www.crestoneeagle.com

Wireless Internet Sites

1-- Shambala Café (see entry under Restaurants)

2—Curt's Olde Country Store and Cafe

3-- Baca Grande Library (www.bacapoa.org/Library~120947~14064.htm), located 4 miles west of Crestone on County Road T; has several hard-wired computers available for surfing the Net (fees apply).

Cell Phone Service; the nearest cell tower is in Moffat, 10 miles west of Crestone as the crow flies. Verizon seems to work best, and AT&T barely. However, a new cell tower will be erected in 2011, 4 miles west of Crestone, which may improve reception for many cell customers.

DOCTORIN'-- *Medical Services*
Emergency Care: dial 911 to summon the Baca Ambulance Service

Medical Services—General Practice

There is only one general-practice clinic in the Crestone-Baca area, the Tiny Little Crestone Clinic, LLC in the Baca Grande subdivision. The TLC Clinic has been providing family health care since 2004, owned and operated by Shawn Quick, FNP Family Nurse Practitioner). Open three days a week by appointment; (719) 256-5118, 76 Camino Baca Grande, 1.0 mile south of the entrance to the subdivision, on the main paved road, and ½ block south of the Baca Fire station. If you need medical services on other days, the next closest family clinic is a part-time one in Moffat, but their hours of operation and providers are constantly changing. If the TLC Clinic is not open, you can call the Moffat Family Medical Center (719-256-4025) and see if they are open. But if they are not, the next medical services are in Alamosa, 50 miles by road south of Crestone via CO 17; or in Salida, 60 miles north via CO 17, US 285, and US 50.

Medical Services—Dentistry

There is only one dentist office in the area, likewise located on Camino Baca Grande in the Baca subdivision. John Percival (DDS, MSc.) practices holistic dentistry out of an office in the Baca Professional Building at 46 Camino Baca Grande, 0.36 miles south of the entrance to the Baca. Call (719) 256-6222 or email jpercival@fairpoint.net. Office hours by appointment.

Medical Services—Physical Therapy

Rebound Physical Therapy; 53 South Baca Grant Road (in the Baca subdivision), Crestone, Co 81131(719) 539-6144; (866) 539-6144.

Alternative Medicine (see Chapter 9, The Community of Healers)

Medical Marijuana Clinics:

High Valley Healing Center; Dispenses pain-relief products to patients on the Colorado Registry for Medical Marijuana; 116 S. Alder, Crestone, CO 81131; (719) 256-4006; www.highvalleyhealingcenter.com

KEEPING THE SABBATH- *Churches*

In its mining days, Crestone boasted more saloons and billiard halls than churches, but now the ratio is reversed. There are two churches in Crestone, and one in the Baca.

The Episcopal Church is the Little Shepherd of the Hills Church, located in downtown Crestone in the 100 block of North Alder Street. It was originally a private log home in the early 1900s, but in 1949 Alfred and Helen Collins (owners of the Baca Ranch) converted the building into the present-day church. The chapel is dedicated to Lady Julian of Norwich, a 14th Century English mystic. The Little Shepherd of the Hills is a mission of the Episcopal Church of the Ascension in Salida. Father John Huffman is the vicar and mass is celebrated the first Sunday of each month at noon. The public is welcome. The chapel is set back from Alder Street, nestled in the trees, and is open for prayer and meditation. (719) 256-4140 or (719) 539-4562 www.mountainregion.org/littleshepherdcrestone.html

The Crestone Baptist Church is located on County Road T, 330 yards west of the entrance to the Baca. It was started as a mission of the Southern Baptist Church, dedicated in 1975 to the memory of Bob Thalmann. Sunday School for adults and youth begins on Sundays at 10am, followed by Worship at 11am. For youth, the church offers Sunday school lessons, children's sermons, Vacation Bible School, and youth activities. The public is welcome. P. O. Box 189, Crestone, CO 81131 (719) 256-4625

Nada Carmelite Hermitage (Catholic) is located in the Baca subdivision. Monks celebrate Mass every Sunday at 9 am. *Driving Directions:* from the entrance to the Baca, drive south on Camino Baca Grande for 1.4 miles to Rendezvous Way where there is a small sign saying "Carmelite Monastery"; turn right (west) and go about ¼ mile on Rendezvous to the Nada parking lot (dirt); walk to the main buildings and the Chapel. (719) 256-4778 www.spirituallifeinstitute.org

READIN', WRITIN', AND 'RITHMETIC-- *Schools*

From the mining days until 1931, Crestone had its own independent school district (#8) and operated a two-room schoolhouse that is the current Crestone Community Center, in the 100 block of North Cottonwood Street. In 1931 the district merged with district #31 in Moffat to become the Moffat Consolidated School District, and by the 1950s the local schoolhouse closed, with all the children being bused to Moffat.

Crestone Charter School

Due to the growth of the Baca subdivision starting in 1971, the number of children being bused from Crestone to Moffat every day (a 24 mile round trip) slowly increased to the point where a large proportion of the Moffat School students were being bused from Crestone and the Baca. By 1994 Crestone area parents resolved to re-institute a school in Crestone, under the aegis of Colorado's newly-enacted Charter School Act. The Creston Charter School (CSC) was officially established in July 1995 as a K-12 school, based a one-year contract with the Moffat Consolidated School District. For the past 15 years CSC has been located in temporary trailers 4 miles west of Crestone on County Road T, on land owned by the Baca POA.

By 2009 CSC enrollment had increased to 65 students in grades 1-12 (about 1/3 of the total enrollment in the Consolidated School District), and was running out of space while the trailers were rapidly deteriorating. Applying in 2009 to a State program for funding new energy-efficient school buildings, CSC surprised everyone by becoming the first charter school in history to be awarded a grant to build a new, state-of-the-art school. As of early 2011 the school is in the advanced planning stage, with construction planned for summer 2011. It will be located on a 10-acre parcel annexed by the Town of Crestone in 2010.

Rahula Community Preschool

Located in the tall trees at the entrance to Crestone, this privately-owned preschool is as much a part of the community as the Crestone Charter School. The school is named after Rahula, the only son of Buddha. Parents have the option of selecting one to five days per week, and full-day or half-day sessions. The main language is English, but many Spanish words and phrases are introduced into the activities of the *muchachos y muchachas*. Contact Vicki Matthews, Director, at (719) 256-5020, email rahula@fairpoint.net; Website: http://rahula.us/index.html.

JUST THE FACTS, MA'AM—*Demography, Economy, Government*

DEMOGRAPHICS

In the latest decadal U.S. census (2000), the Crestone-Baca area (Census Tract 9776, Block Group 3; nearly identical to zip code 81131) had a population of 801 persons, 89% of whom listed themselves as Caucasian. The overall population density of the Crestone-Baca area was 801 persons in 396 square miles, or 2.02 persons per square mile. Compared to other countries in the world, this density would rank as the 3rd lowest out of all 239 countries measured, being less than that of Mongolia (#237), but more than Greenland (#239). If our area were a State, its population density would be lower than all other states except Wyoming (a close tie) and Alaska.

As shown by 2000 Census data (Fig. 7-8), the Crestone-Baca is dominantly a community of single persons, mostly between 50 to 59 in 2000 (Baby Boomers) and 40-49; with some couples without children, and some single parents with 1 child. It contains few (<10%) "traditional" 2-parent, medium-to-large families (4 persons or more). The second smallest age group is 20-29 (post-high school), indicating that most young people leave the community after high school (probably due to lack of jobs). On the older end of the scale, 14% of men and 11% of women are over retirement age (65).

The 2010 Census reports 127 people and 107 houses in the Town of Crestone, an increase of 74% and 35%, respectively, over the 2000 numbers. 38% of the houses were vacant, probably summer cabins. In Census Tract 9776 (Saguache County excluding Center and Hooper), 2011 population grew to 3,143 and houses to 2,509, an increase of 23% in population and 41% in houses compared to the year 2000. In contrast, the population of Saguache County as a whole grew little from 2000 (5,917) to 2010 (6,108), an increase of only 3%, due to population loss in the Center-Hooper area.

The "flip side" of demographics is the Crestone Cemetery, final resting place of 55 people, all listed at http://files.usgwarchives.net/co/saguache/cemeteries/crestone.txt.

JOBS

Crestone is a bastion of small businesses and the self-employed. Additionally, some people live a subsistence lifestyle based on bartering for goods and services. Of the 432 households in the area in 2000, 40% reported receiving no wages or salary that year and 22% reported receiving no earnings of any kind. Likewise, of the 561 adults in the area between school age (18) and retirement age (65), only 386 (69%) reported being employed.

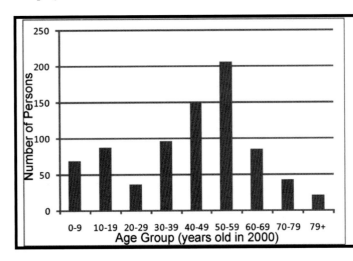

Fig. 7-8. Age distribution of the Crestone-Baca area from the 2000 US Census. Barring significant in- or out-migration between 2000 and 2010, the age groups will have shifted 10 years to the right by 2010.

For men, the largest occupation sector in 2000 was construction (mainly new homes in the Baca), followed closely by management and professional. For women, most employment was in management and professional, followed by sales and office occupations. However, due to the collapse of the real estate lending market in mid 2008, home construction in the Baca has significantly decreased. As many as half the construction jobs have been lost, plunging the community into its own small version of the Great Recession.

Occupation Type	Men	Women
Construction and maintenance	64 (33%)	0
Farming, fishing, or forestry	18 (9%)	0
Management and Professional	62 (32%)	92 (48%)
Production, transportation, moving	7 (4%)	5 (3%)
Sales & office occupations	29 (15%)	59 (31%)
Service occupations	16 (8%)	34 (18%)
TOTAL employed	196	190
TOTAL persons 18-64	257	304
Percent unemployed	76%	63%

INCOME

Crestone was never a place to get rich, even in the mining days, and that fact is still true today. The graph below indicates that *at least* 24% of households in the Crestone-Baca area were below poverty level in 2000.

By 2008, median income in zip code 81131 was $25,154, compared to $56,993 in Colorado. 35% of local residents were below the poverty level, compared to 11% statewide. Median household income in Saguache County increased by 18.4% from 2000 to 2007. However, that increase is almost exactly the same size as the net inflation of the US dollar in the same period (19%), indicating that 2007 incomes had the same purchasing power as 2000 incomes.

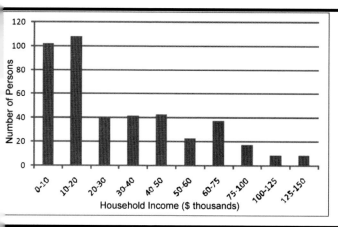

Fig. 7-9. Household income of the Crestone-Baca area from the 2000 US Census. The Federal poverty level in 2000 was $8350 for a 1-person household and $11,250 for a 2-person household; those two sizes comprised 83% of all households in the area.

COMMUNITY SERVICES

Due to Crestone's isolation and small population (and small tax base), local governments can provide very limited social services. The local residents have long understood and accepted this, and have adopted the self-reliant attitude that it "takes a village" to provide social safety net. Services that may be provided by government in a larger town are typically provided by grassroots, nonprofit organizations in Crestone.

As a result, the Crestone-Baca area has an astounding number of tax-exempt organizations (Federal 501c3 designation). For example, TaxExemptWorld.com lists 50 tax-exempt institutions in Crestone, CO. Considering that there are only 432 households in the 81131 zip code, this equals 1 tax exempt organization for every 8.6 households, which may be the highest ratio in the United States! Almost all of these organizations are religious/spiritual in nature (described in Chapter 8), but there are some secular charities (see below) which provide much-needed assistance.

Secular Nonprofits

NEIGHBORS HELPING NEIGHBORS (NHN)

NHN is the strongest and most consistent part of the local social safety net. NHN was founded in 1998 to support "the well-being of families in crisis." NHN is a tax-exempt 501c3 charity and can be reached at P.O. Box 822, Crestone, CO 81131, or at (719) 256-4404.

CRESTONE YOUTH PROJECT (CYP)

CYP runs the Crestone Youth Center (66 Skyview Way, in the Baca subdivision) and the CYP Thrift Store in the Town Center Building (letter A on Town Map). By combating TBS (Teenage Boredom Syndrome) in Crestone, they are doing us all a great favor.

Fire Mitigation; The Urban-Wildland Interface (UWI)
According to the Bureau of Land Management, "an urban wildland interface community exists where humans and their development meet or intermix with wildland fuel." That certainly describes the Crestone-Baca area. We are Federally classified as a UWI community, specifically an "intermix community", meaning that wildland fuels are continuous outside of and within the developed area (Fig. 7-10).

Subsequent to the Great Forest Fire of 1882 (see Chapter 10), there have been no catastrophic fires in the Crestone-Baca area, but there have been some recent scares. In the summer of 2000 wildfires driven by 60 mph winds raced through the Great Sand Dunes National Monument, only 15 miles south of Crestone. In May of 2002 the Million Fire across the valley burned 9346 acres and destroyed 11 homes; Crestone and Baca volunteer firefighters helped fight it, and noticed how a similar fire could easily start here. On July 13, 2007 a lightning-caused brush fire on valley floor near the Baca subdivision burned 20 acres before put out by the local VFDs (Bryant and Haines, 2007). And in June of 2010 the Medano Fire 12 miles south of the Baca burned 6200 acres of the Sangres. Flames 200 feet high erupted from the burning forest, and filled the Valley with smoke.

To lower the risk of fires the Bureau of Land Management performed two mitigation projects on BLM land near Crestone in September of 2003 (Fig. 7-10), covering 320 acres of BLM land northwest of Crestone near the cemetery, and 190 acres east of Crestone (Crestone Eagle, 2003).

Fig. 7-10. Map of the Wildland-Urban Interface area (thick dash-dot line) of the Town of Crestone Areas with diagonal lines were "mitigated" (trees were thinned) by Bureau of Land Management crews in September of 2003. The Baca subdivision contains similar fuels. Light rectangles in the mountains show private mining claims within the Rio Grande National Forest.

142

Fire protection is guided by the Community Wildfire Protection Plan developed by the Baca Grande Volunteer fire Department and Kundalini Fire Management, Inc. (see http://csfs.colostate.edu/pages/documents/BacaGrande_CWPP_2005.pdf). Fire Bans can be announced by government agencies, including the Rio Grande National Forest (parts or all of Forest); Bureau of Land Management (all or part); Saguache County (all of County) and/or Town of Crestone (all of Town). Violations are punishable by fines, but those fines are actually negligible compared to the cost of burning down your house (or your whole neighborhood). Recent fire bans were in 2002, 2004, 2006, and 2010.

The Baca Grande Volunteer Fire Department; is a part of the Baca Grande Property Owner's Association and provides fire protection for the 10,000-acre developed portion of the Baca Grande subdivision managed by the POA.

THE CRESTONE END-OF-LIFE PROJECT (CEOLP)

CEOLP assists locals who are dying to get their affairs in order and to leave this planet in the way they want. They work with families and relatives in weaving a final safety net for their loved ones. They offer the unusual service of an open-air cremation (Fig. 7-11).

This local practice evolved from several factors. The first is economic: 35% of Crestone households earn less than the Federal poverty level. The average cost of a traditional funeral in the USA is $6,500, which is more cash than many Crestonians earn in an entire year. The second factor is sociologic. Crestonians have deliberately stepped out of the mainstream and fend for themselves in many ways (locally-grown food, wood heat, solar electricity) in a pioneer manner. After decades of living this way, they don't want the final act of their life to be manhandled and packaged by the corporate funeral system. They would prefer to go locally, laid in state at home for 3 days and then consumed in a funeral pyre like Viking royalty. Following age-old traditions, the body is consumed by burning ½ a cord of firewood over a 5-6 hour period.

For details, go to **www.crestoneendoflifeproject.org**, or P.O. Box 1238, Crestone, CO 81131.

Fig. 7-11. Family and friends gather at a dawn open-air cremation of a local resident. Since receiving approval from the County in 2008, CEOLP has provided 7-8 such services per year at its permanent site west of Crestone. Photo by Bill Ellzey

8. ACTIVITIES AND EVENTS

Crestone is not really a tourist town, it is more of a portal. Activities here are powered by the interests of the locals and the muscles of visitors, rather than being tourist-oriented entertainment driven by large commercial interests. You can enjoy commercial tourism in any standard Colorado tourist town. But what you can get in Crestone is not widely available even in Colorado anymore, at any price: uncrowded trails, pristine lakes, spectacular scenery, and a calming quietude. This is Nature in its unspoiled state, and a community of people trying to live with it in sustainable, respectful harmony.

Due to the low profile of activities, visitors often ask "What is there to do in Crestone"? Actually, there is quite a lot.

BIKING

Mountain Biking and Road Biking; First, the Bad News: mountain bikes are not allowed in the Sangre de Cristo Wilderness (see boundaries on Fig. 3-2). The Good News; there are still plenty of trails and roads outside of the Wilderness suitable for your stump-jumper or road cruiser. These roads fall into two categories: (1) trails & roads in the Rio Grande National Forest and in BLM land outside the Wilderness boundary, and (2) public roads in Crestone and the Baca subdivision (some paved, most not).

Mountain Biking

Mountain Bikes on the Liberty Road: the longest backcountry route is the 8 mile-long Liberty Road that extends along the base of the mountains from the southern boundary of the Baca subdivision, to Sand Creek at the northern edge of the sand dunes. This two-track road is well-used, because the National Park Service, Forest Service, and private inholders drive it to access the backcountry. But for mountain bikes, there is a problem.

The northernmost 1.2 miles of Liberty Road, south of Liberty Gate, is in Great Sand Dunes National Park. As of early 2011, mountain bikes were prohibited on this short stretch of the road. But after the first 1.2 miles, the road enters the National Forest (Forest Road 952) and bikes are permitted there, as well as on two spur roads that lead uphill towards the range front (Forest Roads 952.1a, 953). These roads are shown on Fig. 4-1. Thus, bikes will be prohibited on Liberty Road until the Park Service upgrades the road, opens it to motor vehicle traffic, and builds the Cedar Creek public parking lot, hopefully in summer of 2011.

Mountain Bikes On Jeep Roads East of Crestone;
East of Crestone, there are four sandy side roads that lead off to the left (north) from Forest Road 949 (the extension of Galena Avenue). These roads were built in the mining days, and are now two-tracks used by jeeps. The first two roads (labeled "A" in Fig. 8-1) merge to form "Road A", which goes to the mouth of Burnt Gulch. **Road A** is sandy for the first 0.35 miles, then turns rocky at the crux, and remains so for the next 0.4 miles to

he mouth of Burnt Gulch. The rocky portion is seldom driven, so rocks and trees may have to be moved, but the grade is gentle for the next 0.4 miles to Burnt Gulch.

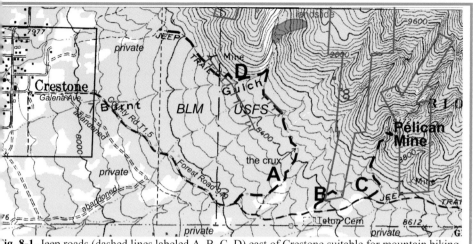

ig. 8-1. Jeep roads (dashed lines labeled A, B, C, D) east of Crestone suitable for mountain biking. ll four roads splay off Forest Road 949 to the South Crestone/Willow Trailhead.

rom the mouth of Burnt Gulch proceed 0.1 miles up along the creek on a low-gradient ep road. The road then turns to the left (NW) and begins to diagonal up a very rocky, oderately steep stretch 75 yards long. Prior to 2004 this section was drivable by most WDs, but that year a thunderstorm caused heavy gullying and rilling of the road. This eep stretch is the front of a large landslide that came off the east valley wall, at some me in the geologic past.

Once the road attains the surface of the landslide, it abruptly flattens out and egins to travel across a nearly-level grove of giant aspens through which the creek eanders lazily. This flat is the filled-up basin of a lake that was dammed by the ndslide when it blocked Burnt Gulch. The landslide has not been dated, but it may have id down during the last major earthquake to occur on this part of the Sangre de Cristo ult, dated at about 7700 years ago (McCalpin, 1982). Uphill from the aspen grove the ad narrows and becomes rocky. This part of the road has not been driven much since 004, and is becoming overgrown by vegetation.

Road B is only 215 yards long and ends at an informal camping spot on the orth lip of an unnamed gully (called Garfield Gulch in the mining days).

Road C is 0.35 miles long and ascends a gulch to the historic Pelican Mine. The rst 0.2 miles is passable by 2WD vehicle, but then the road turns left (west) and eepens in a sloping-outward section. Past this section the road becomes gentler and ays in the gulch bottom until it reaches the Pelican Mine. The mine buildings have long nce been removed and the workings have collapsed, but you may be able to pick up a ece or two of blue-green copper ore there.

Road D travels downslope from the mouth of Burnt Gulch, on the north side of e creek. About 330 yards downstream from the canyon mouth, the jeep road makes a airpin turn to descend the young fault scarp of the Sangre de Cristo fault. If you walk ver to the creek at this point, you will see that the creek is incised about 15 feet into the

145

fan on the upthrown (east) side of the fault, but only about 5 ft into the fan on the downthrown (west) side of the fault. Burnt Gulch is a perennial stream to the east of this scarp, which explains the dense growth of cottonwoods and aspens there. Once the stream crosses the fault line it begins to rapidly leak water into its bed. At some times of year the entire flow of the creek leaks into its bed and disappears in only a 15 ft-long stretch overlying the fault zone; this indicates that the fault zone must be very permeable.

Past the scarp, Road D continues another 220 yards to a small branch road to an old mine entrance. The mine entrance has collapsed and is now covered with dirt, so there is little to see here. Road D continues another 330 yards west, becoming increasingly gullied and overgrown with vegetation, until it hits the boundary of private lands around Crestone. You cannot bike or drive into Crestone on this road without trespassing, so turn around and return to the mouth of Burnt Gulch and Road A.

Mountain Bikes On Jeep Roads North of Crestone (map on Fig. 8-2)
As you approach the North Crestone Campground from Crestone, the paved road (County Road 71) turns sharply NE just before entering the National Forest, 0.8 mi N of Crestone. 0.1 mi later the road crosses over a cattle guard at the Forest Boundary. *NOTE: land to the south of the road is private.* Directly north of the cattle guard is an unmarked dirt road heading west; this is Forest Road 951, open to the public (but land west of the road is private). Much of FR 951 is 4WD only (due to deep sand), but the first 200 yards are usually passable. FR 951 gives quick access to a little-visited area of backcountry.

A Counter-Clockwise Loop Ride Between Crestone and San Isabel Creek, Using County, USFS, and BLM Roads (for mountain bikes, ATVs, or 4WDs)

Mileage	Feature (on Fig. 8-2)
0.0	downtown Crestone (Alder & Galena); ride north toward N. Crestone Campground on paved road
1.3	Forest Road 951 turns off to the left (west), just after the cattleguard, and before the mouth of N. Crestone Canyon. For the next 0.5 miles th roadbed is deep sand.
1.8	to continue on FR 951, turn hard left (west); the lesser-used trail straight ahead leads to mouth of Dimick Gulch (0.8 mi); FR 951 to the west descends the slope and becomes less sandy
2.2	junction with old gravelly jeep road; turn hard right (north); jeep road to south is closed to travel
2.5	FR 951 reaches a property corner with private land to the SW, marked by an old fence and water trough; continue straight ahead on to BLM land, where road is called VG16002
3.1	junction with BLM trail VG16003 to NE; continue straight
3.6	reach County Road 66T (also called BLM road VG16010)
5.3	junction of County Road 66T with BLM road VG16008; turn left (south)
6.3	junction to left (north) with BLM road VG16009; no full-size vehicles allowed.
6.6	similar junction with VG16009 as it loops back to main road
7.3	junction with BLM road VG16002 to left (north); there is no through access to San Isabel for full-size vehicles on this road

7.8   entrance to Crestone cemetery
8.3   Crestone city limit

Road Biking

There are many roads in the Baca, but only a few suitable for road biking. Mile markers are measured from the entrance to the Baca subdivision.

Paved Roads (shown as thicker lines on Fig. 8-3):

Camino Baca Grande, 2.2 miles long, gains 280 feet; this is the entrance road to the Baca subdivision; most of the road follows the old railroad grade to the Independent Mill. It is paved for the first 2.2 miles, to just south of Willow Creek and the intersection with Camino Real. The first 0.4 miles ascends from the valley floor up to the old railroad grade and is the steepest section, gaining 80 ft of elevation (200 ft/mile). Once on the old grade, the gradient is an absolutely uniform 110 ft/mile for the next 1.8 miles to Mile 2.2, its intersection with Camino Real (locally called Two Trees Road).

Camino Real, 4.0 miles long, loses 400 feet; Camino Real is the longest paved road in the Baca subdivision and lies mainly in the grassland part (the Grants Unit). The first 2/3 mile from Camino Baca Grande is in the trees and descends straight down the alluvial fan of Willow Creek. The road loses 210 feet of elevation in this stretch, which almost equals the elevation previously gained on Camino Baca Grande. In the next 1.0 mile (to Mile 2.85) through the grasslands the road loses another 130 feet of elevation in getting to the valley floor, which is here 7760 ft elevation, or 80 feet lower than the entrance to the Baca. At Mile 4.2 the road crosses the valley of Spanish Creek and then ascends 20 ft to regain the valley floor. For the next 1.4 miles the road gently descends 50 ft until it reaches the intersection with Camino del Rey, the main southern road in the Grants, at Mile 5.6. You can continue south for another 0.6 mile (to Mile 6.2) on Camino Real, where the paved road ends at the north edge of the Cottonwood Creek greenbelt [as of 2011].

     The National Park Service announced plans in 2009 to extend Camino Real southward into the National Park, and then to the Liberty Road 2.75 miles to the east (the east-west black line in the pink zone at the bottom of Fig. 8-3). This road (Camino Chamisa) would be a low-standard gravel road. But in 2011 the plans were cancelled.

Badger Road shortcut, 1.4 miles long, loses 160 feet; To avoid gaining elevation on Camino Baca Grande only to lose it again on Camino Real, you can use Badger Road as a shortcut. At Mile 1.6 on Camino Baca Grande (measured from the entrance), turn right (south) onto Badger Road. There is a large sign here saying "Stables." From this point Badger descends for 0.75 miles, dropping 160 feet before reaching Willow Creek and the driveway to the Stables. Cross the creek and continue another 0.3 miles to the intersection of Wagon Wheel Road (Mile 2.65), and turn left (southeast). Continue 0.35 miles on Wagon Wheel to the intersection (Mile 3.0) with Camino Real. This shortcut, all on paved roads, eliminates 60 feet of elevation gain.

Unpaved Roads

Southern Camino Baca Grande and Dream Way, 3.1 miles long, gains 240 feet;

147

From Willow Creek, Camino Baca Grande continues as a County-maintained road for another 0.7 miles. Past Mile 0.7 the road enters privately-owned spiritual retreat land and becomes a private road. However, the road is used by the public to access the retreats. At Mile 1.6 the road forks, with the left (east) fork staying on the old railroad grade (now called Dream Way), and the right fork descending in a rough road (Camino Baca Grande). At Mile 2.3 on Dream Way you reach the Shumei Center, a large religious complex at the site of the historic Independent Mill. South of Shumei the road narrows to one lane and continues traversing along the range front on a gentle upgrade for another 0.8 miles to the mouth of Cottonwood Creek (Mile 3.1).

Road to the Big Stupa, 1.1 miles, gains 360 feet; This 0.7 mile-long, dead-end road extends from the mouth of Cottonwood Creek to the Big Stupa. The total elevation gain is modest (160 feet), and the view of the valley from the Stupa is spectacular.

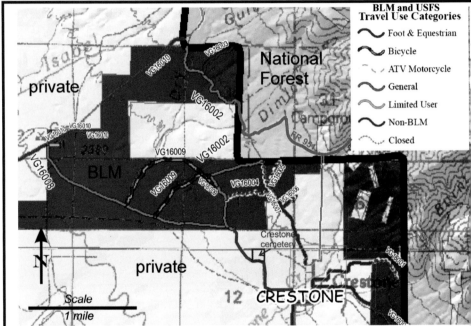

Fig. 8-2. Jeep roads between Crestone and San Isabel Creek. These roads are all open to bike although there are some stretches of deep sand in places. You can use this road network to make a loop ride from and back to Crestone, passing by the historic Crestone Cemetery (in red).

BIRDWATCHING

Birdwatching is not a popular pastime in most of the San Luis Valley, where the valley floor is irrigated crop fields or scrubby rangelands. But the valley margins such as the Crestone-Baca are richer *ecotones*, those transition areas where grasslands, riparian zones, and forest touch and intermingle. Crestone has considerable ecologically diversity so we enjoy the birds of the grasslands, the wetlands, the riparian zones, and the forest a

148

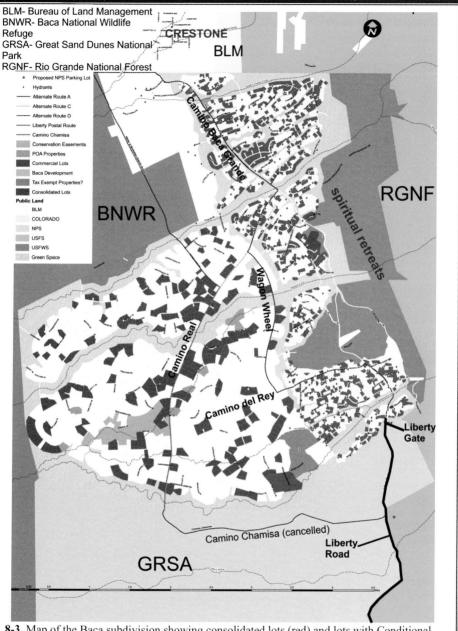

Fig. 8-3. Map of the Baca subdivision showing consolidated lots (red) and lots with Conditional Use permits to operate a home business (dark blue). The "Alternate Routes" in the Legend refer to routes considered by the National Park Service to bring tourist traffic to the North Entrance of the National Park. The NPS preferred alternative was Route A, which utilizes (black lines of short dashes) segments of Camino Baca Grande, Camino Real, and Camino del Rey. As of early 2011 the official Northern Entrance was Liberty Gate in the extreme SE corner of the subdivision. Source: San Luis Valley GIS/GPS Authority, Alamosa, CO.

149

at once (and the raptors that come along with them). Keno (2010) attributes the high bird density and variety in the Crestone-Baca area to the year-round supply of Pinyon Pine nuts and Juniper berries.

For birdwatchers, here is a list of birds commonly observed in Crestone area (compiled by Ryan, Richmond, Gripps, Houston, Picketts, and others).

Marshes and Ponds:
American Avocet
American Bittern
Belted Kingfisher
Black-crowned Night Heron
Black-necked Stilt
Black Tern
Common Snipe
Forster's Tern
Great Blue Heron
Greater Yellowlegs
Killdeer
Lesser Yellowlegs
Ring-billed Gull
Short-billed Dowitcher
Snowy Egret
Spotted Sandpiper
Wilson's Phalarope

American Coot
Blue-winged Teal
Canada Goose
Cinnamon Teal
Green-winged Teal
Lesser Scaup
Mallard
Northern Pintail
Northern Shoveler
Ruddy Duck
Wood Duck

Open Fields and Roadside Areas:
Mourning Dove
Rock Dove

American Tree Sparrow
Chipping Sparrow
Horned Lark
Lark Bunting
Song Sparrow
Vesper Sparrow
White-crowned Sparrow

Bendire's Thrasher
Northern Mockingbird
Sage Thrasher

American Crow
Black-billed Magpie
Brewer's Blackbird
Brown-headed Cowbird
Common Raven
European Starling
Red-winged Blackbird
Yellow-headed Blackbird *(cattails areas)*

Loggerhead Shrike *(also preys on feeder birds)*
Northern Shrike *(winter)*

Common and Lesser Nighthawks *(large numbers arrive during mosquito season in Baca, Crestone, and fields)*

Barn Swallow
Cliff Swallow
Rough-winged Swallow
Tree Swallow *(more common closer to mountains)*
Violet-green Swallow *(along Rd T and also near mtns.)*
White-throated Swift *(rock cliffs)*

Riparian Areas and Feeders * indicates ofte
observed short-term migrants)
Black-chinned Hummingbird
Broad-tailed Hummingbird
Rufous Hummingbird
Downy Woodpecker
Hairy Woodpecker
Lewis' Woodpecker
Northern Flicker
Red-naped Sapsucker
Williamson's Sapsucker
Cedar Waxwing
Brown Creeper
Common Bushtit
Black-capped Chickadee
Mountain Chickadee
Plain Titmouse
Pygmy Nuthatch
Red-breasted Nuthatch (nesting)
White-breasted Nuthatch
American Dipper

Bewick's Wren
House Wren
Rock Wren
Blue-gray Gnatcatcher
American Robin
Hermit Thrush
Mountain Bluebird
Townsend's Solitaire
Western Bluebird
Cordilleran Flycatcher
Olive-sided Flycatcher
Say's Phoebe
Western Wood Pewee
Ruby-crowned Kinglet *(more common than Golden-crowned)*
Golden-crowned Kinglet
Solitary Vireo
Warbling Vireo *(several species of Vireos found along creeks but less common)*
Black and White Warbler
MacGillvary's Warbler
Orange-crowned Warbler
Wilson's Warbler
Yellow Warbler
Yellow-rumped Warbler
Summer Tanager
Western Tanager
Black-headed Grosbeak
Blue Grosbeak*
Indigo Bunting*
Lazuli Bunting*
Northern Cardinal*
Rose-breasted Grosbeak
Dark-eyed Junco
Green-tailed Towhee
Spotted (Rufous) Towhee
Bullock's Oriole
American Goldfinch
Cassin's Finch
Evening Grosbeak
House Finch
Lesser Goldfinch
Pine Siskin
Rosy Finch (winter)
House Sparrow

Pinyon-Juniper and Conifer Forest:
Clark's Nutcracker
Gray Jay
Piñon Jay
Scrub Jay
Steller's Jay
Pine Grosbeak
Red Crossbill
White-winged Crossbill

Conifer forest:
Blue Grouse
Ptarmigan *(frequent high elevations so not likely to be seen by casual observer)*

Raptors: Generally observed around open areas)

Turkey Vulture – *spring into summer (not a true raptor)*
Bald Eagle – *generally in winter*
Cooper's Hawk *(found year round among forest and housing areas)*
Golden Eagle – *year round*
Red-tailed Hawk – *year round*
Rough-legged Hawk – *year round*
Sharp-shinned Hawk *(year round among forest and housing areas)*
Swainson's Hawk – *nesting*
American Kestrel – *year round*
Northern Harrier (Marsh Hawk) – *year round*
Prairie Falcon – *year round*
Burrowing Owl – *year round near Prairie Dog villages*
Great-horned Owl – *year round*
Western Screech Owl – *year round*
Northern Pygmy Owl – *any season but not every year in Riparian & P/J areas*

North Crestone, South Crestone, Willow, and San Isabel creeks contain cutthroat, rainbow, and brook trout less than 10" long, according to Carey (2003). The alpine lakes at their heads (and also the Deadman Lakes) offer good to excellent fishing for trout up to 16", courtesy of periodic stocking by the Colorado Division of Wildlife. In contrast, the shallow alpine lakes are typically barren; these include Cottonwood Lake, Pole Creek Lake, and the western of the Deadman Lakes. For a bird's-eye view of all the high lakes in the Sangres (from aerial photographs of the west and east sides), see Rychlik (2009).

GOLF & TENNIS

Golf (Challenger Golf Course)
The Challenger Golf Course is a 9-hole, 1881-yard, par 31 "executive" golf course on County Road T, 4 miles west of Crestone (Fig. 8-4). It was one of the original amenities built for Baca lot buyers back in the early 1970s (originally named the Las Cumbres Golf Course). It might have been more successful if the Baca had been populated by military retirees, as was the original plan. But the urban refugees and spiritual seekers who moved to the Baca, especially after 1979, were generally not golfers. So the course has continued to be maintained by the Baca POA year after year, even though it loses money.

The fairways and greens are in decent shape considering the above, but by late summer the greens may become somewhat desiccated. And in the first week of August the course is taken over by the Crestone Music Festival, so is temporarily closed. For information on course status call the Baca POA at (719) 256-4171.

Tennis
The Baca POA tennis courts lie west of the Challenger Golf Course and the Charter School trailers, and next to White Eagle Village (4 miles west of Crestone on the north side of County Road T). They are another POA amenity built in the early 1970s and are occasionally locked. Members can get the key from the POA Office, located about half a mile east on the north side of County Road T.

Fig. 8-4. Left: Looking east down Fairway 1 of the Challenger Golf Course toward the clubhouse, from above the first green. Right: the tennis courts between White Eagle Village and the Crestone Charter School.

The rugged Sangres are not the only place to hike near Crestone; it is also possible to hike through open space on the valley floor in the Baca subdivision. There are two types of Open Space lands: (1) the greenbelts that follow each major creek through the Baca, and (2) wetlands acquired or managed by the Crestone-Baca Land Trust.

Greenbelts Within the Baca Subdivision

When the Baca subdivision and its 10,000 original lots were laid out, the planners created continuous greenbelts along the major creeks. Within the Chalets Units these POA-owned greenbelts are 120-180 yards wide and in the grasslands of the Grants Unit they widen to about 250 yards. For those wishing to hike in these greenbelts there is some good news and some bad news. The good news is that no development has ever taken place in the greenbelts, and they offer an unspoiled walk through the rare cottonwood-juniper woodland community. Some of the greenbelts have been thinned by the Volunteer Fire Department, and there are informal trails in many greenbelts, particularly near the major roads. The bad news is that, in the absence of any forest thinning or trail building, the greenbelt can be a rather impenetrable thicket. Most greenbelts contain a rarely-used foot trail that may be blocked in places by fallen trees. The POA covenants prohibit the use of motor vehicles within the greenbelts. Without being able to use ATVs and small trailers within the greenbelts, it is difficult to thin them very far from the road, or to build long trails. As a result, the trails in the greenbelts are rather primitive compared to the well-used trails in the National Forest. But the primitive state of the foot trails does have one advantage; you may not see another person while walking these trails, and you can come across some fascinating natural features seldom visited (see below).

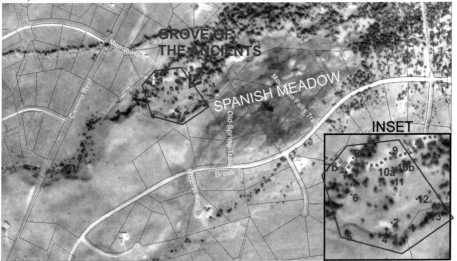

Fig. 8-5. Map of the Grove of the Ancients and vicinity in the Grants Unit of the Baca subdivision. Purple lines show lots in the Grants Unit of the Baca subdivision. In the west part of Spanish Meadow all lots are zoned Open Space. The Grove of the Ancients lies entirely within the POA-owned Spanish Creek greenbelt. Inset shows trees numbered by Crestone Science Center, and the location of the greenbelt trail (green dotted line).

Grove of the Ancients

The oldest living things in the Crestone area are ancient, gnarled Rocky Mountain Juniper trees. Although Junipers are scattered throughout the pinyon-juniper woodland, they reach great age only in special microenvironments. One such environment is the "Grove of the Ancients" on Spanish Creek west of Spanish Meadow, discovered and named by USGS botanist Jim Erdman in 2002. There are at least a dozen Junipers in the 8-acre Grove with trunks larger than 2 feet in diameter. The trunk of the largest (no. 9) measures 43" to 53" in diameter at breast height (DBH).

Many of the old trees have limbs or sub-trunks that were sawed off in times past, exposing tree rings to be counted. On tree no. 6, a 14"-diameter sawed subtrunk showed between 25 and 30 annual rings per inch. By applying this crude growth rate to a tree's measured radius (half the diameter), one can estimate a tree's age.

Wetlands and Meadows of the Crestone-Baca Land Trust (CBLT)

The Crestone-Baca Land Trust (www.crestonelandtrust.org) preserves environmentally sensitive lands such as wetlands, riparian belts, and wildlife corridors from future development, particularly in the Crestone area and Baca Grande subdivision. CBLT protects such lands either by outright ownership, by rezoning to Open Space, or by placing or holding Conservation Easements on the land.

In the past 15 years CBLT has preserved Open Space in four areas of the Baca:
1—Spanish Meadow, a 55-acre meadow south of Spanish Creek (Figs. 8-5, -6)
2—White Wing Wetland, an upland area of high water table and greasewood
3—Oxbow Pond and Wetland, a 170-acre wet meadow that was inadvertently subdivided into (unbuildable) lots (Fig. 8-7)
4—Spanish Creek Wetland, where Spanish Creek exits the Grants Unit of the subdivision (described in Chapter 2).

Fig. 8-6. Spanish Meadow lies on the south side of Spanish Creek (the line of trees in background), west of Wagon Wheel Road in the Baca subdivision. During operation of the Baca Ranch (1860-2004) the water flowing down Spanish Creek was diverted at Wagon Wheel Road to flow through this meadow after mid-summer. This diversion dried out lower Spanish Creek so the large hayfields there could be harvested.

However, since the Ranch was bought by the Federal government in 2004, the US Fish and Wildlife Service has discontinued this seasonal diversion. That action has dried up

Spanish Meadow, Oxbow Pond, and the Oxbow Wetlands, which were previously the key wetlands acquired and preserved by the Crestone-Baca Land Trust.

OXBOW WETLAND AND POND

The Oxbow Wetland is the largest tract of protected open space in the Baca, outside of the streamside greenbelts. It is a 1 mile-long, 0.2 mile-wide wetland meadow located in the southwestern grants between Heatherbrae Road and Camino del Rey, west of Camino Real (a paved road locally called "Two Trees Road"). Most of this 120-acre meadow is public open space land (shaded light gray on Fig. 8-7) owned by the Baca Grande Property Owner's Association, but there are about a dozen privately-owned lots (white) that encroach on the edge of the meadow. The meadow is a good place to watch wildlife.

The principal attraction is Oxbow Pond on the western edge of the meadow, a seasonal lake listed on the National Wetlands Inventory. The pond occupies the deepest part of an ancient, abandoned river meander (an "oxbow bend"), a relic of when Spanish Creek flowed down this channel from the Sangres toward a confluence with Cottonwood Creek. The channel was probably last active during the latest glacial episode in the Sangres (15,000-35,000 years ago), and was abandoned when the glaciers melted away. As of early 2011, there were no constructed trails within the wetland. Birdwatchers visiting Oxbow Pond typically park on the shoulder of Birch Road opposite the Pond, or in the entrance to the Bob-O-Link Trail cul-du-sac. Driving north or south on Quail Run Road will take you into the center of the wetland.

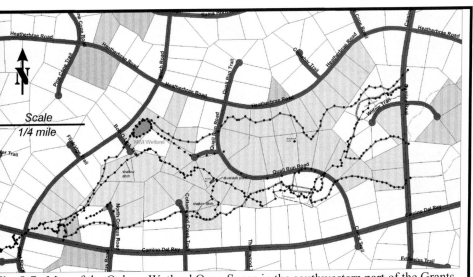

Fig. 8-7. Map of the Oxbow Wetland Open Space in the southwestern part of the Grants Unit, Baca subdivision. The wetland meadow is outlined by the outer line of dots with small hachures. Oxbow Pond, a seasonal lake and NWI wetland, is at upper left. Light gray-shaded lots are open space owned by the Baca Grande POA; slightly darker lots are owned by CBLT; white lots are privately owned. The dotted line at center is the stream channel; dots are GPS waypoints. Map by the Crestone Science Center for CBLT.

155

The Baca Grande Stables (http://bacagrandestables.com) is open all year and offers three types of trail rides, 1-3 hours long, at $20-$25/hr, including the unique "Alternative Architecture Trail Ride." That ride visits many of the alternative building types described in "A Community of Builders" (Chapter 9), and does it in a non-polluting, sustainable way. Children's Group Lessons begin the first week of July and run through the first week of August, also at $20-$25/hr. The Stables will board your horse if you bring your own. Call (719) 256-4756 or email info@bacagrandestables.com

Fig. 8-8. Riders from the big city mount up at the start of their trail ride at the Stables. Photo by Martha Staley.

HUNTING—SEE APPENDIX 3

Crestone has long been a gateway for hunters using the Rio Grande National Forest. With the transfer of private lands in the Baca Grant to the National Forest in 2004, and the opening of the Liberty Road to foot and horse traffic, there is now access to much more hunting in the National Forest. For details on big game species, success rates in this area, and licenses, see Appendix 3.

JEEPING

Motorized vehicles are currently prohibited in the Sangre de Cristo Wilderness, and in the part of Great Sand Dunes National Park accessible from Liberty Gate. Once Liberty Road is upgraded (2011?) vehicles will be allowed on it for 1.7 miles to the Cedar Creek parking lot, but it will be drivable by any 2WD vehicle, so won't exactly qualify as a jeep road. So what does that leave for jeepers?

The jeepable roads are the same two-track roads described earlier in the Mountain Biking section, which lie north of and east of Crestone, partly in BLM land and partly in the Rio Grande National Forest. This includes Forest Road 951 between North Crestone and San Isabel Creeks, and the road up Dimick Gulch.

RAINY DAY ACTIVITIES—*Indoors*

Crestone does occasionally experience a cloudy, drizzly, cold day or two between June and October. It's so unusual that the local photographers all grab their cameras and race outside. But what are the rest of us supposed to do? Aside from washing your socks at the Laundromat, here are some rainy day activities for the greater Crestone area.

PERFORMANCES (Concerts & Lectures)
Crestone Performances, Inc.
CPI arranges musical events both large and small, ranging from the annual 3-Day Crestone Music Festival, to recitals by individual artists in small venues. Concerts will be at venues ranging from Jillian's Studio in Crestone (letter J on Town map) to the Colorado College auditorium. Check local bulletin boards or the *Crestone Eagle*.

Concerts at Hazelrig Music House ($ donation); concerts are held Sundays at 2 pm (as well as at other odd times), and cover every musical genre you have ever heard of, and many you haven't. Since 1999 the industrious Sylvia Hazelrig has hosted more than 225 concerts! If you wait long enough, your type of music will surely come around. Located at 24 Alpine Overlook (Baca subdivision), (719) 256-4371; info@hazelrigmusichouse.com; http://hazelrigmusichouse.com

Concerts AND Free Movie Night at Shumei International ($ donation); irregular schedule; check for events at www.shumeicrestone.org/events/events.html

MUSEUMS:
The Crestone Historical Museum occupies the first floor of the Town Center Building (letter A on Town Map). Exhibits are mainly of a historical nature, highlighting the town's early history as a mining district, the Baca Ranch, and town's more recent incarnation as a spiritual center. The Museum Gift Shop sells maps, books, and other mementos related to historic Crestone.

VIDEO RENTALS
Before Netflix there were……. Video rental stores! Crestone still retains some of these ancient video stores, for example at Crestone Creative Trade (9 on Town Map, Fig. 7-3).

FITNESS
The Intention Holistic Exercise Studio occupies the ground floor of the Challenger Golf Course clubhouse building, 4 miles west of Crestone on County Road T. Personal trainer Carrie Robertson counsels men and women of all ages on strength training, lifestyle coaching, and nutrition. Short- or long-term memberships are available. Located at 68037

157

County Road T, Crestone CO 81131; (719) 588-3879; info@holisticintention.com; http://holisticintention.com

SHOPPING:
Crestone Merchants believe in recycling. The CYP Thrift Store in the Town Center Building carries recycled treasures of all types, including the largest collection of spiritual books this side of Sedona!

The ultimate in recycling is the Crestone Free Box (letter F on Town map), founded in Nov. 1995. If you are tired of something (and it's not junk), take it to the Free Box; I guarantee that somebody in the community is desperately looking for one. Crestonians like to say "The Universe Will Provide." Yeah, it can, but first it needs a Free Box. For your newer religious icons and an assortment of eclectic gifts, visit Crestone Creative Trade (number 9 on Town Map).

PHOTOGRAPHY

Based on the number of professional photographers who live in Crestone, one might think it is a very picturesque location for nature photography. And one would be right. It's hard to take an ugly picture around Crestone, given the clear air and cerulean skies. Sunrises and sunsets are often spectacular.

But the light is strong, so daylight photos tend to be a bit contrasty. After weeks go by without a cloud in the sky, Crestone photographers begin to yearn for some clouds, some mist, some softer shadows. They pray for brooding weather. In the typical clear weather Crestone is blessed with, photographers tend toward capturing the details of small, evocative objects; a cactus flower, the twisted bark of an ancient juniper, the reflection of the sky in a puddle. Professionals such as Linde Waidhofer (www.westerneye.com) and Bill Ellzey (www.billellzey.com) often search for patterns, for small designs intrinsic in nature, which repeat on scales from the small ripples in a stream bottom, to the giant ripples of clouds in the jet stream at 35,000 feet. The repeating patterns are a reminder of the unity of nature, the scale-invariance of its natural laws, and the order imposed wherever the laws of physics battle entropy. The geometry of a mud crack compares to the geometry of a spider web. You might say that Crestone photographers look for scenes that need no captions, that speak in a language understood by all.

PRIMITIVE SKILLS CAMP

One of the greatest gifts you can give a youngster is self-reliance, and Earthknack in Crestone has been teaching life-transforming self-reliance skills for 21 years. Need to learn how to make a fire without matches? Make stone tools? Create string and lashing from plant fiber and rawhide? Make a bow? These are just a fraction of the Stone Age Living Skills you can learn in week-long Earthknack course.

OK, so maybe you are not planning for the end of civilization as we know it, but are more interested in how your grandparents and great-grandparents lived. Earthknack also teaches the lost arts of tallow rendering, soap making, candle making, cobblery (shoe making), basketry, simple blacksmithing, food canning & storage, herbal medicines, butchering, venison jerky, meat smoking, and open fire & dutch oven cooking. You can make your own clothes using hide tanning, buckskin sewing, wool dying, felting, spinning or weaving, earth pigment collection and paint making, and plant dye preparation (see examples at the Earthknack Store, www.earthknack.com/store.html). The abilities will stay with you for a lifetime. And you get some pretty cool clothes, too.

Month-long internships are offered for college-age students and university credit is often available; teachers can receive recertification credits for coursework. Call (719) 256-4909 for current course offerings or visit their website at www.earthknack.com.

SHOOTING

The **Kit Carson Rod & Gun Club** has a shooting range west of Crestone, available during the daylight hours for members and guests. The pistol range has 3 meter to 50 meter setups, and the rifle ranges are 100 and 200 meters. Dues are $40/year for the primary member; NRA membership is required. Call (719) 256-5798 for more information, or mail to P.O. Box 93, Crestone, CO 81131. www.kitcarsonrodandgunclub.org. Directions from Crestone-Baca: from the Baca entrance drive 1.8 miles west on County Road T to the road to Camper Village; turn right (north) onto this road and continue straight, past Camper Village, until you reach the first gate for the Shooting Range.

SWIMMING & SOAKING

Because the SLV is a geothermal valley, there are three hot springs within a half-hour drive of Crestone. Twenty-four miles to the north lies Joyful Journey Hot Springs (www.joyfuljourneyhotsprings.com), with soaking pools at 98°F and 108°F. From Crestone, drive west to Moffat and then 12 miles north on CO 17. For a more rustic retreat (and clothing-optional), try Valley View Hot Springs, operated by the Orient Land Trust (www.olt.org). VVHS contains numerous rock-lined pools on the mountainside connected by walking trails, as well as an 80 ft-long pool; temperatures range from the mid-80s to high 90s F. You can reach VVHS by driving on paved roads to Joyful Journey, then 6 more miles on County Road GG on dirt. Or for the more adventurous, drive the back roads from Crestone, turning north from Road T onto CR 65 and winding 6.7 miles to CR GG. To the south of Crestone lies the Sand Dunes Swimming Pool (www.sanddunespool.com), with a huge pool at 98-100°F and a therapy pool at 105-107°F. This aquatic resort offers RV camping, swimming lessons, and aerobics classes. From Moffat, drive 14 miles south on CO17 to CR D, then east 1 mile, then south 1 mile.

As of 2011 there are two tour oufits in Crestone, willing to lead you around and give you a "peek under the tent" into Crestone's cultural and natural history, plus a self-guided tour. They are listed below in order from the sedate and civilized, to the wild and wooly.

Walking Tour of Historic Crestone; Then and Now
Because Crestone never suffered a devastating fire (unlike most mining towns), many historic wooden buildings still survive. For details about the history of each building, see Sisemore (1983), or visit the Town of Crestone website http://townofcrestone.org/crestone_history.html. Excellent line drawings of historic and modern buildings in Crestone/Baca can be found in Kucin (2000), a book sold locally.

Fig. 8-9a. Looking east up West Galena Avenue, at the block between Cottonwood Street (where photographer was standing) and Alder Street in late spring, 1901. The bank building still exists as the Town Center Building.

Fig. 8-9b. View east up West Galena Avenue, but closer to Alder Street, in winter of 1914. Note that the bank's northern façade is visible at right.

Windhorse Transportation & Tours offers five tours of the Crestone-Baca area, each with a different emphasis and duration (basic, spiritual, sustainability, artist, full-day). Tour guides are long-term Crestone residents. Call (719) 256-4091 or browse http://windhorse.crestonecolorado.com

Fig. 8-10. *Left*: The San Luis Valley Bank on the SW corner of Galena and Alder, built in 1901 when the mines were booming. This was the first and only bank in Crestone in the mining days, and one of few mining-era banks that was: (1) built of wood, and (2) that did not burn down. Once this bank closed, Crestone was without a bank for nearly 100 years, until 2008. *Right:* The same building in 2010, now the Town Center Building. The old bank lobby (bottom center) holds the Crestone Historical Museum, which features the original Diebold bank safe made between 1876 and 1880. This safe got away from Crestone sometime after the bank closed, but was retrieved from Saguache in the 1970s in a bold move by the intrepid Frank and Katie Snider.

Chokurei Ranch Tour

The Cho-Ku-Rei Ranch is a 2400-acre ranch that lies 1.5 miles east of Moffat on County Road T. Not only is this one of the largest ranches in the region, it is one of the most diverse, including a geothermally-heated greenhouse operation, locally-grown foods, and their 43-head yak herd. Yaks are native to Tibet and seem to feel right at home in the San Luis Valley. To schedule a tour, write to P.O. Box 207, Crestone, CO 81131; or call 24 hours ahead to (719) 256-4599; or email <u>chokureiranch@yahoo.com</u>.

Fig. 8-11. A herd of curious yaks heads toward a tour group on the Chokurei Ranch. Public tours visit the yak herd as it roams across 4 square-mile ranch. From the back of a vintage Army troop carrier, visitors can safely feed the yaks, as ranch hands explain how fur is collected from these friendly creatures and spun into yarn.

SPECIAL EVENTS

MAY (Memorial Day): Crestone Volunteer Fire Department Dance
Memorial Day fundraiser dance with live music at the Crestone Firehouse. For info, call CVFD at (719) 256-4765.

LATE JUNE THROUGH MID SEPTEMBER— Crestone Saturday Market, Every Saturday, 9am to 3 pm; vendors selling fresh local produce and dairy, hot meals, bedding plants, handmade crafts, minerals specimens & crystals, etc.; located in the street (the west 100 block of Silver Avenue) adjacent to Little Pearl Park and the Bliss Cafe. Call (719) 256-6400.

JULY: Fourth of July Celebration
Old-fashioned Fourth of July with a parade, soapbox derby, the 5K Run, Walk, or Crawl Race, a pancake breakfast, and all day activities at the two Crestone Town parks. For info, call the Town of Crestone at (719) 256-4313 or email crestone@fairpoint.net

Fig. 8-12. *Left*: Spectators line Galena Avenue in downtown Crestone during the 4th of July Soapbox Derby; *Right*: Clueless out-of-town guests head toward the infamous Wet Zone in 2008.

AUGUST: The Crestone Music Festival (www.crestfest.org)
The Crestone Music Festival is probably the smallest festival in Colorado to consistently offer big-name acts, and certainly the one with the best mountain backdrop. Inaugurated in 1999, it has morphed into a 3-day, multi-genre festival with two stages and continuous acts, plus all sorts of vendors (care for some tie-dye?), jugglers, clowns, acrobats, and fire dancers. It's also one of the cheapest summer festivals in Colorado, with on-site camping offered for a mere $25 for the whole 3-day weekend. Think of it as a smaller Woodstock without the mud.

Past headliners (Fig. 8-13) include rockers such as Leon Russell, Dave Mason, Edgar Winter, John Sebastian, Dan Hicks and the Hot Licks, and Richie Havens. Bluesmen have included John Mayall and the Bluesbreakers, John Lee Hooker Jr., and Booker T (sans the MGs). The Festival is held in early August at the Challenger Golf Course, 4 miles west of Crestone. For info, call (719) 256-4533, visit www.crestfest.org or email crestfest@crestfest.org. And get ready to rock.

ig. 8-13. Headliners from past years of the Crestone Music Festival. Clockwise from upper left: eon Russell spins his magic; Dave Mason and his trusty Telecaster; John Lee Hooker Jr. bestows me mojo; Dan Hicks and the famous Hot Licks. Photos courtesy of Crestone Performances, Inc. 007 photos by Seth Bullington.

EPTEMBER (Labor Day): Crestone Volunteer Fire Department Dance
abor Day fundraiser dance with live music at the Crestone Firehouse.

**EPTEMBER (Labor Day weekend): San Luis Valley Energy Fair
www.slvenergyfair.com)**
egun in 1990 as the Crestone Energy Fair, this is the oldest grassroots fair in Colorado evoted to renewable energy and sustainable lifestyles. It is a volunteer-driven non-profit ir. Presentations and vendors span the spectrum of sustainable living: Straw bale home nstruction, earth bag construction, earthen plasters & pigments, spray foam insulation, tal solar home design, solar thermal and solar PV, solar water pumping systems, uilding a solar oven, geothermal energy, electric vehicles, biofuels, , home-made wind enerators, etc. A unique aspect is the Home Tours, which visit local green homes; in 010 there were three such tours, each led by a different local builder.

CTOBER 31: Baca Fireman's Halloween Ball
eld every year at the Desert Sage Restaurant near the entrance to the Baca subdivision. costume ball with live music, combined with a silent auction fundraiser for the VFDs; izes given for best costumes.

OVEMBER: Winterfest (first weekend after Thanksgiving)

Winterfest is an annual town-wide celebration of the arrival of winter, but also coincides with the Christmas gift buying season. Four simultaneous craft shows at different venues, featuring holiday food, one-of-a-kind gifts, entertainment, and Santa.

WATCHING WILDLIFE

Watching The Big, Mostly Harmless Animals (Deer, Elk, Bear, Bison)
Deer are the most ubiquitous big animal in the Crestone-Baca area and can be seen any morning or evening. They prefer to graze in grassy openings and meadows in the pinyon-juniper woodland, but can also be seen in the forest. The local mule deer have become so acclimated to humans and their cars they hardly even look up when you drive by. In fact, deer have become so acclimated they will walk right in front of a moving car and expect it to stop.

So……..Please use extra caution driving the roads of Crestone and the Baca, especially at twilight when deer are browsing on the shoulders of the roads. Deer often cross the road in groups, so if one crosses in front of you, look in the direction it came from to see if its buddies are about to step onto the roadway. At night PLEASE slow down to at or below the posted speed limit, to avoid a collision. The deer thank you.

MAMA, WHEN DO THE DEER TURN INTO ELK?-- The Elk vs. Deer Controversy

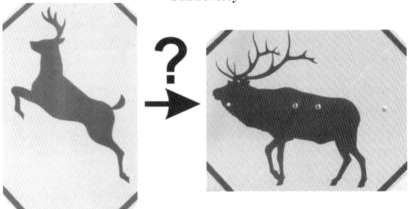

Fig. 8-14. Nobody has ever seen this happen, but many still ask the question.

This oft-quoted tourist question conceals a real interspecies competition between the species, and between their hunters. It may come as a surprise, but elk hunters and deer hunters have been in subtle competition since the 1950s, each claiming that proliferation of the other species is ruining the hunting and habitat of their favored species. Their idea of interspecies competition in the National Forests is that it is a zero-sum game; any changes that increase the number of one species must decrease the numbers of the other.

Thus, elk hunters decry any management or land-use changes that seem to favor deer, and vice-versa. According to Western Association of Fish & Wildlife Agencies www.createstrat.com/muledeerinthewest/elkandmuledeer.html), development of the wildland-urban interface, habitat fragmentation, and grazing practices since the 1950s have generally favored the grass-eating elk over the shrub-browsing deer. Mule deer populations reached a peak in 1950s and have declined since, which supports this claim.

Elk are considerably more skittish than deer so you rarely see them in suburban areas with traffic and dogs. Elk stay away from roads and act unpredictably when cars come by; they may run away, or they may run right across the road in front of you. The best place to see elk is in a meadow that is at least 200 feet away from a road. A good example is along Road T, or Spanish Meadow in the Baca Grande subdivision.

Black Bears

A healthy population of black bears inhabit the Sangre de Cristo Range above Crestone. When savvy hikers camp overnight there, they hang their food high from tree branches and don't leave food (or food smells) in their tents, just to avoid any unpleasant midnight encounters. This situation is common in most Colorado mountain ranges.

What is different about the Sangre de Cristo range here is the presence of a town and subdivision at the foot of the mountains, complete with trash cans and dumpsters. In drought years (such as 2000-2002), when bear food becomes scarce in the mountains, the bears stand up, sniff the wind and often head down to sample the nearest dumpster. If they can't find a dumpster, they might try your kitchen.

Bear incursions into the Crestone-Baca metroplex continued through the summer of 2004 (Keno, 2004a; Quillen, 2004), but then thankfully the drought broke in 2005 and the bears returned to the National Forest and their normal feeding habits. Well, except for..... on Aug. 12, 2007 in the Baca Grande subdivision (Lowers, 2007), when a bear pried open a car containing food. And on June 26, 2008, when a bear tried to break into an occupied house in the Baca (Quillen, 2008).

Ralphie the Buffalo

As the good reader knows, Ralphie the Buffalo is the mascot of the University of Colorado (the Buffs). But you may also run into a bison (correct name) if you wander south into the Great Sand Dunes National Park from its Northern Entrance. A herd of 2000 bison (Fig. 8-15) roams the northern part of the 103,000-acre Medano-Zapata Ranch owned by The Nature Conservancy, which lies directly west of the National Park and south of BNWR. Normally the bison should be inside the Ranch fence...but ya never know. For a real up-close look at the herd, arrange a guided ranch tour www.zranch.org).

Fig. 8-15. The North American Plains Bison numbered about 50 million in the mid 1800s. Now there are about 500,000 bison (1% of their peak population) in captive commercial herds, scattered among roughly 4000 private ranches in the USA. The 2000-head herd in the Medano-Zapata ranch is the third-largest remaining herd in the United States. Adult bulls such as the one shown can weigh up to 2000 pounds. Photo by NPS.

The winter months in Crestone are a magical time, with brilliant blue skies, snowclad mountains, and … silence. This is a level of silence unknown to the city dweller, a silence from when the world was new. The crowds of summer have long since departed and the town reverts to a sleepy, isolated village of neighbors. You can walk right down the middle of Crestone's main streets at noon with only a dog or two for company. Stop by the Town Hall and have a cup of coffee with the mayor. There is all the time in the world. Time to watch the snowflakes falling, time to sit in front of the fire and watch flames dance like small auroras. Even time to dream of plans for next summer.

Fig. 8-16. Downtown Crestone in the still of winter, with snowpacked East Galena Avenue in the distance

Cross-Country Skiing and Snowshoeing
The most popular cross-country route is Liberty Road, starting at Liberty Gate. The route is gentle and rolling and has great views, but is exposed to afternoon sun so is best skied immediately after major snowstorms. In contrast, the Forest Trails such as North Crestone lie in deep shadow and retain skiable snow throughout the winter, but are relatively rockier and steeper, and so perhaps better suited to snowshoeing.

Sledding; The best sled run, snow conditions permitting, is down East Galena Avenue beginning east of the Crestone city limits (Figs. 8-16, -17). This run comes into prime condition only a few weeks per year, typically in January or February, when temperature remain below freezing all day, and car traffic has packed down the snow. In these conditions, a sledder can make it from the McAlpine Ranch all the way into downtown Crestone (if you don't wipeout at the bend at the City limits).

Fig. 8-17. A Flexible Flyer is perched for a run down East Galena Avenue (just beyond the section visible in Fig.), east of the City limits in the McAlpine Ranch .

"The Jewish Santa Clauses of Crestone"

Every town needs a Santa Claus, even those (or especially those) in the middle of nowhere. But a good Santa can be hard to find. He has to be big, jolly, love children, and be able to listen. In other words, he has to be….a *mensch*.

From 1990 to 2009 Crestone's Santa was Ed Rosenberg, a real New York mensch. His brother is a rabbi. Ed was born in NYC and came west in the early 1960s to get a degree in psychology at the University of Colorado. After a colorful past in Colorado communes and in Taos, New Mexico, Ed landed in Crestone in 1988 and got stuck here. He owned the Mountain High Woodstove Company and made sure that every family in Crestone with a wood stove made it through each winter. And he insured that all their chimneys were clean, especially around Christmas, for old Santa. For 19 years he donned his Santa suit (Fig. 8-18) and made sure all the little boys and girls were good. For goodness sake.

Fig. 8-18. In 2008 Ed's health began to decline and he realized a replacement Santa must eventually be found. After searching the town for someone with the aforementioned qualifications, he found a replacement: his younger son, Abram Rosenberg, age 19 (shown at left as Santa's elf, age 8). So, in 2009 Ed hung up his Santa Suit and bid farewell to the elves and reindeer, passing the torch to a younger generation. Crestone preserved its tradition of the Jewish Santa Claus.

TOO CLOSE FOR COMFORT: Bear Breaking and Entering

The Statewide drought of 2000-2004 was severe in southern Colorado, and hard on the wildlife. Black bears in particular were forced down out of the mountains in search of food, and into populated places like Crestone and the Baca subdivision. Because our area has few dumpsters (a bear's normal in-town dining venue), they decided to go right to the food source; people's kitchens.

On May 12, 2002 the Crestone Science Center had just hosted a field trip for 39 international geologists. We had treated them to a traditional Western-style dinner of BBQ ribs. Without thinking, the next day I dumped the leftover rib bones in an outdoor trash can. This was Mistake #1.

The next morning at 5 am I was awakened by the sound of a trash can going over. Looking down from my 2nd-floor window, I observed a black bear with its body 2/3 of the way in the 55-gal drum, rooting happily away. He would emerge with a rib, then sit back on his haunches and leisurely crunch it up; then dive back in for another one. This went on for about 15 minutes, until all the ribs were gone from one barrel. For good measure, he spread all the other trash from the barrel around in a wide circle, to make sure he hadn't missed anything. Once he finished with the first barrel, he started tipping over the second one. That was enough for me, so I ran downstairs, opened the door about 20 feet away from him, and yelled. He instantly took off at a gallop and disappeared into the trees in about 5 seconds.

Later that night Mr. Bear returned and triggered the outside floodlights. I looked down at him as he was worrying my front door knob. Opening the window, I yelled down at him, thinking that had worked earlier. But in the nighttime, a bear knows he is KING and you are just prey. He glared at me, and disdainfully sauntered off into the dark at his own pace. Next morning I found paw- and nose-prints on every first-floor window.

As wildlife experts will tell you, once a hungry bear has gotten food at your place, he will continue coming back. A week or so later I returned home just after sunset and as I parked outside the kitchen I noticed the screen was missing from a kitchen window. Earlier in the day I had left this casement window cranked open, covered only by a screen (Mistake #2). Now the screen was gone. I thought, that's funny; what could have knocked the screen off? And where is the screen? It wasn't lying on the ground below the window. The window just gaped open.

Looking in the kitchen door, I noticed the screen lying on the kitchen floor; it had been pushed inward. Also the door to the freezer compartment of the refrigerator was standing wide open. The bowl of ripening peaches that had been on the kitchen counter was upside-down on the floor in front of the fridge. The peaches were gone, replaced by smear of yellow peach slime all over the floor. There were large paw-prints of yellow peach slime on the front of the fridge. An ice-cream container from the freezer lay upside–down on the floor, licked clean. All signs pointed to....... Mr. Bear having been (or still being) inside the house. I crept up to the bedroom, grabbed my blunderbuss, and went room-by-room through the house, looking for Mr. Bear. But no bear was there.

The next morning I circled the house, and found two empty tortilla bags behind the house. These had also been in the freezer. Based on the physical evidence, it appears that the bear had heard my car coming up the driveway, grabbed two bags of frozen tortillas as a "to-go" snack, and climbed out the kitchen window with them. Then he went around back and finished them off, while I was inside hunting for him.

9. THE COMMUNITIES OF CRESTONE-BACA

...it is hard to be pessimistic about the West. This is the native home of hope. When it finally learns that cooperation, not rugged individuals, is the pattern that most characterizes and preserves it, then it will have achieved itself and outlived its origins. Then it has a chance to create a society to match its scenery.
Wallace Stegner, 1997, *The Sound of Mountain Water*

Few communities in the world can claim to have taken Stegner's challenge literally, to "create a society to match its scenery." But Crestone, a former mining town and ghost town, is trying. The impetus for its utopian effort was ultimately two Institutes formed by Maurice and Hanne Strong in the early 1980s. The Manitou Foundation & Institute still exists and is responsible for many of the spiritual centers as well as for protecting the foothills from overdevelopment. The Aspen Institute was brought to the Baca from Aspen in 1981 by Maurice Strong, and stayed until 1984, after which it returned to Aspen. Its legacy lives on as the Baca Campus of Colorado College.

THE REVISIONING OF THE BACA GRANDE (for more details see Pearson, 2008) In 1977 Maurice Strong (a Canadian businessman) and partner acquired AZL Resources and along with it the Baca Ranch and the unsold parts of the Baca Grande subdivision. Maurice and his wife Hanne Marstrand Strong moved to the Baca Ranch in 1978, with Hanne's mother (Karen Marstrand) and daughters. Once the Strongs arrived on site, however, they soon became aware of two things: (1) the original plan for the Baca subdivision as a retirement community had largely failed, and (2) the area had potential for another type of use.

In October of 1978 an elderly local mystic named Glenn Anderson arrived at Hanne's door and said "I have been waiting for you to arrive." He then proceeded to inform her that it was "long known that the Native American people who visited and inhabited this area, for thousands of years, recognized it as a place for spiritual growth and healing—where all aspects of life are more easily permeated by the sacred, and people of awareness can flourish" (Manitou Foundation, 2005). His source for this astounding statement was the "oral transmissions from various wisdom keepers." His challenge to Maurice and Hanne was this: to use their holdings in the Baca to create an oasis to preserve endangered wisdom traditions from around the world.

Before embarking on such a radical revisioning of the Baca development, Hanne invited a number of Native American elders to the Baca to confirm Anderson's prophecy about the Baca being a place of historical refuge and holy power. The elders visited in 1979 and 1980 and confirmed the prophecy. So in the early 1980s the Strongs began "revisioning" the Baca Grande subdivision to transform it from a retirement community to a spiritual oasis. The original 14,000-acre subdivision had contained about 10,000 lots. The Strongs soon realized that if those lots were all built on and occupied with 2- to 4-person households, the Baca would be by far the largest city in the San Luis Valley!

169

Clearly the local utility infrastructure and water supply could not handle such a population, nor could the tiny Town of Crestone provide sufficient services. But worse, the "full build-out" would destroy the local ambience necessary for quiet contemplation and meditation. So they immediately attempted to reduce the potential density by consolidating over 5000 lots in Chalet 3 and in the steeper foothills that they controlled.

In the early 1980s the Strongs invited several religious and contemplative organizations to locate in the Baca. The first organizations included the Lindisfarne Association; The Aspen Institute for Humanistic Studies; The Spiritual Life Institute of the Carmelite Order; and Karma Thegsum Tashi Gomang, a Tibetan Buddhist group headed by the 16th Karmapa. The Haidakhandi Universal Ashram of the Hindu tradition received land in the mid-1980s.

By the late 1980s the Strongs were receiving so many requests for land that in 1988 they established the Manitou Foundation to manage the land grant program. "Manitou" is a Native American word for the animistic spirit-gods that pervade the natural world; every plant, every stone has its own Manitou. Once established as a nonprofit organization, the Manitou Foundation received major support from Laurance and Mary Rockefeller, friends of the Strongs who loved the Baca and visited it many times.

THE STRONGS

Maurice and Hanne Strong think big. Their stage is the world stage, and their local base for a time was Crestone and the Baca Grant. From their past and ongoing activities, their personal mantra must be something like the quote attributed to Mahatma Ghandi: "You must BE the change you want to see in the world."

Maurice Strong—The Wizard of the Baca Grande

If you search the Internet for 'Maurice Strong" today you will find thousands of Web pages about him, most identifying him as one of the secret architects of the New World Order. But back in 1978 when he arrived at the Baca Grant he was a Canadian oil developer and an ex-UN diplomat. In 1972 he organized the UN Conference on the Human Environment in Stockholm, which recommended creation of the UN Environment Programme. Maurice became that agency's first Executive Director.

Fig. 9-1. Maurice Strong at a United Nations press conference in 2009. UN photo.

Later in the early 1990s Maurice was appointed Secretary General of the UN Conference on Environment and Development (better known as the Earth Summit) held in Rio de Janiero in 1992 (see Wood, 1990). In 2001 he published a book explaining his environmental activities and beliefs (Strong, 2001). His list of international awards is impressive and continues to grow; for more information on Maurice go to www.mauricestrong.net

Hanne Marstrand Strong
A native of Denmark, Hanne is the driving force behind the evolution of the Crestone-Baca area into a spiritual and ecological center. Along with her mother and sister, she founded the Manitou Foundation, the Manitou Institute, the Earth Origins Seed Bank, the Baca Center for High Altitude Sustainable Agriculture, the Quinoa Project, the Earth Restoration Corps, the Youth Peace Journey, and the International Educational Center for Indigenous Peoples. Through the Manitou Foundation she developed the Manitou Habitat Conservation Plan which manages and protects the scenic mountain backdrop above Crestone and the Baca. These days Hanne spends much of her time in China, a colossus whose emergence will mold much of 21st-Century life on earth. As of 2011 she still resides in the Baca.

THE MANITOU FOUNDATION & MANITOU INSTITUTE

The Manitou Foundation was created in 1988 to put Glenn Anderson's prophecy into action in concrete terms:

(1) To donate land in the Crestone/Baca area to representatives of world religions, particularly those with unbroken lineages, for the establishment of retreat Centers that perpetuate their ancient wisdom traditions.

Fig. 9-2. A Buddhist monk meditates in one of the area's monasteries. Nine of the 15 retreat centers are Buddhist. These include Tibetan Buddhist (6) Bhutanese Buddhist (1), and Zen Buddhist (2). Most centers have small cabins for rent for personal retreats which range from primitive to luxurious. Photo by Bill Ellzey.

(2) To donate land for the establishment of Centers offering educational programs & projects that facilitate Earth stewardship activities of conservation, community sustainability, environmentally appropriate building, and agricultural technologies.

3) To administer a land preservation program, including setting aside as open space the majority of land (900 of 1,400 acres) held by Manitou Foundation in the foothills of the Sangre de Cristo Mountains, to preserve their pristine quality and protect the natural plant and wildlife ecosystems.

The Manitou Habitat Conservation Program –
In the mid 1990's, Manitou and specialists of The Conservation Fund, with generous support of Laurance Rockefeller and the Jackson Hole Preserve, devoted several years to ecological studies of Manitou's mountain properties, culminating in 1995 with the creation of the Manitou Habitat Conservation Plan (MHCP). Comprehensive assessments were made of the terrain, slope, soil types, drainage and erosion patterns; botanical studies and wildlife patterns - corridors, birthing areas, human interface issues; forest health and wildfire concerns, etc. The result was a master conservation easement being laid on almost all of the Manitou Mountain Tract to the east of the Baca Chalets (Fig. 9-3). During this same period the Manitou Institute, a tax-exempt charitable organization

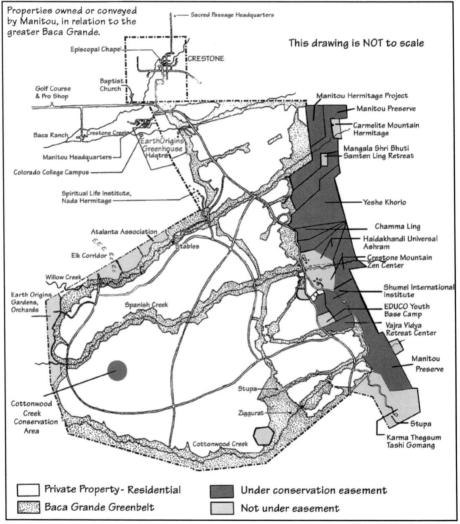

Fig. 9-3. Map of lands in the Baca Grant owned or conveyed by the Manitou Foundation. From http://manitou.org.

172

was created, to support local spiritual and environmental projects and programs, and to administer the MHCP conservation easements. The Institute launched the Earth Restoration Corps (now its own organization; www.earthrestorationcrops.org), and sponsors programs of Earth Origins Seeds and the Youth Peace Journey.

THE ASPEN INSTITUTE IN CRESTONE (1981-1984)

The Aspen Institute for Humanistic Studies was conceived in Aspen, Colorado in 1950 by Walter Paepke, president of the Container Corporation of America (see Hyman, 1976). Through reading and discussing selections from the works of classic and modern writers, Institute members would "better understand the human challenges facing the organizations and communities they serve." Aspen Institute events have attracted presidents, statesmen, diplomats, judges, ambassadors, and Nobel laureates over the years, enriching and enlivening the Institute as a global forum for leaders. To conspiracy theorists, however, the Aspen Institute is a key component of the New World Order.

By the early 1970s the Institute wished to expand its campus in Aspen, and in 1972 applied to build a 356-room hotel and a 56,000 square-foot conference facility in Aspen Meadows. After 7 years of negotiations with City and County officials, the Aspen City Council turned down the application in 1979. The Institute's Board became disgruntled and voted to sell the entire West End campus to a local land developer for $5.9 million, and to accept a donation of 320 acres of the Baca Ranch from Institute trustee Maurice Strong as a replacement (in 1981). On that acreage the Institute built a Seminar Building (Fig. 9-4), 18 townhouses, a French restaurant (originally named The Bistro; now the Desert Sage, owned by Tshering Dorji from Bhutan), and jogging trail. The Institute also bought the Inn at the Baca Grande (built to host prospective lot buyers in the early 1970s) and added a 2nd story to it (source: New York Times, Dec. 13, 1981).

The Baca campus was a good venue for concentration and undistracted study of seminar topics. However, its isolation soon proved to be a drawback to global leaders and captains of industry, and their accompanying wives and significant others. In one instance, someone's glasses broke and they needed a small screw to repair them. No such crews could be purchased in Crestone, so they had to drive 50 miles to Alamosa and return (L. Eickhoff, pers. comm.). A 100-mile drive was required, just to get a small crew.

The Bistro restaurant next to the Townhouses was about the only amenity in 1981. There was no Internet, no cell phones, no satellite TV, no video rental, no Federal Express or UPS deliveries. In a sense that may be hard to understand today, seminar attendees in Crestone were cut off from the world. The nearest "shopping" required a 100-mile round trip to the small farming supply towns of Salida or Alamosa. And what was for sale there paled in comparison to the glitzy designer shops of Aspen. As reported in the Aspen Times (2005), *"The Institute began moving its executive seminars and conferences to an isolated campus near Crestone, Colorado, which turned out to have little appeal to high-powered executives accustomed to Aspen."*

In 1984 the Institute decided to return to Aspen and try to re-acquire its campus here. It concluded that *"The [1979] sale proved devastating for the Institute's reputation and fund-raising capabilities both here and beyond, ... and for the next seven years it hobbled along, renting the space it once owned..."* (www.aspeninstitute.org). The Strong's generosity in donating the 320 acres and building the facilities is nowhere mentioned in the Aspen Institute's documents. This seems an odd historical omission,

173

somewhat like rewriting history to omit "inconvenient truths." In the matter of bringing the Aspen Institute to the Baca, the Strongs were guilty only of being 30 years ahead of their time, a trait they have exhibited in many other endeavors as well.

Fig. 9-4. Kit Carson Mountain reflects in the windows of the Seminar Building built by the Aspen Institute. This building was designed in a pseudo-Bauhaus style to mimic those on the main campus of the Aspen Institute in Aspen, Colorado. It is now part of the Baca Campus of Colorado College, and is a common venue for community events.

The Legacy of the Aspen Institute: The Baca Campus of Colorado College
1984 was the last year the Aspen Institute used its center at the Baca, but in 1987 Colorado College (CC) rented a single classroom for one class. The next year CC leased three townhouses and the Seminar Building from the Aspen Institute, and started a fundraising campaign to purchase all the facilities. In March 1990 CC purchased one townhouse, the Seminar Building, and 293 acres of adjacent land. These purchases created the Baca Campus of Colorado College, the anchor for the college's Hulbert Center for Southwest Studies. From April to September of 1992 the 7000 square foot Lodge was built (student housing).

Since 1987, "*more than 30,000 students have been involved in the campus………… Nearly 2000 students and faculty utilize the Baca each year*" (www.coloradocollege.edu/dept/sw/baca.asp). The impact of CC alumni is felt far beyond the borders of Colorado. For example, CC alumnus Ken Salazar ('77) is currently Secretary of the Interior; Marcia McNutt ('74) is director of the U.S. Geological Survey; Diana DeGette ('79) is an 8-term member of Congress; figure skater Peggy Fleming ('70) won Olympic gold in 1968 and was a commentator for ABC Sports for 28 years. And the list goes on. So, the CC students you see walking from the Baca Campus into downtown Crestone, or sitting around town with their sketch pads, may just become the leaders of the next generation.

174

Crestone is a place where the physical and spiritual worlds overlap. The physical setting is certainly conducive to contemplation, undistracted by urban sound, light, and busyness. Foothill summits and high peaks beckon as sites for breakthrough meditation.

> *Along with the geographical clarity that comes from elevation gain, I sense a new orientation in my being. In a few lucid moments, it is as if the boundary that defines my sense of "self" has become more permeable. I feel less contained, less isolated, more like a moving part in a greater entity called mountain..."*
> Anderson, 2005, *First Church of the Higher Elevations*

Fig. 9-5. *Left:* A benevolent Buddhist appears to bless the Sangres, rising from the courtyard of the Dragon Mountain (Zen) Temple. *Right:* The spiral ramp of the Ziggurat forms a "Stairway to Heaven" to Crestone Peak and Needle.

The Manitou Foundation recognized this aspect early on and has capitalized on it, drawing 21 retreat centers to the foothills of the Baca Grande. The religious traditions now represented in Crestone (mainly Buddhist, Hindu, and Native American) have always incorporated a respect for the unspoiled natural world. Recently there have also been movements within the Judeo-Christian religions to include ecology and an appreciation of Nature in their doctrines, in an attempt to soften the Bible's stern admonition to "multiply and subdue the earth." This movement is called "eco-spirituality" and it "originates in the basic belief that the earth is a divine expression and, as such, is sacred and holy." (Colorado Ecospiritual Center; www.ecospiritual.com). Crestone could be a poster child for this new doctrine.

Many people come to Crestone hoping that the isolation and physical beauty alone will infuse them with spiritual enlightenment. However, enlightenment requires work and discipline wherever you are. As Crestone Mayor Ralph Abrams says: *"Soulful truths aren't to be found in a physical place, and those who look for instant spiritual gratification probably will find something else"* (Welsch, 2009).

The religious centers of the Baca may differ from what Americans are used to, relying more on the teachings and interpretations of living teachers ("Rinpoches" in Buddhism; "Gurus" in Hinduism) than on an ancient written body of dogma such as the Bible or Talmud. The religious hierarchy that grants these teachers status is not as rigid as, say, the Pope and the Roman Catholic Church. Rinpoches can be proclaimed by other Rinpoches, or in some cases self-proclaimed. Most spiritual centers are open to the public, at least for part of the year; in some cases they like visitors to call ahead. For a more in-depth survey of spiritual centers, see *A Sacred Earth Journal*, for sale at local restaurants, grocery stores, and at the ashram gift shop (http://shop.babajiashram.org).

Fig. 9-6. Not your average Colorado road sign, this one at Camino Baca Grande and Willow Creek lists several of the spiritual centers located in former Manitou lands on southern Camino Baca Grande and Dream Way. Distances are measured south from Willow Creek; the sign is also the beginning of the Mileage Log below. Proceeding south on Camino Baca Grande, land to your left (east) belongs to spiritual centers of the Manitou Foundation; land to your right is mainly privately owned lots in the Baca Grande subdivision.

MILEAGE LOG FOR THE OLD RAILROAD GRADE (Camino Baca Grande and Dream Way) (see Fig. 9-8 for map)

Point	Mileage	Feature
1	0.0	Camino Baca Grande (paved) crosses Willow Creek, following the old 1902 railroad grade southward
2	0.4	pavement ends
3	0.5	driveway on left leads to the Yeshe Khorlo center (call for appointment)
4	0.8	driveway on left leads to the Chamma Ling retreat cabins
5	1.2	driveway on left leads to the Haidakhandi Universal Ashram and Lakshmi Gift Shop
6	1.5	Camino Baca Grande crosses Spanish Creek; old trail up Spanish Creek is on south side of creek, but is closed now by the Crestone Mountain

		Zen Center
7	1.7	fork in road; continue straight on the old railroad grade (now called Dream Way) to reach Crestone Mountain Zen Center and Shumei International; the right fork is the continuation of Camino Baca Grande into the subdivision, and leads to Dharma Ocean (no. 17), White Jewel Mountain (no. 18), and Vajra Vidya (no. 16)
8	1.85	driveway on right leads to a private home
9	1.9	driveway on left leads to the Crestone Mountain Zen Center; call for appointment, since the Center is closed some months
10	2.1	driveway on right leads to private home
11	2.2	enter the northern boundary of the Shumei International center; this is the southernmost spiritual center on the railroad grade
12	2.6	leave the southern boundary of the Shumei center; road narrows to a single lane
13	3.1	"T" intersection with Tranquil Way; turn left (east) for the mouth of Cottonwood Creek, trailhead parking, and the road to the KTTG "Big Stupa"; turn right to head down and west into the Baca Grande subdivision
14	3.2	water tank owned by the Baca Grande Water and Sanitation District; *No Parking or Camping here*
15	3.3	road crosses Cottonwood Creek; an informal parking area for hikers has arisen between the water tank and the creek crossing; the Cottonwood Creek Trail starts opposite on the north side of the creek; HOWEVER, please note that the first 0.5 mile of the Trail crosses private land owned by the Manitou Foundation (see Chapter 3).

Fig. 9-7. A Tibetan prayer flag at the entrance to Yeshe Khorlo flutters in the wind, seeming to carry its prayers up into the blue skies of the San Luis Valley.

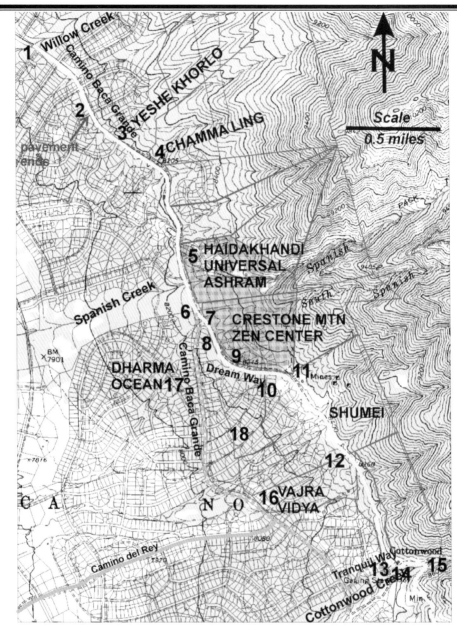

Fig. 9-8. Route to the spiritual centers along Camino Baca Grande/Dream Way (thick white line) to Cottonwood Creek. The road separates spiritual retreat lands (to the east, large outlined polygons) from the lots of the Baca subdivision (to the west). Numbers 1 through 15 refer to the Mileage Log. Solid medium gray line shows Camino del Rey (paved). The medium gray dotted line is the unpaved southern part of Camino Baca Grande, site of Dharma Ocean (17), White Jewel Mountain (18) and Vajra Vidya (16). South of point #15, the road continues to the KTTG center and the Tashi Gomang Stupa (the "Big Stupa").

TIBETAN BUDDHIST

1-- Dharma Ocean Foundation

Dharma Ocean offers Buddhist training and sitting meditation programs in the lineage of Chogyam Trungpa Rinpoche. The Director is Dr. Reginald Ray (PhD, Univ. of Chicago Divinity School, 1973). In the spring of 1974, at the invitation of Chögyam Trungpa Rinpoche, he moved to Boulder, Colorado where he became the first full-time faculty member and chair of the Buddhist Studies Department at Naropa University.

> *"To be awake, to be enlightened, is to be fully and completely embodied. To be fully embodied means to be at one with who we are, in every respect, including our physical being, our emotions, and the totality of our karmic situation."*
> Reggie Ray

Dharma Ocean offers training in Buddhist meditation through retreats entitled *Meditating With The Body*, typically 6 days long for beginners and 17 days long for advanced practitioners. Winter Dathun is also offered, a 26-day intensive retreat for advanced practitioners (every Dec-Jan.). The Foundation maintains a retreat cabin rental ("luxurious solitary space") next to the Retreat Center on North Carefree Way.

The Retreat Center is also open to rental groups at various times of the year. It has one of the largest public rooms (3000 square feet) in the area which can seat up to 150 people, as well as a full-service kitchen and dining area. A 68-bed Residence Hall is under construction (2011).

Fig. 9-9. The new 12,000 square-foot Dharma Ocean building huddles beneath Kit Carson Mountain. Since its completion in 2010 the building has become a popular venue for large community gatherings and events.

Founder:	Reginald Ray
Date Founded:	2005
Retreat cabins for Rent?	YES (1); residence hall under construction
Operations Manager:	Amulya Ananda
Location:	Willow Creek and Spanish Creek
Contact:	P.O. Box 159, Crestone, CO 81131; (719) 256-4335; (877) 342-7629; 2541 N. Carefree Way; info@dharmaocean.org; www.dharmaocean.org

2-- Karma Thegsum Tashi Gomang (KTTG)

KTTG was founded in 1980 by His Holiness the XVI Gyalwa Karmapa, head of the Kagyu order of Tibetan Buddhism. "Karmapa" means "He who performs the activity of a Buddha." Since the 12th century, the Karmapa has held the position of supreme head of the Kagyu Order of Tibetan Buddhism, the lineage known as the "sacred word." The 16th Karmapa visited the Baca in 1980, at the invitation of the Manitou Foundation, and chose the land now occupied by KTTG. However, he died in 1981, and the present facilities were built by his followers.

KTTG is dedicated to working to fulfill His Holiness' vision that this beautiful and remote location would be an auspicious place for the preservation and continuation of the Buddhist religion and culture of his Tibetan homeland

Fig. 9-10. The Tashi Gomang Stupa of KTTG looms over the SLV. It was dedicated to the 16th Karmapa in 1996, 15 years after his death

KTTG is best known for its Tashi Gomang Stupa (aka the Big Stupa) at the south end of the Baca Grande subdivision. Construction was begun in May 1991 and the stupa was consecrated on July 6, 1996. The stupa was filled with 100,000 tsa-tsas (miniature stupas made by volunteers. Within each tsa-tsa is a roll of prayers and mantras. The tsa-tsas were blessed and consecrated by visiting lamas before being placed inside the stupa. Visitors often walk around the stupa in a clockwise direction 3 times during their meditation. The Stupa is open to the public.

Founder:	16th Gyalwa Karmapa
Date Founded:	1980
Retreat cabins for Rent?	YES (2)
Resident Lama:	Zoe de Bray
Size:	200 acres south of Cottonwood Creek
Contact:	P. O. Box 39, Crestone, CO 81131; (719) 256.4694; www.kttg.org

3-- Mangala Shri Bhuti

Mangala Shri Bhuti is a sangha of the Longchen Nyingthik tradition of the Nyingma Lineage of Tibetan Buddhism. The organization was founded in 1990 by Dzigar Kongtrul Rinpoche in Boulder, CO. In 1989 Rinpoche moved to the United States with his wife and son, and in 1990 began a five-year tenure as a professor of Buddhist philosophy at Naropa University in Boulder. For many years the sangha gathered in the basement of a house owned by a number of students in Boulder.

Simply being in the natural beauty of retreat causes a person to reflect more deeply. Reflecting deeply, you gain a bigger perspective rather than seeing only what is in front of your nose. Your greater intelligence comes out of what is almost a dormant state. Once activated, this intelligence leads you to that which will be of true, lasting benefit to your life.
Dzigar Kongtrul Rinpoche

In 2000 the Manitou Foundation granted Mangala Shri Bhuti a 15-acre site that straddles the ridge south of Willow Creek between elevations of 8800 and 9000 feet. This retreat land was named the Longchen Jigme Samten Ling retreat center. The land does not contain a large central building, but instead a dozen small wilderness retreat cabins, each sponsored by an individual donor. These are occupied year-round by both long-term retreatants and an on-going rotation of students in 100-day retreat. Kongtrul Rinpoche guides each individual at his or her own level. A local retreat master on site is available to support and help clarify any of the instructions.

Mangala Shri Bhuti has been somewhat eclipsed in Colorado by the acquisition of the Phuntsok Choling site near Ward, CO in 2000, which contains a central retreat building as well as cabins.

Rinpoche has published two books that outline his philosophy and practice for Westerners (Kongtrul, 2006; 2008).

Founder:	Dzigar Kongtrul
Date Founded:	2000
Retreat cabins for Rent?	YES (12); but only for members of the sangha
Retreat Master	Elizabeth Mattis Namgyel
Location:	between Willow Creek and Spanish Creek
Contact:	P.O. Box 4088, Boulder, CO 80306; (303) 459-0184 or (719) 256-4807; www.mangalashribhuti.org
Other Practice Centers	Boulder, CO; Ward, CO; Vershire, VT; Bir, India

4— Pundarika Foundation

Pundarika Foundation was founded in 1994 and supports the spiritual and humanitarian work of Tsoknyi Rinpoche, son of the late Dzogchen Master Tulku Urgyen Rinpoche. It relies on its 2000 volunteers/students who attend retreats, practice Dharma under the inspiration of Rinpoche, and contribute time, money and prayers to its success. Approximately 40 of Rinpoche's students have already come to live in Crestone, many in close proximity to the Retreat land, forming a growing sangha.

Pundarika Foundation's primary mission is to:
-Keep alive the wisdom of the Dharma
-Sustain practitioners who preserve the teachings of the Buddha as a vital tradition
-Help people experience inner peace, to better face the challenges of modern life with
    compassion and sanity

Tsoknyi Rinpoche is a teacher of Buddhist meditation and has written two books on the subject, *Fearless Simplicity* (Rinpoche, 2003) *and Carefree Dignity* (Rinpoche, 2004). His latest book on bodhicitta will be released in 2012. Rinpoche's humanitarian projects include the spiritual and physical support of 2,100 nuns in Tibet and Nepal, ensuring that female practitioners are accorded the same opportunities as their male counterparts. Through Pundarika he also supports the rebuilding of nunneries and monasteries destroyed by earthquakes in Asia.

Yeshe Rangsal retreat land

Pundarika purchased 55 acres in the Baca Chalet 1 area, just east of Camino Baca Grande between Rendezvous Way and Hilltop Way. This land is called Yeshe Rangsal , or "self-cognizant wakefulness." On this land lies the Enlightenment Stupa dedicated to Tulku Urgyen Rinpoche, located 1.7 miles south of the entrance to the Baca Grande. A shrine to Dorje Yudronma (protectress of Yeshe Rangsal) is essentially complete. The long-term plan is for the Stupa to be accompanied by a three-year retreat facility and retreat cabins. As of 2011, the main event at Yeshe Rangsal is the month-long Practice Retreat from mid-August to mid-September.

My vision for Yeshe Rangsal is a place where practice and study will
be the means for us to become sane human beings. From the ground of
basic sanity, deepening our practice in retreat, we develop into
accomplished yogis and yoginis on the path to enlightenment.
Tsoknyi Rinpoche

Founder:	Tsoknyi Rinpoche
Date Founded:	1994
Retreat cabins for Rent?	none (2011); 10 planned
Director	Estaban Hollander
Location:	east of Camino Baca Grande, between Rendezvous and Hilltop Ways
Contact:	P.O. Box 57, Crestone, CO 81131; (719) 256-4011; www.pundarika.org

The Vajra Vidya Retreat Center is located on southern Camino Baca Grande downslope of Dream Way. The retreat center was founded in 2003 by Khenchen Thrangu Rinpoche, a Tibetan lama of the Kagyu sect of Buddhism. It is dedicated to the 16th Gyalwa Karmapa. Teaching and practice are overseen by Lamas Karma Wangdu and Khenpo Jigme, both highly trained lamas sent by Thrangu Rinpoche. They are available for guidance, teaching, and private interviews. There is always at least one Lama in residence, though each of them travel several times during the year to teach at other centers.

Unlike many retreat centers, each meditation practitioner performs his or her individual practices of varying lengths with the help of one of the resident lamas. Thrangu Rinpoche's vision of providing all the elements needed for successful practice have come together in this special place. In general, retreatants determine with their own teacher what practices are appropriate and which texts to be used on their retreat. Most short and long-term retreats are under the guidance of Khenpo Jigme. Khenpo has completed the five-year monastic college (Shedra) program and a three-year retreat.

The above arrangement allows for practitioners of all levels of experience to engage in an authentic practice with complete support. The daily schedule includes one hour of morning and evening group practice (optional), as well as the traditional four sessions a day for individual practice. The Morning Group Practice includes a lineage supplication, a short Manjusri practice, and one hour of sitting meditation. The Evening Practice alternates between Chenrezig and White Tara practices with closing prayers. Silence is observed most of the day.

The Vajra Vidya Retreat Center has a newly-built North Wing that contains eight retreat rooms, a shrine room, and a living space, all of which support focus on practice itself. The Center also features a modern kitchen, showers and laundry facilities, a small Buddhist library, and WiFi. Three meals a day are provided in the dining room. Participants and the Lamas eat together at all meals; all food is vegetarian.

Founder:	Khenchen Thrangu Rinpoche
Date Founded:	1998
Retreat cabins for Rent?	NO (but 8 rooms inside main lodge)
Resident Lama:	Khenpo Jigme
Director:	Ani Seltong Dronma
Size:	35 acres between Dream Way and Camino Baca Grande
Contact:	P.O. Box 1083, Crestone, CO 81131; 3203 Camino Baca Grande; (719) 256-5539; www.VajraVidyaRetreatCenter.org; khenpojigme@VajraVidyaRetreatCenter.org

6-- White Jewel Mountain Dharma Center

White Jewel Mountain is the Sangha of Adzom Rinpoche's students in Crestone. Its goals are: 1—To create a permanent facility for monastic training and retreat in the Nyingma tradition of Tibetan Buddhism; 2—To be a year-round seat in the West for Adzom Rinpoche and his Dharma activity; 3—To provide highly accomplished monastics from Tibet as resident teachers and retreat masters; 4—To offer hospice care for conscious dying available to those of all faiths, in collaboration with other retreat centers; 5—To provide traditional full cremation services appropriate for Buddhist practitioners and available to all

Adzom Rinpoche was born in 1972 in eastern Tibet, and first visited Crestone in 2001. After meeting with the Manitou Foundation he was granted 48 acres for a retreat center. Rinpoche envisioned a "grand mandala" of a spiritual retreat center, monastery, and hospice/crematory where people would come to die in a conscious fashion.

He said "We are all together in the fact that we shall all die. To have a center here in Crestone that engages the death process with the compassion and wisdom learned from the traditional Tibetan methods would be of great benefit to many."

Dorje Trollo Practice and Tsok:
Every Sunday, 10-noon, at the retreat land on southern Camino Baca Grande, about halfway between Dharma ocean and Vajra Vidya..
Tsok (food offering practice) once a month (on the Sunday closest to the 29th of the lunar month). For that, participants are invited to bring some unopened or freshly prepared finger food.

Founder:	Adzom Rinpoche
Date Founded:	2008
Retreat cabins for Rent?	2
Land Manager:	Leanna Bradbury
Size:	48 acres on Camino Baca Grande
Contact:	P.O. Box 813, Crestone, CO 81131; (719) 256-5773; www.whitejewelmountain.org; whitejewelmountain@fairpoint.net

BHUTANESE BUDDHIST

7-- Yeshe Khorlo (*The Wheel of Wisdom*)
A retreat and meditation center of the Nyingma tradition of Bhutanese Buddhism. The Crestone retreat center was founded in 1998 by Gangteng Tulku Rinpoche and named the Choying Dzong Lhakhang retreat center.

Yeshe Khorlo was founded in 1995, and in 1996 Gangten Tulku visited Crestone for the first time. After receiving a land grant from the Manitou Foundation in 1998, he invited one of his senior lamas from Bhutan to live in Crestone and begin the work of building a retreat center here. The center, named Choying Dzong (*The Fortress of Basic Space*), was completed in 2001.

Yeshe Khorlo is dedicated to sharing the teachings of the 14th-century Buddhist saint and King Tertön (treasure revealer), Pema Lingpa. The termas (treasures) revealed by Pema Lingpa were instructions and blessings hidden in the 8th century by Guru Rinpoche who prophesized that they would be revealed at a future time when they would be of greatest benefit to the beings of that time.

The center is also a place for all people to come and deepen their spiritual practice and awaken their inner goodness through meditation and retreat. Yeshe Khorlo facilities include Choying Dzong, a Bhutanese style Lhakang (temple) and teacher's residence, an outdoor gathering space for teachings and empowerments, and four retreat cabins for solitary-contemplative retreat. Retreat cabins are about 200 square feet; two have electricity. Future plans call for a three-year retreat compound. Yeshe Khorlo offers weekly teachings, meditation instruction, and twice-monthly feast gatherings.

Founder:	Gangten Tulku Rinpoche
Date Founded:	1998
Retreat cabins for Rent?	YES (4)
Resident Lama:	Lopon Phurba Dorji
Size:	320 acres between Willow Creek and Spanish Creek
Parent Organization:	Yeshe Khorlo USA (founded 1995)
Other Centers:	Austria, Bhutan, Canada, France, German, Poland, Russia, Slovenia, Switzerland, Taiwan
Contact:	P. O. Box 87, Crestone, CO 81131; 2282A Happy Day Overlook; (719) 256-5224; www.yeshekhorlo.org; info@yeshekhorlo.org

Zen Buddhist

8-- Crestone Mountain Zen Center (*Dharma Sangha*)
The Crestone Mountain Zen Center is a monastic community that offers residential training in Zen meditation and practice under the guidance of Abbot and Head Teacher Zentatsu Baker-roshi, Dharma Heir of Shunryu Suzuki-roshi. During the Summer Guest Season the retreat facilities are available for a variety of retreats, workshops and conferences, including meditation from different wisdom traditions, yoga, music, dance, bodywork and psychotherapy. From May through December the Center is open for individual guests and retreatants to enjoy the beauty, quiet, and isolation of the Crestone mountains and practice with the residential community. In winter the Center is closed to outsiders, and Zen practitioners join in the residential practice for Ango (the annual 90-day winter Practice Period), Sesshin, Seminars and Work Practice.

Fig. 9-11. *Left:* Abbot Roshi Richard Baker; photo by Bill Ellzey. *Right:* Entrance to the Zen Center's heavily-wooded 80 acres at the foot of Kit Carson Mountain, visible at upper left. Besides the Lindisfarne Dome and the Zendo, the campus includes the Main House with kitchen, community space and large dining hall, a Japanese style tea house, a Guest House and a workshop with a former pottery studio that was converted into a dormitory.

A yurt and a number of small cabins are also available, including a 300 square foot cabin for retreat leaders that has a separate bathroom. Currently, the Center can accommodate a maximum of 26 retreat participants, but for larger groups, participants can use the Dome for "camping" at a reduced rate or stay at local inns. For an in-depth look at life inside the monastery, see Winson and Sagan (1999).

Founder:	Roshi Richard Baker
Date Founded:	1985
Retreat cabins for Rent?:	YES (numerous)
Size:	80 acres
Contact:	P. O. Box 130, Crestone, CO 81131; 2000 East Dreamway; (719) 256.4692; www.dharmasangha.org; cmzc@dharmasangha.com;

The Lindisfarne Association—One of the First Manitou Grantees (1979)

The Crestone Mountain Zen Center is located on land originally granted to the Lindisfarne Association, including its unique chapel dome (pictured below). Lindisfarne was founded by writer/philosopher William Irwin Thompson in 1972, as "an alternative way for the humanities to develop in a scientific and technical civilization." Originally based in New York, Lindisfarne moved to Crestone in 1979, to a 320-acre site granted by the Strongs. Mr. Thompson lived on site until illness caused him to return to New York in 1983. Lindisfarne eventually gave up the land in 1988 and granted 80 acres to the Crestone Mountain Zen Center (see previous page). Mr. Thompson retired from the presidency of Lindisfarne in 1997, but still meets with Lindisfarne fellows at their annual meeting in Santa Fe, New Mexico.

The most enduring legacy of Lindisfarne in Crestone is the Interfaith Chapel, or dome (Fig. 9-12). The dome was conceived by Thompson and designed by Keith Critchlow. It was constructed by bending in place and laminating 2x4s into 12" thick beams to span 2800 square feet; then another web of smaller beams were shaped and laminated behind the main beams. The chapel's geometrical lattice was deliberately designed to make no spiritual tradition or religion feel unwelcome or out of place. It follows the principles of "No decoration, only proportion; no iconography, only geometry." The center skylight is about 24 feet high; beneath it lies the altar, a 300 year-old millstone from San Luis, Colorado (the State's oldest town).

Fig. 9-12. Interior of the Lindisfarne Chapel, built in 1980 using the principles of sacred geometry. The dome is now part of the Crestone Mountain Zen Center and open to the public except when the Zen Center is closed from January 15 through April 15. Photo by Martin Macaulay.

Lindisfarne and Sacred Geometry

Robert Lawlor first visited Crestone in 1980 to attend the Lindisfarne Institute's Summer Program in Sacred Architecture. In 1981 he attended another Lindisfarne gathering here called *Homage to Pythagoras*, the proceedings of which were later published by Barnford (1994). Based on his experiences in Crestone, Lawlor went on to write a book on sacred geometry (Lawlor, 1982), which has become a standard reference in this field.

Fig. 9-13. Dragon Mountain Temple is a small, experimental, zen temple in the Shunryu Suzuki-roshi lineage. Its focus is the intensive meditation life (sesshin). Kijun Tenryu Steven Allen, the founding Abbot of Dragon Mountain Temple, began his zen practice at the San Francisco Zen Center in 1971, studying with Suzuki-roshi.

Abbot Allen was ordained in 1975, and remained at the San Francisco Zen Center until 1984. In 1986 he began teaching and has worked with various zen groups in California, New Mexico, Colorado and South Africa. His current focus is bridging the gap between Eastern and Western spiritual thought and practice, by studying texts both from the traditional Zen Koan system and the Western literary tradition.

The Temple offers three types of retreats, ranging from solitary to structured. The solitary retreats can occur at any time of year and be any length, with retreatants attending any parts of ongoing more structured retreat programs. The Creative Arts Retreats are 5-day retreats that focus on one of four topics: The Creative Arts, The Healing Arts, The Scientific & Ecological Arts, and The Spiritual (Transformative) Arts. In these retreats attendees meditate on and discuss the relevant issues that face us all in the modern world. Creative Arts retreats occur in the beginning of February, May, August, and November.

The most structured and traditional retreats are the 7-day zen sesshins, which are held four times a year and end on each solstice and equinox. The form of these more rigorous meditation retreats is derived from the San Francisco Zen Center, the birthplace of Zen Buddhism in America, where Abbot Allen studied in the early 1970s.

Founder:	Kijun Tenryu Steven Allen
Date Founded:	2006
Retreat cabins for Rent?:	YES; 2 solitary huts, plus additional rooms in the Temple
Contact:	P. O. Box 583, Crestone, CO 81131; (719) 256-5092;
	www.dragonmountaintemple.org;
	info@dragonmountaintemple.org

BON

Bon is the ancient (pre-Buddhist) indigenous religion of Tibet, thought to have originated west of modern Tibet about 17,000 years ago and spread outward by Lord Tonpa Shenrab. Many of its teachings were later incorporated into Tibetan Buddhism.

10- Chamma Ling Retreat Center

Origin of the center: Tenzin Wangyal Rinpoche founded Ligmincha Institute in March of 1992 to introduce to the West the wisdom traditions of the Bonpo which are concerned with the harmonious integration of internal and external energies, and most importantly with the spiritual path to enlightenment. He resides in Charlottesville, Virginia, but travels and teaches extensively throughout Europe, the United States, Mexico and South America. Rinpoche founded Chamma Ling in Crestone in 2002 as a solitary retreat center to support practitioners in this tradition throughout the country. The primary goal of Chamma Ling is to provide a support for serious practitioners to go into solitary retreat for weeks or months. Any member of its sangha can apply for use of the retreat cabins. While use of the facilities by people outside of the sangha will be considered, first priority will be given to those who have previously practiced and studied with the Rinpoche.

Chamma Ling Retreat CenteR
Preserving the Bön - Buddhist Tradition

"Letting them be in their nature is the method. To find the non-dual state of Liberation. Overcoming hope and fear is the result."

From *"Wonders of the Natural Mind"* by Tenzin Wangyal Rinpoche (Wangyal, 2000)
Self-arising wisdom is the base.
The five negative emotions are manifested energy.
Seeing emotions as mistaken is an error.

Wangyal Rinpoche has published five additional books, including Tibetan Sound Healing (Wangyal, 2007), and Awakening the Sacred Body (Wangyal, 2011), making him easily the most prolific author in Crestone.

Founder:	Tenzin Wangyal Rinpoche
Date Founded:	2002
Resident Lama:	Lhari-la Kalsang Nyima
Size:	51 acres on the south side of Willow Creek
Retreat cabins for Rent?:	YES (4)
Parent Organization:	Ligmincha Institute (founded 1992)
Contact:	P.O. Box 608, Crestone, CO 81131; www.chammaling.org
Other Centers:	Charlottesville, VA (Ligmincha); Houston, TX; Santa Monica, CA; Warsaw, Poland; Mexico City, Mexico

HINDU

11-- Haidakhandi Universal Ashram (HUA)

HUA is a spiritual community and pilgrimage center inspired by Haidakhan Baba (a Hindu mystic, also known as Babaji) and dedicated to the Divine Mother, who embodies the totality of all that is to be known. Life at the Ashram is guided by Babaji's teachings of truth, simplicity, and love. Although the worship activities are based in Indian ritual, Babaji taught that all religions lead the sincere devotee to God.

Fig. 9-14. Entrance to the Lakshmi Vedic Temple. . Lakshmi is the Hindu goddess of prosperity and beauty, and the consort of Vishnu, the supreme deity of classical Hinduism.

Service is the ongoing aspect of the community, to provide facilities for pilgrims and seekers to pray, meditate, worship and serve. The daily schedule of the Ashram is built around this service (called karma yoga), plus the morning and evening devotional services (aarati), simple living, and repetition of the name of God. A fire ceremony is scheduled at 10:08 am on the Full Moon and New Moon of every month, and is open to the public.

HUA has created one of the most environmentally sustainable spiritual centers in the Baca. It has an organic garden, an orchard, its own water system, photovoltaic-derived electricity and solar heating. The Maha Lakshmi Gift Shop (http://shop.babajiashram.org/) is located within an Earthship, built of earth-rammed tire and sunk into the earth. To visit, please call for directions and for the aarati schedule.

Date Founded:	1986
Retreat rooms for Rent?:	YES (dormitory with 5 rooms; plus one yurt)
Resident Director:	Ramloti
Size:	101 acres at the mouth of Spanish Creek, near the site of the historic mining camp of Spanish City Contact:
Contact:	P. O. Box 9, Crestone, CO 81131; phone (719) 256-4185; (719) 256-4108; www.babajiashram.org; info@babajiashram.o

190

12-- Sri Aurobindo Learning Center

The Learning Center was founded in 1986 by Seyril Schochen, to honor the work of Sri Aurobindo and The Mother. Sri Aurobindo (1872-1950) was a Mahayogi of India, and was held by some to be India's foremost spiritual teacher of modern times. His followers founded Auroville, India, the "City of Human Unity", in 1968. Sri Aurobindo was later recognized on his Birth Centenary as "The Apostle of Human Unity" by all the Member Nations of UNESCO. The Learning Center consists of the main retreat house (Savitri House), a library, a meditation dome, and the new Solar Bridge guest house. The library contains all of Sri Aurobindo's writings and those of The Mother (1878-1973), his spiritual co-worker and co-founder of Auroville.

Fig. 9-15. Attendees of the Savitri immersion Workshop (June 2009) flank photographs of The Mother (left) and Sri Aurobindo (right). The Workshop includes intensive reading of Aurobindo's 24,000-word epic poem "Savitri." (Sri Aurobindo, 2010).

At Savitri House and Savitri Solar Dome, the emphasis is on transcultural exchange, enrichment for universal peace, consciousness healing and evolution, and a new education for a new world. The Center seeks to become an Indo-American collaborative center for educational, scientific, cultural and spiritual researches for "a living embodiment of an actual human unity," as described in Auroville's Charter. Events hosted include musical performances, plays, dramatic readings, traditional, Indian and Native American dances, and guest lectures and presentations. All community members and visitors are welcome to attend the presentations. The Center is located at 80 North Baca Grant Way in the Chalet 1 section of the Baca subdivision.

Founder:	Seyril Schochen (1915-2006)
Date Founded:	1986
Retreat cabins for Rent?:	YES (1); contains 3 bedrooms
Manager:	Kathryn Van Note
Other Centers:	Auroville, India
Contact:	P. O. Box 88, Crestone, CO 81131; 80 North Baca Grant Way; (719) 256-4917; http://sriaurobindolc.org

13--Spiritual Life Institute (SLI)
The Spiritual Life Institute was founded as a small monastic community of men and women monks of Roman Catholic origin. Their main center is Holy Hill Hermitage in Skreen, County Sligo, Ireland. But on the western margin of the Baca subdivision, SLI created a 104-acre center in 1983 named the Nada Hermitage ("nada" means "nothing" in Spanish). The community moved here from Sedona, Arizona, where development was encroaching on their monastery and making quiet contemplation impossible. In past years Nada has moved away from its original monastic affiliations, but continues to offer Mass.

Fig. 9-16. The Nada Hermitage sprawls on 104 acres of grasslands, just west of the Baca Grande subdivision.

Most of the monastery grounds are closed to the public, to avoid disturbing solitary retreatants. However, the Sangre de Cristo Chapel is open to the public and Mass is held every Sunday at 9am.
Directions: from Camino Baca Grande, turn right (west) on Rendezvous Way, at the sign "Nada Carmelite Hermitage." Continue ¼ mile to the dir parking lot on the right. Walk to the chapel, which is open to the public.

The central focus of Nada is individual retreats to regain communion with God. Retreatants can participate in Nada's monastic lifestyle or choose solitary retreats in their own hermitages, located near the center on the valley floor, or in remote cabins high in the mountains. Unlike most other spiritual centers in the area, Nada offers the retreat experience to everyone: men and women, young and old, married couples and singles, clergy and laypeople, Christians, practitioners of other spiritual traditions, and those without any religious affiliation. The key is to take advantage of the quietude, isolation, and proximity to Nature to escape distractions and focus the mind.

For more information, read the "Desert Call", the quarterly magazine of SLI tha has been published for 40 years, or read Slattery (2004) for one retreatant's experience.

Date Founded:	1983
Retreat cabins for Rent?	YES
Size:	104 acres
Other Centers:	Skreen, Ireland
Contact:	P.O. Box 219, Crestone, CO 81131; 1 Carmelite Way; (719) 256-4778; www.spirituallifeinstitute.org; nada@spirituallifeinstitute.org

INDEPENDENT CENTERS

14-- Shumei International Institute (SII)

Shinji Shumeikai, informally known as Shumei, is a spiritual organization dedicated to elevating the quality of life. Shumei advocates an ideal state of health, happiness, and harmony achieved through the wisdom and insights of the spiritual leader, Mokichi Okada (1882-1955; also called Meishu-sama). Inspired by his philosophy, SII helps people of the world realize that they are world citizens able to act for the common good (mission statement). Okada taught that a world free from sickness, poverty, and discord is possible through: (1) the spiritual exercise of Jyorei, (2) the appreciation of art and beauty, and (3) the practice of Natural Agriculture.

Jyorei (also spelled johrei), which translates as "purification of the spirit", is a healing art that "by focusing spiritual light, gradually penetrates and dissolves the spiritual clouds that cause physical, emotional, and personal dilemmas." Mokichi Okada developed this healing practice as a treatment for physical infirmities during the 1930s, but it assumed its final form in 1947 a few years before Okada's passing. It is estimated that 1 million people around the world practice Jyorei.

Fig. 9-17. At SII, Shumei architects have seamlessly blended old stonework from the mining days, with modernistic buildings.

"If we want to establish eternal peace on this earth of ours, we must first eliminate the feeling of discomfort from each individual and replace it with a feeling of ease and comfort. Everybody who has this feeling of comfort will loathe war and love peace. This is an indisputable fact."— Mokichi Okada

Shumei International Institute built its complex starting in 2001 between Spanish Creek and Cottonwood Creek, on land granted by Hanne Strong in 1999. It includes the former site of the historic Independent Mill. SII hosts many concerts, movies, and art exhibitions throughout the year (see their website for upcoming events). Shumei master gardeners have created an impressive organic garden using traditional Japanese gardening techniques and the principles of Natural Agriculture (see Fig. 9-27). As far back as the 1930s, Okada had warned about the dangers of synthetic chemicals in agriculture.

Founder:	Mokichi Okada
Date Founded:	2001
Retreat cabins for Rent?	NO
General Manager:	Matthew Crowley
Size:	40 acres
Other Centers:	in 13 countries
Contact:	3000 East Dream Way; P.O. Box 998, Crestone, CO 81131; (719) 256-5284; www.shumeicrestone.org; matthew@shumei.org

SPIRITUAL MONUMENTS: STUPAS, THE ZIGGURAT, STONE CIRCLES AND LABYRINTHS

Sometimes the best way for a novice to approach a new creed is to visit its concrete symbols. In Buddhism such symbols include prayer flags and shrines called stupas. A stupa is a symmetrical Buddhist religious shrine that contains relics of revered teacher(s) (Rinpoches), prayer scrolls, and other religious items. After its dedication a stupa is sealed, preventing entrance by the public. Visiting pilgrims circle the stupa clockwise three or more times (circumambulating), while performing walking meditation or reciting mantras. Although there are eight types of Tibetan stupas, two of the three in Crestone (the middle-size and small stupas) follow the style called the "Stupa of Enlightenment," while the Big Stupa is in the style of "Stupa of Many Doors or Gates" (Fig. 9-18).

THE TASHI GOMANG STUPA (LOCALLY CALLED THE BIG STUPA)

Fig. 9-18. The Tashi Gomang Stupa looms over the valley floor and southern Baca Grande subdivision, with the San Juan Mountains in the far distance.

The Tashi Gomang Stupa, consecrated in 1996, is the stupa of "many auspicious doors, "symbolizing the 84,000 paths taught by the Buddha to reach enlightenment. This style of stupa commemorates Buddha's first turning of the Wheel of Dharma in Deer Park at Sarnath, near Varanasi, India.

The Big Stupa is dedicated to the 16th Karmapa and contains his relics and those of many Buddhist saints. It also contains relics from Tilopa, Marpa, Milarepa, Rechungpa, Longchenpa, Lodro Thaye, Dilgo Khyentse, Tulku Urgyen, and Trungpa Rinpoche. Sealed inside are wood from the Bodhi tree, the four elements, stones from the eight pilgrimage sites in India, 100,000 tsa-tsas, and many medicinal herbs (Source: www.rinpoche.com/crestone/hhk visit3.htm

THE STUPA OF ENLIGHTENMENT

The Jangchub Chörten lies just east of Camino Baca Grande, 1.7 miles south of the entrance to the Baca Grande, on lands of the Pundarika Foundation. It is easily visible from the road and is the most accessible of the three local stupas. In 2005, a preliminary consecration was held on the site. This ceremony was presided over by several Rinpoche and lamas and attended by hundreds of people. The stupa was constructed to very precise specifications and filled in the traditional way with 30,000 tsa-tsas (a miniature replica c a stupa containing relics of the Buddha, and mantra scrolls; Fig. 9-19). Relics of Tulku

194

Urgyen Rinpoche and many other great masters were placed inside, along with sacred texts from the Buddhist canon.

The stupa is dedicated to Tulku Urgyen Rinpoche and was built in the style of The Stupa of Enlightenment, a design that commemorates Buddha's conquest of Maras (demonic forces) before he attained complete enlightenment under the Bodhi Tree in Bodhgaya, in the present state of Bihar, India. The stupa creates the opportunity for pilgrims to accumulate merit by making offerings and circumambulating the sacred site. Many feel that the environment around the stupa provides a particularly auspicious and peaceful place to meditate.

ig. 9-19. *Left*, the Stupa of Enlightenment with the Sangres in the background; *Right*, a a-tsa.

THE PADMASAMBHAVA STUPA (LOCALLY CALLED THE LITTLE STUPA)

Fig. 9-20. The unassuming "Little Stupa" is only slightly taller than a person, but has outsize significance; it was the first stupa ever built in Colorado (1984). It was erected in the yard of a private home on South Carefree Way, about ¾ of a mile south of Camino del Rey. The home was then owned by Canadian diplomat James George. Mr. George had discovered the Baca as a member of the Aspen Institute, when it was headquartered here from 1981-84. The site was selected by the eminent Nyingma lama Dilgo Khyentse Rinpoche, and the stupa was dedicated on Sept. 10-11, 1984 by Sogyal Rinpoche and Lama Urgyen. Padmasambhava lived in Tibet in the 8th Century and is known as the second Buddha. For more details, go to: www.padmasambhava.crestonecolorado.com

195

THE ZIGGURAT

In ancient history, a ziggurat was a temple mound built in Babylon with a temple at the top. The most famous ziggurat was the Tower of Babel, built in the time of King Nebuchadnezzar (605-562 BC). These lofty structures (up to 300 feet high) could be seen for miles on the flat plains of Mesopotamia. Rising above the plains of the southernmost Baca Grande is the smaller version pictured below, the Halaby ziggurat.

Fig. 9-21. The Halaby ziggurat spirals toward heaven at the base of the Sangres. To get there: Take Camino Real (aka Two Trees Road) south until nearly its end; turn left (east) on Cottonwood Creek Road; drive 0.63 miles and turn right (south) on Rainbow Trout Trail. Ignore homemade signs that say this is a private road (it is not). After 0.8 miles Rainbow Trout Trail ends in a T-intersection with North and South Alpine Falls Trail. Park here and walk up a jeep road 0.3 miles to the east, which ascends the crest of a ridge to the ziggurat. The ziggurat in the Baca can be seen for many miles, perched on a ridge just north of Cottonwood Creek

How the ziggurat came to be there is a story in itself. It was built by Najeeb E. Halaby (1915-2003), a business leader, government official, and American success story. Halaby's father had emigrated to America in 1891 from Syria, and Najeeb was born in Dallas. He became a Navy test pilot in WWII and flew the first operational American jet plane. In 1945 Najeeb made the first nonstop transcontinental flight in a jet. President John Kennedy appointed him as head of the Federal Aviation Administration (1961-65), and he later became CEO and Chair of Pan American Airways (1969-72). His government and industry service led him to join the Aspen Institute for Humanistic Studies, which was headquartered at the Baca from 1981-1984. He purchased a large plot of land in the southernmost Baca Grande during those years.

His oldest daughter Lisa (b. 1951) obtained a B.A. in Architecture and Urban Planning from Princeton in 1974. In the late 1970s she worked on an urban planning project in Tehran, Iran, and may have picked up the idea of building a ziggurat there, and later communicated it to her father. Lisa later became more famous than her father. In 1978 she married King Hussein of Jordan and became Queen Noor.

Two items are copiously abundant in the Crestone area; spiritual devotion, and rocks. Given that combination it is not surprising to find many religious monuments made of rocks, such as the ubiquitous stacks of balanced "Zen stones" (Fig. 9-22).

Fig. 9-22. In their simplest form, stacked rocks are merely small cairns only 1-2 feet high. Such stacks can be found throughout the Baca, although like earthly pleasures and desires, they are temporary. This Buddhist trashcan reminds us to rid ourselves of burdensome attachments.

More ambitious and permanent are large arrays of rocks such as labyrinths. The easiest labyrinth to see is the "Garden of Love" at I Am Harmony Bed & Breakfast, located right off Camino Baca Grande, 1.1 miles south of the Baca entrance. This rock garden is open to the public at 1361 Chaparral Way.

For a more remote and powerful experience, visit Crestonehenge (Fig. 9-23) in the Grants Unit of the southern Baca Grande. The layout includes small standing stones, concentric rings, and radial avenues aligned with astronomical directions. Its history is chronicled at www.angelfire.com/co/StandingStones/index.html.

Fig. 9-23. Crestonehenge was begun in 1999 and underwent several different arrangements, before being declared "finished" in 2003. The line of stones at center points due east, to the spot on the crest of the Sangre de Cristo range where the sun rises on the Spring and Autumn Equinoxes. Directions: South on Camino Baca Grande to Camino Real, then 3.8 miles south to Cottonwood Creek Road. Turn left (east) and drive 330 yards to Allot Trail. Turn left and park; Crestonehenge is visible to the west.

THE PARANORMAL COMMUNITY:
UFOS, EXTRATERRESTRIALS, AND ANCIENT STONE STRUCTURES

The San Luis Valley of Colorado and northern New Mexico is unique in the USA for its numerous reports of UFOs and cattle mutilations (known as Unexplained Animal Deaths, or UADs). The incidents began in 1967 with the celebrated case of Snippy the Horse (see below) and have continued to present (e.g., Denver Post, 2009). As mentioned by O'Brien (1996), *"The Snippy case and the San Luis Valley's apparent corresponding UFO activity provided a "guilt by association" scenario which led to the inexorable linking of UADs with UFOs...."* This association has been capitalized upon by the construction of the UFO Watchtower near Hooper, surely the only facility of its kind in the country (Messoline, 2005; also see ufowatchtower.com). The valley's paranormal history from 1948 (first film of a UFO made by an amateur) to date is chronicled in detail in several books by former Crestone resident Christopher O'Brien, under the general heading of "The Mysterious Valley" (O'Brien, 1996, 1999, 2007).

Flying Saucers Killed My Horse
The modern paranormal history of the SLV really begins with the mysterious mutilation of a horse in 1967 (Doty, 2007). Although the horse is widely known as Snippy, its true name was Lady (Snippy was its mother). Lady lived on the 2000-acre King Ranch, at the western foot of Blanca Peak, 10 miles south of the Great Sand Dunes.

On September 8, 1967, Lady did not show up for her morning feeding. Harry King found the horse ¼ mile north of the ranch house, "missing all the tissue from her shoulders to the tip of her nose, the exposed bones glistening , bleached white, like they had been in the sun for thirty years" (O'Brien, 1996). The Kings found no predator or scavenger tracks around the body, but did notice four "burned areas." Harry's sister Nellie, who considered Lady "her horse, "called the Alamosa County Sheriff, who concluded that Lady was hit by lightning (however, he never came to view the body). Nellie was aware of several UFO sightings near the Ranch in previous weeks, and was convinced there was a connection. Lady's mysterious mutilation was widely reported (as the Snippy incident) in national and international media, and was even investigated as part of the Condon Report undertaken for the Air Force's Project Blue Book on the origin of UFOs, in 1967. This was the first of dozens of such UAD incidents reported in the San Luis Valley over the next 35 years.

UFOlogists have been visiting the San Luis Valley and the Crestone area ever since. For example, the Center for the Study of Extraterrestrial Intelligence (CSETI) has held field trips and conferences in and near Crestone for the past 18 years. A continuing event is the CSETI "Ambassador to the Universe Trainings" in Crestone, held up through July 2011 (see www.cseti.org/trainings.shtml). In addition, the Paranormal Research Forum (www.paranormalresearchforum.com) has held a late-summer UFO Trip to the

San Luis Valley, annually since 1998. And the UFO Watchtower near Hooper is open year-round.

The San Luis Valley Crystal Skull (aka the Crestone Crystal Skull)

Fig. 9-24. The famous "crystal skull" of Crestone.

In February of 1995, Moffat rancher Donna Koch was riding the fence line of her newly-acquired ranch. At the base of one corner fence post lay an enigmatic 6.5 inch-high skull, apparently made of glass or crystal. A few months later she showed the skull to the Saguache County assessor, merely as a curiosity. The assessor soon contacted Christopher O'Brien, a writer and paranormal researcher who lived in Crestone. On June 6, 1995 O'Brien videographed the skull and interviewed Ms. Koch. She reported strange, unexplained happenings when people handled the skull or were near it.

Many believers in the paranormal claim that crystal skulls, carved from quartz by unknown people, can produce miracles (en.wikipedia.org/wiki/Crystal_skull).The Crestone skull was later exhibited at the Light Reflections shop in Moffat, where people experienced strange powers coming from it. O'Brien took the skull to various UFO/paranormal meetings, where it was presented as the only crystal skull found in North America.

Then, on Nov. 10, 1996 the Rocky Mountain News newspaper in Denver ran a story about the skull. The story was read by relatives of Brad Chavez, a Denver glass artist working for Blake Street Glass Company, who told him about it. It turned out that Mr. Chavez had made this skull, as well as about one hundred other ones, for Day of the Dead festivals in Colorado and New Mexico. His parents owned the ranch adjacent to Koch's, and he had left the skull at one of their fence corners as a cornerstone. He remarked "I'm really sorry it went so far, I had no idea all this was going on down there."

Stone Meditation Seats

Another strange phenomenon is the "stone meditation seats" located between Crestone and the mouth of North Crestone Creek. The seats are large boulders that appear to be shaped to form chairs or seats. The seats are protected by Sacred Passage and The Way of Nature Fellowship (www.sacredpassage.com), who provide the following description: *In the late 1970s John P. Milton moved to Crestone and was the initial discoverer of the ancient stone meditation seats that fill the land there. An estimated two thousand such sacred stone meditation seats cluster on the Sacred Land Trust area, the largest aggregation of such sacred sites in the world.... These special sites have been used for millennia of vision questing, ceremony, and prayer."* To my knowledge, no scientific study has been performed on these seats by independent observers, and the seats have no known counterparts elsewhere in North America. Their origin remains a mystery.

Ancient Stone Huts

In the southern part of the Baca Grande subdivision there are four enigmatic stone structures, which have been the cause of much local curiosity and speculation. Each

199

structure is a stone igloo about 6 feet in diameter and 4-5 ft high (Fig. 9-25). The stones are dry-stacked and contain no mortar or other trace of modern construction. However, they are located only 200 ft downslope from the old railroad grade to the Independent Mill (now Dream Way), so were certainly noticed by the miners (beginning in 1870) and railroad men (beginning in 1900). They do not have any openings at the top to permit smoke to escape, and do not appear to be fire-blackened inside.

Several possible origins have been proposed: 1—built by Native Americans prior to arrival of the Spanish, as sweat lodges, to quarantine the ill, or for meat storage? 2—built by Spanish miners in the 1700s as bread ovens ; 3—built by gold miners after 1870 as a cache for blasting powder; 4—made by Chinese railroad workers ca. 1901; 5—built by New Age visitors after the Baca Grande subdivision was created (1971) for some ceremonial purpose. The mystery remains and is still being investigated.

Fig. 9-25. Photo of one of the mysterious stone huts in the Baca Grande subdivision. At present the huts lie on private land that is for sale. The huts are being studied by the Native American Research and Preservation, Inc. (stonequest.org). They ask that you respect the private property and scientific significance of the huts, and do not damage them if you visit.

The Pyramid of the Arcturians

On March 30, 1992, Dr. Norma Milanovich of the Trinity Foundation (Albuquerque, NM) held a community meeting in Crestone to describe her plans for building a pyramid here. The pyramid would be 396 feet high, made of pink granite, and cover a footprint of more than 40 acres, this being slightly smaller than the Great Pyramids of Egypt at Giza.

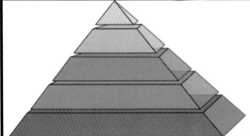

Dr. Milanovich had been instructed to build the pyramid by Kuthumi, an Ascended Master from Arcturus (the star system 37 light-years from Earth), who began channeling via her computer in the late 1980s in order to save mankind from destruction (Milanovich et al., 1990).

In order to save mankind, he instructed Dr. Milanovich to build the pyramid, which would function as a "standing columnar wave of tachyon energy" to communicate with the Ascended Masters. As reported by Quillen (1994), *"Initial plans called for a lower floor 30 cubits high [53 ft], a capstone of obsidian imported from Jericho, seven* levels, four entrances, and thirty chambers, including a crystal chamber. Preliminary plans also specified carved ceilings and pillars and numerous sculptures to depict all of the major religions of our world and the six golden ages of man, and also 12,000 pictures to detail the building of this great wonder, and to honor the 144,000 spiritual warriors who will work on it." The purpose of the pyramid was to allow the "enlightened" to move from the third to the fifth dimension, by changing the structure of their RNA and DNA.

At this initial public meeting there were few objections from the Crestone community. They were probably a bit overwhelmed. However, once the shock faded, locals began to critically consider numerous aspects of the project and how it might impact their quiet life in Crestone. For example, where would the 144,000 pyramid workers live? (Saguache County then had a population of 4,000). At the follow-up meeting on April 18, 1993, locals countered with a suggestion for a more modest 40 ft-high pyramid, but this scaled-down version was evidently unacceptable to the Ascended Masters (Nealson, 1994b).

After the initial excitement in 1993-94, local resistance, and the lack of funds to build the pyramid, combined to make the project fade away. As of 2011 the pyramid has not been built, like many projects proposed for Crestone (see below). The Trinity Foundation no longer exists, and Dr. Milanovich has moved on to other projects. She was last sighted in Colorado at the Galactic Gathering conference in Denver (September 2009), organized by the Institute for the Study of Galactic Civilizations (www.galacticcivilizations.org).

Shirley MacLaine and "Ariel Village"

Oscar-winning actress Shirley MacLaine is a personal friend of the Strongs and shares many of their progressive beliefs. A few weeks after the 1987 worldwide "Harmonic Convergence," Shirley's autobiographical book "Out on a Limb" was shown on TV as a two-part, made-for-television movie. In January 1988 she announced that the Crestone/Baca area represented "the center of the universe" (Wyckoff and Dilsaver, 1995). She went on to teach a set of well-attended and expensive New Age classes based on her book, the income from which was used to purchase 180 acres in the southern Baca Grande subdivision in December 1989. This large parcel was one of those consolidated by the Strongs in the mid-1980s, and was to host Ms. MacLaine's New Age center to be named "Ariel Village" (Mills, 1994).

The New York Times (May 1, 1988) reported that Ariel Village was to include a large alternative healing center (a "metaphysical fitness center"). However, many Crestone and Baca residents were leery of the projected hordes of New Age visitors that would swamp the area to visit MacLaine's mega-Village. Local residents sent her a petition opposing the scale of the Village. When she visited Crestone in May 1991 she declined to give an interview with the local paper, but later remarked that "if Crestone doesn't want me, I don't want it." Subsequently she withdrew her development plans and sold the land.

201

Early promoters of the San Luis Valley extolled its healthful properties, basically claiming that nobody ever became sick here.

"There is no use for the practice of professional pharmacy. Chronic health and longevity characterize animal life. The envelope of cloud-compelling peaks; the seclusion from the oceans; the rarity of the air inhaled, and the absence of humidity; disinfect the earth, the water, and the atmosphere of exhalations and miasmas. Health, sound and interrupted, stimulates and sustains a high state of mental and physical energy. All of these are burnished, as it were, by the perpetual brilliancy and salubrity of the atmosphere and landscape; whose unfailing beauty and tonic taste stimulate and invite the physical and mental energies to perpetual activity"
William Gilpin; *Mission of the North American People*, 1860

But at present, Crestone possesses what must be the largest per capita number of alternative "healers" of any place in Colorado. So what happened? First, the alternative-type people who moved here naturally gravitate toward "complimentary & alternative medicine" and away from mainstream, allopathic medicine. Prior to the creation of the TLC Clinic in 2004 there were no allopathic clinics in Crestone anyway; the nearest was in Moffat, 12 miles away. Second, few Crestonians have health insurance, and many distrust the "industrial" medical/insurance industry. Third, the Eastern religions transplanted here also brought with them ideas about Eastern medicine, including traditional Chinese medicine and herbalism, and Indian ayurvedic medicine. These ideas have been embraced by many in the community. Fourth, many area residents moved here from some more urban (and less healthy) place, often at a fairly advanced age, so they brought various ailments with them. Finally, despite the natural setting, many Crestonians get little physical exercise like walking, and use their cars for even short trips. The healthiest local habit is probably a high incidence of vegetarianism.

Local healers offer a wide range of health-related services, which are advertised monthly in the Crestone Eagle newspaper. These services span the spectrum of alternative medicine and New Age energy work:
--"Bodywork" (Massage, Accupressure, Acupuncture, Rolfing, structural integration, Feldenkrais)
-- Yoga (Hatha, Kundalini, Ashtanga), and Tai Chi
-- Ethnic and Herbal Medicine (Chinese, Hindu-ayurvedic)
-- Hydrotherapy and Colonics
-- High Valley Healing Center, A medical cannabis compassion club
--"Energy Work" (Sound Healing, Biofeedback, Reiki)
-- Naturopathic Medicine

For more information about the area-wide Crestone Healing Arts Guild, see Frank (2008) or contact the Crestone Healers group at www.crestonehealers.com.

Throw a rock into a crowd in Crestone, and you will hit an artist, or a musician. Maybe both. Historically artists were rare in the town of Crestone, devoted as it was to mining (1870-1930s) and cattle ranching (1930s-1970s). But all that changed with the creation of the Baca Grande subdivision in 1971. Part-time and full-time artists discovered that the Crestone-Baca area had many qualities they were looking for: clear light, quietude, picturesque setting, low cost of living, and a stress-free environment. Few distractions could derail the creative process (except of course, the lure to take a walk outside on a beautiful day).

Fig. 9-25. The Crestone-Baca art community is an anomaly in the predominantly working-class San Luis Valley, one of the poorest areas in Colorado. Curious ranchers and farmers may envision a typical day in Crestone to resemble the cartoon at left. *Courtesy of Monika Griesenbeck, Salida, CO.*

Today the Crestone-Baca area is home to painters, sculptors, photographers, jewelry artists, various craftspersons, and eccentric artists uncategorizable (e.g., Darnell, 2000).

Most of these artists produce works at home and sell them at galleries in Crestone (primarily the Crestone Artisans Gallery) and elsewhere in the Southwest. However, some artists do sell out of their home studios. Check a current issue of the Crestone Eagle newspaper for studio hours.

Retail Galleries

Fig. 9-25. The Crestone Artisans Gallery, a cooperative gallery of local artists; water colors, photography, handmade elk/deer hide bags, jewelry, fiber arts, scarves, place mats, handpainted journals, woodcrafts, pottery, prints, gourds, books, CDs, cards. Located at 20 S. Cottonwood St. (SE corner of Galena Ave. and Cottonwood St.), in Crestone, CO 81131; (719) 256-5280.

Ceramic Art
　　Clay Art Center; gallery/studio at Sangre de Cristo Inn, 116 S. Alder St.; (719) 256-5537.

Shumei International Institute; hosts different Artists Exhibitions/Symposia about every 2 months; various media; 3000 East Dream Way Road (the old railroad grade to Cottonwood Creek), P.O. Box 998, Crestone, CO 81131; (719) 256-5284; fax (719) 256-5245; info@shumeicrestone.org; www.shumeicrestone.org/events/Art_S.html

Musicians

CRESTONE: THE ALBUM
Paul Winter certainly has credibility in the New Age world; his Winter Solstice Celebration at New York's Cathedral of St. John the Divine has been held every solstice since 1969. But he is no newcomer to Crestone, either. He first visited in 1979, to take part in the annual conference of the Lindisfarne Fellowship. He returned to Crestone often over the next 15 years for these yearly meetings. In 2004 he was invited back to play for an event at the Shumei International Institute, 25 years after his first visit.

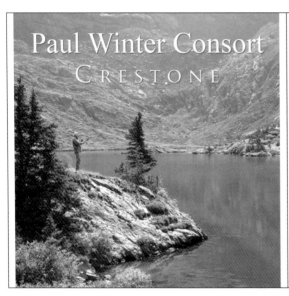

Fig. 9-26. His album *Crestone* won the 2007 Grammy in New Age category. *"Looking out once again at the breathtaking panorama of this valley and these mountains, and reflecting on my twenty-five year relationship with Crestone, I felt a calling to make music about this remarkable realm"* (Winter, 2010). Photo by Bill Ellzey.

Most of the album was recorded in September 2006 at North Crestone Lake at 11,800 ft elevation, with the help of a few local residents (see May, 2008).

The local live music scene currently centers around the Laughing Buddha Lounge in downtown Crestone, where various bands perform weekly. An even wider spectrum of acts appears at the Hazelrig Music House in the Baca subdivision (Classical, Celtic, Folk, Country, Bluegrass, New Age, Jazz, Indian, and Middle Eastern). Since 1999 more than 225 concerts have been held there; go to hazelrigmusichouse.com for concert schedules. The House is located at 24 Alpine Overlook; drive south on Camino Baca Grande to North Baca Grant Way, turn left (east), and Alpine Overlook is the second cul-du-sac on the left (north).

Both local and visiting musicians can take advantage of Crestone's Wunderground Studio for rehearsal, live demo recording, or multitrack recording. The Studio is a stand-alone, 1000 square-foot building located on Cedar Street east of the liquor store. For more information or to schedule a session, go to http://wundergroundstudio.com or call 719-256-5073.

The Crestone-Baca area probably has a higher percentage of owner-built homes than anywhere else in Colorado. The primary reason for this is that Saguache County has never had a building code. If a building will stand, it's legal… This unusual situation has determined much of the character of the Crestone-Baca area.

Prior to 1997 even building permits were not required in Saguache County. All an owner-builder had to do was file a free "Notice of Intent" with the County, describing where and what he or she was going to build. The building's electrical and plumbing systems had to be approved by State inspectors, but otherwise there were no codes and no inspections. This *laissez-faire* situation left local residents free to build basically any type of structure they wanted, with some very ingenious results (Nealson, 1994a). One result was a large number of straw bale homes, which led to Crestone's informal title as "Straw Bale Capitol of Colorado."

In 1997 Saguache County proposed initiating a mandatory Building Permit and Building Code system, similar to that in most Colorado Counties. The County-initiated proposal ignited a firestorm of protest in the Crestone-Baca area, where the right to build one's home free of "government interference" was held dearly and deeply. The County ended up choosing a compromise solution, by adopting the Building Permits but not the Building Code. The result is that now Building Permits must be obtained and paid for, but there are no structural standards or inspections. With this Solomon-like solution, the County is able to track where building is occurring, while local owner-builders are still free to design and build the dwelling of their dreams (Koko, 2005).

Although there are conventional 2x4 frame ("stick-built") buildings in the Baca, they make up only about half the inventory. The other half are non-traditional building styles such as A-frame, straw bale, Southwestern stucco, round, octagon, dome, free-form ferrocement, earthship, and even a pyramid and a full sphere. Typical additions to houses not common elsewhere are a "meditation tower," detached artist's studio, and/or guest house. A selection of alternative house styles can be visited during the "Home Tours" held every September during the San Luis Valley Energy Fair (www.slvenergyfair.com).

Strawbale Homes: The straw bale house has become very popular in the Crestone-Baca area for several reasons. First, it is considered "green building" because the strawbales are basically an agricultural waste product (it's straw after all, not hay). Second, strawbale homes are inexpensive in the smaller sizes, 900-1500 sq. ft. Third, the 18-24"-thick strawbale walls have great insulating properties and considerable thermal mass, compared to a wall of 2x4 studs. As in the traditional adobe homes of the American Southwest, the walls have enough thermal mass to buffer the extreme daily and seasonal temperature variations.

Walls are composed of standard small bales of straw (18" to 24"W x 14"H x 36" to 40"L), stacked with the short dimension up. There are at least three methods of construction: (1) a post-and-beam or balloon frame structure (Fig. 9-27) with the walls filled in with non-load-bearing strawbales; (2) 2x4 studwall construction with the bales passively stacked inside the walls, and then stuccoed; or (3) load-bearing strawbale walls where the bales are tightly pressed together by pulling down on a solid header at the top of the wall. The walls are thus 18"-24" thick, yielding an insulation R-value of about 30

205

neglecting any interior facing. With the owner-builder providing all the labor over a two-year period, the final cost can be as low as $30 per square foot.

In an extreme continental climate like Crestone's, the high R-value and thermal mass of strawbale walls keep the interior temperature relatively constant, obviating the need for expensive heating or cooling. Most strawbale walls are covered with stucco on the outside (natural color or stained). In the high desert environment stucco is a low-maintenance exterior finish, since it resists the withering effect of ultraviolet sunlight at 8000 ft elevation. A video showing strawbale construction is available from RMPBS (2000), Spirit of Colorado; Mi Casa es Su Casa: VHS video cassette, Rocky Mountain PBS (Public Broadcasting System).

Fig. 9-27. This 2-story strawbale home was built with a "balloon frame" composed of vertical 18" plywood columns (the width of a strawbale) spaced 4 feet apart (the length of a strawbale). The columns bear the weight of the roof and of the interior second-floor. The strawbales are non-load-bearing infill which provide some racking resistance, plus a lot of insulation and thermal mass. The final exterior finish will be earth-toned stucco applied over tar paper (partially attached at left) and a wire mesh.

Other types of homes in the Baca include:
1-- A-frames (the original design of choice back in the 1971-80 period)
2-- Underground homes and Earth Ships (e.g., the Haidakhandi Universal Ashram on Dream Way)
3-- Domes and spheres (e.g., the 32 ft-diameter sphere built in 2003 in Baca Grants Unit, on Beaver Trail off Homestead Road; Chernin, 2003)
4-- Earthbag and papercrete houses (most famously, Kelley Hart's former house; see Hart, 2003b)
5-- AerBlock (aerated autoclaved concrete, or AAC); go to www.aerblock.com and look under "Projects" for 8 Crestone structures; also see Hart, 2003a)
6-- Pyramids (e.g., 1131C Badger Road)
7-- Free-form ferrous-cement structures (examples on Cottonwood Creek Road, and on Pine Cone Way high in the Baca Grande subdivision)

All things are connected. Whatever befalls the earth befalls the sons of the earth.
Chief Seattle, 1855 (letter to President Franklin Pierce)

In a way the collapse of the Crestone-Baca construction industry in 2008 had one positive result. It reminded Crestonians (and other Americans) that an economy based entirely on home building (especially retirement- and second-homes), is not sustainable in the long run. That lesson, combined with a growing worldwide interest in sustainability, led locals to reassess the Crestone-Baca economy and lifestyle. In some ways this reassessment has suggested a return to the pioneer ways of Crestone's founders, and to the subsistence ways of the "Quiet Years" (1930s-1970s), when Crestone was an isolated, self-reliant semi-ghost town. Self-sufficiency might be attained in three areas: Energy, Food, and Transportation.

ENERGY

Most of the energy used in Crestone is imported, either via propane trucks, gasoline tankers, or via power lines from the San Luis Valley Rural Electric Co-op. However, many homes in the Grants Unit of the Baca subdivision were built to be self-sufficient in energy. These "off the grid" homes were never connected to the power grid, but instead generate all their electric power by solar photovoltaic panels, and heat by solar thermal panels (with backup from wood or propane). Crestone has a wide reputation in the solar energy field, as shown by Grudowski (2011), with institutes like the Crestone Solar School (www.crestonesolarschool.com).

In the past few years the San Luis Valley has become a hotbed of activity in solar energy, following the national trend. Industrial-scale solar electricity is being generated in Alamosa County, and projects are proposed for Saguache County. Local homeowners already connected to the power grid have installed "grid-tied" solar photovoltaic systems that feed excess produced power back into the grid, for which they are credited by San Luis Valley Rural Electric Co-op.

Many Crestonians believe that solar electric power can be more efficiently generated by a distributed, rooftop approach rather than centralized, industrial-scale solar power plants. However, in Crestone-Baca nearly everyone in the area who can afford to buy a solar photovoltaic system has already done so, utilizing Federal and State tax credits. Several fanciful schemes have been proposed to loan homeowners money who cannot afford solar systems. However, lending agencies are understandably reluctant, having just experienced the catastrophic results of giving home mortgages to under-qualified borrowers. So at least for the present, industrial-scale solar will remain an important component of the valley's economy.

FOOD

Prior to the railroad coming to Crestone, the town's food supply came from local sources. But along with the rest of America, Crestone became increasingly dependent in the 20th Century on food imported from far away. Given that, and the short growing season in Crestone, is it realistic to think that we could ever become self-sufficient in food? It is possible in theory, but requires three changes: (1) a change back to eating mainly non-processed foods, (2) eating locally-produced foods in season (near harvest), rather than (say) South American avocados in mid-winter, and (3) exploiting every opportunity for growing foodstuffs locally.

There is little the community can do about changing a person's eating habits. But on the production side, some advances are possible. The Grandmother of all local food organizations is the Atalanta Association (www.atalanta.org), founded in 1994 by members of Subud USA on 44 acres granted by the Manitou Foundation. They offer what is now termed Community Supported Agriculture (CSA; see del Amor, 2003), broadly defined as individuals and families buying a share of the farmer's harvest at the beginning of the season. Atalanta uses the Cooperative version of CSA, wherein people become members and work in the garden to earn their share of produce. Atalanta is also a founding member of the High Valley Dairy Goat and Sheep Cooperative.

More recently, Shumei International Institute has become a major player in CSA, through their organic garden (Fig. 9-28). Two privately-owned enterprises provide locally-grown food, Living Arts Institute (livingartsinstitute.net) in Crestone and Chokurei Ranch near Moffat. LAI's Chokecherry Farm offers the traditional form of CSA where locals buy a share of the farmer's harvest at the beginning of the season. The arrangement is a way to nourish farmers economically while providing a weekly box of fresh farm goodies to the CSA member throughout the entire growing season. Chokurei Ranch provides produce, dairy, and meat mainly through sales at the Crestone Saturday Market. For information about locally-produced food, go to www.slvlocalfoods.com.

Fig. 9-28. Shumei master gardeners debrief elementary students from the Crestone Charter School, in a meeting of generations and cultures. They had just finished their joint planting of the organic potato garden (right background). Photo by Bill Ellzey.

FOOD FROM TREES

Sometimes overlooked by the proponents of Local Food production is food already being produced every year by trees. Production comes from two trees: (1) the wild Pinyon Pine, and (2) fruit trees in Crestone, many planted 100 years ago.

Part 1; The Economics of Pinyon Nuts

Nearly every autumn, you will pass many cars parked on road shoulders in the Crestone-Baca area. If you look beyond the cars into the pinyon-juniper woodland, you may notice people sitting on the ground, patiently picking up tiny brown objects off the ground. These people are engaged in the age-old tradition of harvesting pinyon nuts (also called pine nuts).

The pinyon nut has long been a staple for the Native Americans, and later Hispanic settlers, of New Mexico and southern Colorado. Pinyon nuts are higher in protein and carbohydrates than pecans, but lower in fat. They keep well; if unshelled they can go a year without turning rancid . The taste is *"pine and sunshine and popcorn, and peanuts too in a way"* (Long, 1986). Shelled pine nuts are an ingredient in foods such as pesto. But locals often eat them unshelled, cracking the shell with their teeth and spitting it out while consuming the soft nut inside.

> *"Even U.S. Americans become expert at cracking the shells with their teeth. But it takes an old Indian or native to show what can be done. Pinyons go in one corner of the mouth and the shells come out the other. Sitting against a warm wall in the winter sun, people can keep it up for hours."* Long, 1986.

According to the USDA Forest Service (2010), *"Colorado pinyons may start bearing cones at 25 years. Good seed production occurs on trees that are 75-100 years old, with maximum seed production occurring on trees 160-200 years of age. Large seed crops are produced every 3 to 7 years and are adversely impacted by water stress. Cones require 3 years to mature."* In a good year an acre of pinyon-juniper woodland can yield up to 300 pounds of nuts! Gathering pinyon nuts is a family activity. The adults may spread a sheet beneath the tree and beat the nuts down with sticks or brooms.

> *"Cars and wagons lie like beetles along the highways and byways. You hear people and children chattering not far way, with as much noise as the pinyon-jays whose blue wings flash among the branches. The dwarf trees are suddenly a vineyard; the barren land turns fruitful and calls for pickers. Little children run from tree to tree picking up the nuts that have fallen. Sometimes they find the cache of a squirrel and get ten to fifteen pounds at a stroke.....*" Long, 1986.

In good years the nut crop from northern New Mexico and southern Colorado may be worth a million dollars, and the pickers get perhaps a third of this amount. According to Long (1986), *"About four-fifths of the crop is sold outside the state [New Mexico], most of it going to the east side of New York. There the pushcart vendors sell the nuts to people who miss the Russian pine nuts and the Italian pistachios of their homelands...."* (Long, 1986). However, since the 1980s the pinyon market has slowly been flooded with cheap pinyon nuts imported from China; these now comprise 80% of the pine nuts sold in America.

As of this writing, residents of Crestone-Baca have made no attempt to organize the nut harvest from the tens of thousands of pinyon trees here, even in the years of bumper crops (e.g., 1992, 1996, 2005). However, on the basis of weight alone the pinyon crop probably exceeds all other locally-grown foods put together.

Part 2; Fruit Trees, Young & Olde
Crestone's pioneers planted numerous apple trees in the 1880s, and many of those trees are still alive and producing old-fashioned varieties of apples. In 1909 consulting engineer Robert McF. Doble, writing about the eastern Baca Grant (present site of the subdivision) to the Baca Grant Development Company, said: *"I feel confident that the "Fruit lands" of the Baca Grant will become famous and will handsomely reward the owners... The soil and the general topography are particularly favorable for orchards. The lands are sheltered by the high mountains lying easterly and northerly of them and by the same means are protected from the early rays of the sun. The lands slope toward the west and the south and therefore have the full benefit of the afternoon sun which warms up the ground and the mountain slopes and provides a store of heat which is given off during the night, to the great benefit of the fruit bearing trees."* (quoted in Sherer, 2005, p. 11-12).

The cultivation of fruit trees is being reinvigorated by members of the Crestone Fruit Tree Project. Since 1996 they have added about 200 new fruit trees to the Crestone-Baca area (for example, the McAlpine Ranch added a 40-tree multi-fruit orchard in 2010). Apples, apricots, cherries, and plums grow well here, despite the temperatures as low as -26°F in winter. Fruit production could be even greater, if those property owners and renters lucky enough to have these old fruit trees would get them pruned, water them in dry seasons, and manage them for fruit production. In the Crestone-Baca area fruit trees should be considered a fundamental part of any plan for Local Food production.

WHERE TO BUY LOCALLY-PRODUCED FOOD
From June to mid-September local food can be purchased at the Crestone Saturday Market, in the 100 W block of Silver Avenue. At other times local food is sold at Curt's Olde Country Store (directly southeast of the Market); the Bliss Café (directly north of the Market); Crestone Mercantile (100 E block of Galena Ave.); and the Chokurei Farm Store at Challenger Golf Course.
Vendors sell local plant starts, vegetables, fruits, eggs, goat dairy products, yak meat, etc.

TRANSPORTATION
When the Baca Grande subdivision was laid out in 1971, gasoline cost about 35 cents a gallon. So the planners had no qualms about siting the development's infrastructure out on the valley floor, 3-4 miles west of the closest part of the subdivision (and up to 9.5

road miles from the southern edge of the subdivision). But after 2008 and $4.50/gallon gas prices, Crestonians began to question the efficiency of this arrangement, and to think how to bring these facilities (particularly the Crestone Charter School), closer to the population centers and downtown Crestone. After all, how sustainable is burning a non-renewable fossil fuel that is 70% imported? That practice currently costs Americans *$750 million per day (10 million barrels per day @ 75/barrel)* of American's hard-earned money going overseas, much of it to countries that do not have our best interests at heart. The engine exhaust is also a major contributor to greenhouse gases. Realistically, Crestone will never achieve "sustainability" as long as people are burning imported gasoline to drive to the Post Office and Charter School every day.

An encouraging trend is the increased local use of low-emissions gas-electric hybrid vehicles and zero-emissions vehicles (ZEVs) such as Low Speed Electric Vehicles (LSVs; see the Sunmobile, below). LSVs with the proper safety equipment are licensed in Colorado for use on roads with speed limits of 35 mph or less, which means they can be used throughout the Crestone-Baca area. As infrastructure slowly migrates from the valley floor to the Town of Crestone, we should see increased use of quiet, plug-in electric transport on the roads of Crestone. ZEVs are recharged with locally-produced, all-American, zero-emissions solar electricity. What could be wrong with that?

Alternative Transportation in 2011: ATVs and LSVs

An unusual aspect of Crestone is that it's legal for licensed drivers to drive unlicensed ATVs and golf carts on town streets, as well as to drive licensed Low-Speed Electric Vehicles (LSVs). The Town passed an ordinance to this effect in 2009, to encourage quieter, more fuel-efficient local transportation. Although the ordinance officially applies only within the City limits of Crestone, it has been extended by locals to include the two dead-end Forest Roads that extend from Crestone north (1.3 miles) and east (2.3 miles) to the two Forest Service Trailheads. Thus, one could drive the 3.6 mile trip between the trailheads, through Crestone, on alternative vehicles. Although Crestone is still a long way from catching up with Peachtree City, GA with its 9000 electric golf carts, it has started down that road.

Kelly Hart and the Sunmobile

Nine years before the gas price "blowup" of 2008, Kelly Hart of Crestone was already thinking about sustainable modes of local transportation. In 1999 he invented the "Sunmobile" (www.sunvee.com). This 2-person vehicle could travel at up to 25 mph and had a sufficient range to travel back-and-forth between the Baca subdivision and Crestone. Like all full-electric vehicles, it emitted no greenhouse gases and was eerily quiet. The problem was, it was 9 years ahead of its time and the $5/gallon gas prices of 2008. By 2008 Kelly had moved on to other things and the Sunmobile had been dismantled and recycled into other projects.

10. HISTORICAL TIMELINE OF THE CRESTONE-BACA AREA

(*events compiled from Harlan, 2002; Sisemore, 1983; Sherer, 2005; Pelton, 1891; coloradohistoricalnewspapers.com; the Crestone Eagle newspaper; and other references as cited*)

Prior to 1870

1694: Don Diego de Vargas pioneers the East Fork of the North Branch of the Old Spanish Trail. The trail goes north from Santa Fe through the eastern San Luis Valley (see Kessler, 1998). Recent research suggests that the Trail passed very close to the present Town of Crestone (Krall and Martorano, 2011).

The 1700s: The Crestone area was included in "New Spain", the Spanish Empire in the New World. Spanish miners advanced up into the San Luis Valley from what is now Mexico, and extracted gold at Cedar Creek and Pole Creek. They left behind *arrastras,* circular pits carved in bedrock in which gold ore was crushed. The base of the arrastra at Pole Creek is a large rock of Precambrian schist that had been carved in place. A center hole for the rotating shaft is over 6" in depth and evidently supported a heavy pine timber rotated by means of poles lashed to the shaft. The poles would have had drag stones ("mullers") tied to them and were rotated by manpower. The large flat drag stones, weighing several hundred pounds each, would crush the ore as they passed over it. The arrastra at Pole Creek is about 6 feet in diameter (see photo in Sisemore, 1983, p. 74). It was probably built between 1700 and 1765, a period in which numerous Spanish parties passed through the San Luis Valley prospecting for gold (Geary, 1997).

1807: Jan. 27, Lt. Zebulon Pike crosses Medano Pass from the east and descends into the San Luis Valley at the sand dunes, before continuing south.

1823: The government of newly-independent Mexico grants **Luis Maria Cabeza de Vaca** a 500,000-acre land grant in "New Spain" (near Las Vegas, New Mexico). The Baca family moves there and lives on the land from about 1824-1827, but is then driven away by Indians. When the family returns to their land from Mexico in 1835, the land had been settled and claimed by US citizens (for more details, see Martin, 2005).

1824: Antoine Roubideau (or Robidoux), a French trapper and merchant, builds a wagon road across the Sangres south of Medano Pass (then called William's Pass); this pass is now called Mosca Pass.

1820s to 1840s: The three prominent and sharp peaks of the Crestone Group (probably Kit Carson's summit pinnacle, Crestone Peak, and Crestone Needle) are named the *Les Trois Tetons* by French trappers, probably in the heydey of beaver trapping in the Sangre (1821-1840).

1830-1848: Crestone lies on the North Branch of the Old Spanish Trail, which connects Santa Fe with California. The trail hugs the eastern margin of the San Luis Valley near Crestone, in order to avoid the marshes (lakes?) in the valley center (see Figs. 10-1, 10-2). See www.oldspanishtrail.org.

1836: The area that will later contain Crestone and the Baca Grant is included in the self-proclaimed Republic of Texas.

1845: The United States annexes the Republic of Texas and makes it the 28th State of the Union; this is considered an "act of war" by Mexico.

1846-1848: The Mexican-American War. It is ended by the Treaty of Guadalupe Hidalgo in 1848, which provides for the Mexican Cession, in which Mexico cedes 525,000 square miles to the US in exchange for US$15 million. The ceded area contains the future site of Crestone. The Treaty of Guadalupe Hidalgo also guarantees the pre-existing property rights of Mexican citizens in the transferred territory. [*This provision later becomes the source of many land disputes in the 20th Century SLV, regarding Spanish land grants, mineral rights, and communal use-rights to land.*]

1848: Dec. 3, John C. Fremont crosses Roubideau Pass (now called Mosca Pass) on his Fourth Expedition. They turn north onto the Old Spanish Trail, and a few days later arrive near the present site of Crestone, on what is now called Crestone Creek (then called Riviere des Tres [or Trois] Tetons). For more details, see Richmond (1992).

Fig. 10-1. Lithograph of the Sangre de Cristo Mountains east of Crestone, from Fremont (1886). The high flat-topped peak is clearly Kit Carson Mountain, showing both the notch and separate true summit on the right, and the Northwest Ridge and Pt 13,151 on the left (compare to Fig. 5-12). However, the remainder of the scene is impressionistic.

1850: The Compromise of 1850; the US Congress agrees to pay the $10 million debts of the former Republic of Texas, in exchange for the State of Texas relinquishing its claim to land in (present-day) New Mexico and Colorado. This includes the Las Vegas Baca Grant, and much of central Colorado. The ceded land (including where Crestone and the Baca will founded later) becomes part of the Public Domain of the United States.

1853: On Aug. 25, the Gunnison-Beckwith Expedition enters the San Luis Valley via Roubideau's Pass, looking for a route to build a railroad to the Pacific coast. They travel north on the Old Spanish Trail, camping on Chatillon Creek [*Cottonwood Creek*] on Aug. 26 and Leroux Creek [*Rito Alto Creek*] on Aug. 27 (Cooper, 2003). Beckwith (1855) reports "prarie-grass fields" along Crestone Creek, and extensive marshes farther west (in the present BNWR). The party described the peaks east of Crestone as follows: "The sharp edges and needle forms of the summits of the Sierra Blanca [*Sangre de Cristo Mountains*], rising 3,000 feet above the valley, attract much admiration at our camp tonight." Later that same year, the 5th Fremont Expedition passed by Crestone on the Old Spanish Trail on Dec. 4, going from Medano Pass to Rito Alto Creek. Fremont wrote: "*We selected a campground in an immense natural deerpark, and raised our tents under the shelter of wide-spreading cedars.*" (Fig. 10-1)

1859: The Baca family sues the United States to honor its obligations under the Treaty of Guadalupe Hidalgo, i.e., to honor their land grant from the King of Spain.

1860: The U.S. Congress declares that the original 500,000-acre Baca Land Grant land grant, having been homesteaded by others in good faith, should be retained by the homesteaders. However, in exchange, an Act of Congress dictates that the Baca family can choose five new grants of 100,000 acres apiece from the public domain of the United States in the western territories. They chose #1 and #2 (in the present State of New Mexico), #3 and #5 (in the present State of Arizona), and #4 (the one near Crestone).

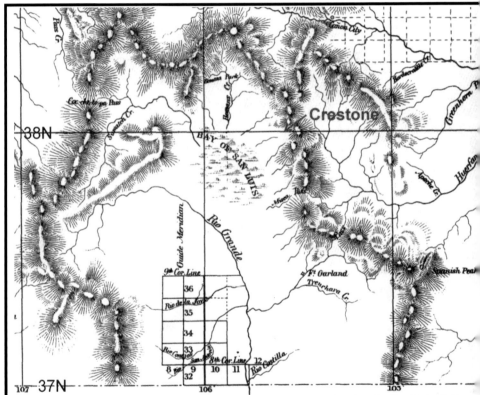

Fig. 10-2. Part of the Map of Colorado Territory made in 1861, showing the San Luis Valley (Source: 37th U.S. Congress, 2nd Session, Senate Executive Document No. 1). This map was made only two years after the beginning of the Colorado Gold Rush (1859). None of the valley's present towns existed at this time (e.g. Alamosa, Monte Vista, etc.). In fact, the Baca Grant did not exist yet either; it was granted to the Baca family in 1864.

1861: The Territory of Colorado (with boundaries the same as the later State of Colorado) is created out of parts of the Territories of Kansas, Nebraska, and New Mexico.

On official government maps, the floor of the northern San Luis Valley is labeled the "Bay of San Luis" (Fig. 10-2). The term "Bay" is probably a corruption of the French-American word "bayou", meaning a marshy lake or wetland. The mountains fringing the San Luis Valley were visited by French-American trappers in the early 1800s and they gave names to several other landmarks, including the Crestone Peaks, which they named "Les Trois Tetons" (see maps in Wheeler, 1877).

1862: The Baca Grant is first surveyed, and on Dec. 12 the survey is filed with the Territory of New Mexico, who then forwarded it to the surveyor general of the newly-formed Territory of Colorado. This is the first attempt to lay formal claim to the land.

1864: after 5 years of wrangling with the Colorado Surveyor General and the Land Office, the Baca family formally receives approved title to the 100,000-acre Baca Grant #4; it then sells the Grant to attorney John S. Watts for $3000 (his attorney fee); Mr. Watts was the family lawyer who had secured them the land exchange starting in 1860. From 1864-1869 the Grant is leased and run by Mr. Lily and Mr. Joe Coberly of the L&C Rough and Ready Flour Mills of Littleton, Colorado.

1866: The U.S. General Land Office issues a map of the Territory of Colorado (Fig. 10-3), to help Congress decide on Colorado's application for statehood in 1865. [Congress denies the application, however, and Colorado does not gain statehood until 1876]. The map shows numerous geographic features in the northern San Luis Valley with French names, which are no longer in use. The stream flowing across the NW corner of the Grant is named "Riviere des trois Teits"; this is now named Crestone Creek. The next major stream to the north is named "Le Croux Creek", named for Antoine Leroux, the guide for Gunnison's 1853 expedition; this is Rito Alto Creek of modern usage. Farther south Cottonwood Creek was called "Chatillon Creek", and at the Sand Dunes, the present Mosca Pass was named "Robidoux Pass", after a French trapper.

Gunnison also named the northern arm of the valley north of Mineral Hot Springs and Villa Grove "Homan Park", and its creek "Homan Creek", after his astronomer Sheppard Homans. That creek is named San Luis Creek on modern maps. The 1866 map also shows a 60 mile-long, unnamed lake on the valley floor, as stated by Gilpin (1860, 1869). The Baca Grant (Baca Claim No. 4) is also shown, for the first time on a Colorado map.

Late in 1866 Saguache County, Colorado is created, encompassing 3168 square miles (larger than the states of Delaware or Rhode Island). In Washington, Congress passes Revised Statute (RS) 2477, which states that any trail or road used by the public prior to that land being withdrawn from the public domain of the United States, has a permanent, irrevocable public right-of-way. This law was used in 2009 to argue that trails crossing the spiritual retreat lands had an irrevocable public right-of-way. The Spanish Creek and Cottonwood Creek trails may have been used prior to 1864 (when the Baca Grant was withdrawn from the public domain), but that withdrawal occurred 2 years before passage of RS2477, and Federal laws generally are not held to be retroactive.

215

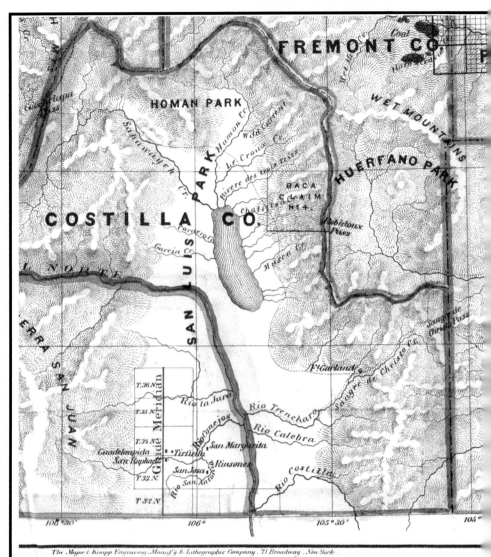

Fig. 10-3. Map of the "San Luis Park" from 1866, just prior to the creation of Saguache County from parts of Costilla County. From the U.S. General Land Office (1866).

1869: Lily and Coberly purchase the Grant from John Watts; DeWitt and Joe Travis build a cabin on North Crestone Creek, but find out later the land had already been claimed by the Baca Grant, so they move north to San Isabel Creek.

1870: Lily and Coberly sell the Grant to Alexander Hunt, 4th Territorial Governor of Colorado. The Wales Ranch is homesteaded by the Wales and Shellabarger families in July 1870 (Harlan, 2002, p. 30), 2.7 miles downstream from the mouth of Rito Alto Creek (7 mi NW of Crestone); [*this site is still owned and inhabited by the Shellabargers*

216

140 years later; see Shellabarger, 1923] San Isabel is homesteaded by the Travis family, 2.0 miles downstream from the mouth of San Isabel Creek. [*This is the site of the present Boyce Ranch* (3.1 miles NW of Crestone; Harlan, 2002)].

1870-1886: The First Mining Boom and Bust

1870 (or slightly earlier): gold is discovered in Pole Creek by John Duncan and other prospectors. This was the beginning of what later became the El Dorado Mining District, which extended from Short Creek northward to South Crestone Creek.

1872: "By 1872, the land bordering San Isabel Creek was nearly all claimed by homesteaders, and a young, thriving community was in the making." The San Isabel Post Office opened on July 7, 1872. (Harlan, 2002)

The "Crestonie Post Office" opens Feb. 7, 1872, probably in the oldest adobe house at the Baca Ranch headquarters, which is still standing (Harlan, 2002). The Ulysses Herard family homesteads the mouth of Deadman Creek in 1872, only to discover three years later they are trespassing on the Baca Grant; they soon move to the mouth of Medano Creek, east of the Great Sand Dunes (Geary, 1997).

1873: The Crestonie Post Office is officially closed on Oct. 29, 1873; however, mail continues to be dropped off there as a "mail shelter." (Harlan, 2002). William Gilpin (future owner of the Baca Grant) re-publishes "Mission of the North American people" (Gilpin, 1873), touting the agricultural potential of the San Luis Valley to Eastern US and foreign investors.

1874: The El Dorado Mining District is organized, composed of the mines in the Baca Grant between South Crestone Creek and Pole Creek. The main mining camp is called Sangre de Cristo and is located just downstream from the mouth of Cottonwood Creek, on the north bank; its site thus lies within the present Baca Grande subdivision. According to "D.I." (1875), the first gold discoveries near the mouth of Cottonwood Creek were made in September 1874 by the Horne brothers. He reports that by March of 1875, Sangre de Cristo camp was "a thriving little burg of some dozen cabins, and about forty rustling prospectors."

1875: The 1st potatoes are grown in the northern San Luis Valley by DeWitt Travis at San Isabel; 70,000 pounds are harvested and sold to miners in Leadville (Harlan, 2002).

1876: Colorado is admitted as the 38th State of the Union. The date is the centennial of the founding of the United States of America, explaining Colorado's nickname "The Centennial State."

The mines around Crestone are visited by a party of the Wheeler Geographical Survey of the West, headed by Lieutenant Eric Bergland. He writes the earliest description of the "new" Crestone mining district:

"The first mines visited are situated in the new district, in the vicinity of the headwaters of North Creston Creek. This district was [Oct. 27, 1876] about to be organized under the name of Creston district. First discoveries were made in May, 1875, and a number of prospecting shafts had been opened. But little ore had been taken out up to the time of my visit, as there is no mill at the mines and the ore is not rich enough to warrant the cost of

217

shipment to any distance. Some of the quartz which has been milled gave a yield of $12 to $15 per ton. Three to four thousand dollars have been expended in completing lines of communication to the mines. Timber is convenient and abundant on the slopes and in the gulches where the ore is found, and a sufficient supply of water is also available.
....
El Dorado Mining District: This was visited and reported upon by Mr. Niblack. This district lies between South Creston and Deadman's Creek, and is about 7 miles south of Creston district. It was organized in 1874, and a small town has been built which is called Sangre de Cristo Post Office. Two 5-stamp mills have been erected, but were not in operation when visited, Oct. 29, 1876. The character of the ores is about the same as those of the first district, but the yield has not been sufficient to induce much expenditure in the development of the several prospecting shafts." (from Bergland, 1877).

Also in 1876, the formation of the "Christonie District" was also reported in the *Saguache Chronicle* newspaper as follows:
"The miners on the Christonie Creek organized a mining district Nov. 25, 1876. The boundaries are as follows: On the south, by the northern boundary of the El Dorado district; east, by the summit of the Sangre de Christo Range; north by San Isable (sic) creek; and west by a line running parallel with the summit at an average distance of four miles from the Ohio lode.
Article 2. In working out assessments five dollars per day per man shall be allowed, and an allowance of five dollars per day per man where powder and fuse is used.
Article 3. Regular meetings shall be held on the second Saturday of December, July and October of each year.
Article 4. Any three members may call a meeting, by notifying the president and three written notices, giving day and date of said meeting, shall be posted.
Article 5. That the district shall be governed by the United States and state law, in regard to mining.
John Farrington was elected president and Daniel Warden, secretary. A vote of thanks was tendered Carl Wulsten for valuable suggestions.
We are indebted to Mr. Daniel Warden for the following communication:
"The miners on the Christonie held a meeting pursuant to notice, to organize a district. We had a good attendance, each miner seeming anxious to organize. We were honored with the presence of several distinguished gentlemen, among whom was his honor, the mayor of Pueblo, who is out here in the interests of himself and friends. We regret his short sojourn with us; also Mr. Carl Wulsten of Rosita, United States surveyor of mines and mineralogist. Mr. Wulsten was favorably impressed with the character of our gold ores, the situation of the mining district, its advantageous water power, the abundance of wood, and near proximity to the county seat. Mr. Wulsten is well known throughout southwestern Colorado, as an expert. He came here with Mr. Mitchell as an advisor. Mr. Mitchell is a gentleman from London, England, and represents large capital. He is one who says very little, but has accomplished much. This is his second visit to the gulch. On Mr. Wulsten's recommendations, he has bonded several mines in this district, and starts for England immediately to report to his company the condition of affairs. We have every faith in Mr. Mitchell's ability to bring back with him large capital from London for investment of mines of this range. We do not wish to deceive the public, neither do we wish to deceive ourselves, but are willing to stand on the merits of the mines we own, and if they fail to be good investments to the capitalists, we are willing to fall with them and lose our all.
We have with us Mr. Ira G. Wing, a miner of large experience; also Mr. Smartt, both of whom have spent much time in the mines of Nevada, Idaho, Montana, California, and Colorado. With the assurance of experts Like Mr. Wulsten, and the tenacity with which those old time miners have clung to their opinions from the start, we fell [sic] sure in saying to the community at large, that we have in this district mines that will stand the best, and on their own merits. We are looking each day for a delegation of the business men of Saguache to pay our camp a visit at least. The invitation is a standing one; come and look for yourselves and take no mans word for what we say.

The following are the names of the lodes in Christonie district: Ohio, Desperado, Quien Sabe, Sidney, Terrible, Golden Guinea, Longfellow, Home Stake No. 1, Home Stake No. 2, Red Jacket, Sun Beam, Christonie, Apolo, Laura, Grand View, Highland Mary, Little Mary, Sterling, King of the Mountain, Mountain Lion, and Golden Fleece."
From the Saguache Chronicle, Dec. 2, 1876, vol. 3, no. 9, p.3:
www.coloradohistoricmewspapers.org

Saguache Chronicle, Dec. 9, 1876, vol. 3, no. 10, p.2:
"*Trip to the Mines. We spent five days during the past week at El Dorado and Christonie districts in the Sangre de Christo range, examining the mines and visiting the boys, and next week will report the incidents of a very pleasant visit. Our acknowledgments are due to one and all for courtesies rendered which will be long remembered, especially the house warming ball at Hopkins & Bassett's new hotel in El Dorado district. It was an agreeable surprise to find so many ladies* en fait *in the latest fashions, metropolitan gossip, and not averse to a quiet flirtation. The music was above average, furnished by Mrs. Herrard [sic], organ; Mr. Hopkins, violin, Mr. McCoy, banjo, and Mr. Bassett, triangle. Although the Chronicle has devoted considerable space to the Saguache county mines, we believe that their importance merits all and more than we can say.*"

Saguache Chronicle, Dec. 23, 1876, vol. 3, no. 12, p.2:
"*Geo. H. Adams left some fine looking specimens of free gold ores from the Reliance lead in Christonie district. The lead is one of the early discoveries of the district, but only the assessment had been worked out when Mr. Adams and Joseph Hixon took hold of it, placing Mr. Geo. Marshall, an experienced miner in charge. Mr. Marshall found that the work previously done was on a spur, and after some prospecting struck the true vein, which promises to be a veritable bonanza, for the amount expended in the original purchase.*"

Saguache Chronicle, Dec. 30, 1876, vol. 3, no. 13, p.2:
"*The Sangre de Christo Gold Field. We find the following editorial remarks respecting Saguache County Mines in Mines, Metals, Arts and Railroad Journal, of St. Louis, Ware & Co., publishers:*
This locality in Southern Colorado has attracted very close attention, on account of the prevalence of free-gold milling ore. Compared with the trouble and expensiveness attendant on the working of smelting ores, or ores adapted for wet treatment, all ores that can be worked by simple stamping and amalgamation, are infinitely the most profitable and desirable. Nothing within the range of metallurgical treatment is simpler and less expensive than the recovery of gold from a matrix that holds it in a free or uncombined condition. Many gold mines yield their ores in such a condition that the mining, hauling, and milling costs less than $4 a ton. It would, therefore, be a folly to claim that smelting, concentration, chlorination, or any other system of treatment, could equal sample gold recovery by amalgamation, even at $14 a ton.
We regret to be informed that the free ore of the Sangre de Christo becomes refractory, after reaching a depth of 35 to 50 feet from the surface."

The Crestone Mining District

The Crestone area was divided into two mining districts. In 1876 the younger "Crestone Mining District" (originally Christonie District) was organized, extending from South Crestone Creek north to San Isabel Creek (Fig. 10-4). Together with the older El Dorado Mining District, the two districts produced about $7-8 million in precious metals between 1874 and 1938 (Parker, 1952). For more details on mines and claims, see Sherer (2005).

Claims and Mines (from north to south)

Dimick Gulch: Perthshire; Argylshire

North Crestone Creek, north side: Reed (north of canyon mouth); Spar; Log Cabin; Trout; Lucky Baldwin; Kinney (#1, #2, #3); Blue Beard; Front Lode

North Crestone Creek, south side: Columbia; Detroit; Montreal; Banner (see Lakes, 1902); Iowa (#1, #2);

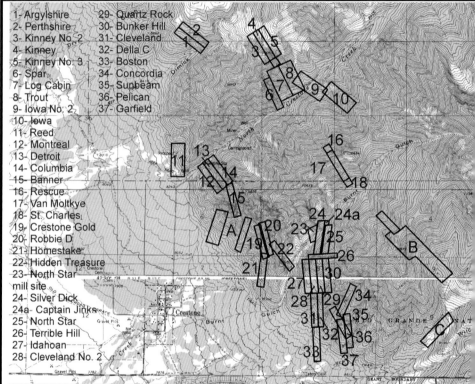

1- Argylshire
2- Perthshire
3- Kinney No. 2
4- Kinney
5- Kinney No. 3
6- Spar
7- Log Cabin
8- Trout
9- Iowa No. 2
10- Iowa
11- Reed
12- Montreal
13- Detroit
14- Columbia
15- Banner
16- Rescue
17- Van Moltkye
18- St. Charles
19- Crestone Gold
20- Robbie D
21- Homestake
22- Hidden Treasure
23- North Star mill site
24- Silver Dick
24a- Captain Jinks
25- North Star
26- Terrible Hill
27- Idahoan
28- Cleveland No. 2

29- Quartz Rock
30- Bunker Hill
31- Cleveland
32- Della C
33- Boston
34- Concordia
35- Sunbeam
36- Pelican
37- Garfield

Fig. 10-4. A partial list of patented mining claims of the Crestone Mining District, which still exist in 2011 as privately-owned parcels ("inholdings") within the Rio Grande National Forest and BLM land. From the Saguache County Assessor's Office. Unlabeled claims at A may be Lucky Baldwin, Blue Beard, and Front Lode. Unlabeled claims at B include the Cap Sheaf, Longfellow, and Cleora. Unlabeled claim C may be Wilcox.

North of Burnt Gulch: Banner (see Lakes, 1902); Homestake; Crestone Gold; Robbie D; Hidden Treasure; Von Moltkye; Rescue; St. Charles.

Mouth of Burnt Gulch: the Pest House (quarantines) and the slaughterhouse, with a big pile of bones behind it; creek water was piped into it to wash everything down.

South of Burnt Gulch: Idahoan; Cleveland (#1, #2); Quartz Rock; Captain Jinks; Silver Dick; North Star; Bunker Hill; Terrible Hill; Concordia; Garfield; Sunbeam; Pelican; Cap Sheaf; Longfellow; Cleora.

The Mining Camp of Teton: Founded in 1877-78, Teton was the first mining camp of what later became the Christonie (Crestone) Mining District, predating the town of Crestone by 2-3 years. It was established by prospectors who discovered gold in Burnt Gulch in the mid-1870s, probably as placer gold in the bed of Burnt Gulch. Like prospectors everywhere, they then followed Burnt Gulch upstream, looking for the bedrock (lode) outcrops from which that alluvial gold had been eroded. They found their first good lode deposit (the Pelican Lode) in 1877, in Garfield Gulch [the 3rd small gulch southeast of Burnt Gulch], and it became the mainstay of Teton.

From its beginning Teton was supported by the income from the mines in and southeast of Burnt Gulch and from Hugo Hykifer's Mill, which treated the ore from the Pelican Mine far up Garfield Gulch (Harlan, 2002, p. 59). Teton was quite a large town, and boasted a boarding house and sawmill. Teton received a U.S. Post office on August 30, 1880, showing it was the main mining camp at that time (this was two months before the town of Crestone was platted). The post office operated not quite one year, closing on June 7, 1881. Its function was then transferred to the newly-established post office in Crestone. Thus by 1881 Teton had already been eclipsed by Crestone as the primary settlement.

Due to the rather transient nature of Teton, the dwellings were either log with minimal foundations or tents. Because of this, there are no preserved foundations (concrete) to be seen today. According to Sisemore (1983, p. 39), the last burial in the Teton cemetery occurred in 1950, and is represented by the largest and best-preserved headstone. Most of the burials evidently date from about 1880 to 1902; see Sisemore (1983, p. 39-40) for a list.

The Mining Camp of Wilcox: Major Mines: Wilcox

THE EL DORADO MINING DISTRICT (ORGANIZED 1874)

The first mining district organized in the Crestone area was called the El Dorado District (aka Sangre de Cristo District), and included all the mines south of South Crestone Creek (Fig. 10-5). John Duncan reported the first discovery of gold in this district about 1870, on the lower slopes of Milwaukee Hill (the ridge separating Alpine Creek from Pole Creek). Duncan was later joined by other miners, who all believed that the Baca Grant did not own the mineral rights. Instead, they believed that the Spanish land grant only conferred on the owners only surface and grazing rights, but not mineral rights, and thus the miners were free to work claims as anywhere else on the public domain of the United States. Duncan went even further, building a town named after himself and encouraging miners to settle and build there, even though the town was clearly ¾ of a mile inside the Baca Grant. Other miners followed his example, and created the mining camps of Willow at the mouth of Willow Creek, Spanish City (aka Lucky) at the mouth of Spanish Creek, Sangre de Cristo (later named Cottonwood) at the mouth of Cottonwood Creek, and Independent at the Independent Mine.

Unlike in the Crestone Mining District, most claims and mines in the El Dorado Mining District lay on the Baca Grant, which was judged in 1900 to have legal ownership of all mineral rights. Therefore, those claims and mines do not exist as patented claims today, and their exact locations are known only from an unpublished map made by the owners of the Baca Grant. (Baca Grant Development Company, 1909).

Spanish City (aka Lucky); located 3 miles SE of Crestone at the mouth of Spanish Creek; "founded in 1889 when rich gold-bearing quartz veins were found nearby; lasted for 25 years." Several hundred people there in 1897, according to Bill Hutchinson. Mail came on horseback from Crestone. Dance hall, dairy at bend in creek; 2 stores, barber shop, dance hall, livery stables. Was abandoned around World War I (1914-1917).

Sangre de Cristo; The mining camp of Sangre de Cristo was founded sometime in the early 1870s. Although nothing remains of the mining camp today, the town sported a post office from April 19, 1876 to 1884 (Harlan, 2002). Sangre de Cristo supported and was sustained by the famous Golden Phantom Mine, one of the first lode deposits discovered in the Sangre de Cristo Mountains. Harlan states "During the height of mining activity in Sangre de Cristo, two small stamp mills—the beck Milling Company and the Bowman Mining and Milling Company—treated ore from the nearby mines, namely the Badger, the Bonanza, and the Jackson. Farther south on Deadman Creek, in Cedar Gulch (1st named canyon south of Cottonwood), and in Davis Gulch (not labeled on modern maps), small prospects such as the El Paso, Silver Hole, and the Golden Phantom, sent ore to the Sangre de Cristo mills for extraction."

The miners in this District leased their claims from the owner of the Baca Grant, George Adams. Because Adams was primarily interested in cattle raising and town promotions, he hired Judge Charles to look after his mining interests. "It was Charles' job to see that the miners and prospectors on the Ranch had properly signed leases and that they paid the required royalties on all the minerals mined" (Harlan, 2002, p. 45). The town was renamed **Cottonwood** in 1893, a name it retained until the last structure was removed in the late 1970s. At its peak (1898) it held 1,000 people (Sherer, 2005, p. 46).

Major Mines: Independent; Midnight; Eastern Star; Alamosa; Bonanza; Badger; Jackson; Golden Phantom

Modern USGS topo maps show a cluster of prospect pits and adits about ½ mile south of the mouth of Deadman Creek (Fig. 10-5). According to Ellis et al. (1983), these include two interconnected, near-surface adits with at least four portals and over 400 total feet of underground excavations. [This may be the Golden Phantom mine]. It appears that these adits intersect the clay zone of the Lexam Explorations, Inc. detachment fault gold target. Of the eight samples from that zone, "*five contain gold in the range of 0.01 oz gold per short ton to 0.06 oz gold per short ton…… Most samples also contain about ½ oz silver per short ton and some have elevated arsenic content (300-600 ppm). (Eliis et al., 1983; US Bureau of Mines field notes, Denver, CO, June 19, 1979)*." The quotation is from www.nature.nps.gov/GEOLOGY/parks/grsa/index.cfm

Town of Duncan (adapted from Slaughter, 2007)

John Duncan was born in Indiana on March 17, 1951. He emigrated to Colorado and arrived in the Sangre de Cristo area in 1874, where he discovered gold on the slope of Milwaukee Hill, the high ridge that separates Alpine Creek from Pole Creek. In 1890 gold was discovered in Pole Creek, leading Duncan to establish a permanent settlement between that claim and his claim on Milwaukee Hill, thus founding the Town of Duncan. The town flourished and it is rumored that approximately 4000 people lived in or near

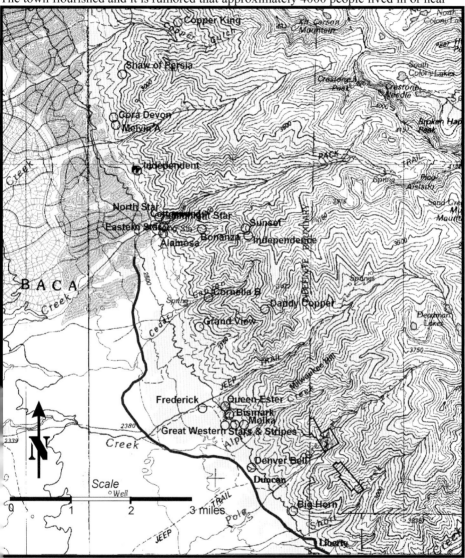

Fig. 10-5. Mines of the El Dorado Mining District. Circles show mines identified on a map by Baca Grant Development Company (1909). Other symbols show prospect pits (X's), adits (Y's), and shafts (squares), from USGS 1:24,000-scale topographic maps. Patented claims east of the Baca Grant between Pole and Short Creeks (rectangles) are from the USDA Rio Grande National Forest map. Liberty Road is shown as a thick black line.

Duncan by 1892, the year the Duncan Post Office opened. Businesses in Duncan included three grocery stores, Liggit & Company (which sold drugs, fine soaps, and perfumes), J.A. Hopkins Dry Goods & hardware (sold mining supplies), two general merchandise stores, a lumber supplier, The Thomas Miles Stage & Express Line (which carried the mail), two saloons, a barber, a shoemaker, boarding house, doctor, attorney, assay office, The Duncan Eagle newspaper, and one school. But no churches.

The Monte Cristo Tunnel, which is caved in but still visible today, is located just above the base of Milwaukee Hill. The mine tunnel was a community endeavor of Duncan townspeople, and unsuccessfully attempted to intersect Duncan's Denver Belle vein. Ores from this vein produced ore containing as much as $1000 of gold per ton (Harlan, 2002).

From 1879 to 1900 independent miners and prospectors erroneously operated on the Baca Grant, assuming that the Grant owners owned only the surface and grazing rights, but not the mineral rights. After the U.S, Supreme Court judged them wrong, they were given a choice; either abandon their claims, or continue working them under lease to the Baca Ranch

Major Mines: Honest Abe; Golden Treasure (Bryon Rolson); Sultan (Frasier brothers)

Liberty: The mining town of Liberty was located 1.5 miles southeast of Duncan, near the mouth of Short Creek. The town was founded in 1900 by miners evicted from their claims on the Baca Ranch. Many of then tried to prospected Short Creek, outside of the Ranch boundaries, but unfortunately only low-grade ore bodies were found along Short Creek. The miners gradually drifted away and the town is said to have been abandoned by 1921.
Major Mines: Yellow Bird

Fig. 10-6. A rusted oyster tin found in a rubbish dump on the Burnt Creek alluvial fan, between Crestone and Teton. The A. Booth's Company shipped oysters by rail as far west as San Francisco, between about 1873 and 1910. This tin was probably brought to Crestone after the railroad arrived from Moffat in 1901, and before it ceased regular operations (1907).

1877: William Gilpin buys the Grant from Alexander Hunt for non-payment of taxes. (Gilpin was the first Territorial Governor of Colorado from 1861-1862). He brings noted mining expert Professor James Aborn to the Baca Grant to determine its mineral potential. Gilpin is a shameless promoter of the San Luis Valley to investors from the Eastern USA and overseas (Gilpin, 1860, 1869).

The high peaks east of Crestone are known by the name *Les Trois Tetons* at least as late as 1877, when that label appears on the topographic maps made by the Wheeler Survey (Wheeler, 1877). Wheeler's 1877 map labels the mountain now named Kit Carson Mountain as "Frustrum Peak", and archaic term for a pyramid or cone truncated at the top.

1879: Big lode gold strikes are made in Burnt Gulch.

1880: E.A. Reser and George Adams (renters of the Baca Grant) buy 160 acres northeast of the Grant (two earlier 80-acre homesteads) and plat a townsite they call "Crestone" on Nov. 4, 1880. The plat covers 120 acres, but does not include the southeastern 40 acres.

1881s: *The Gold and Silver Extraction Mining & Milling Co.* (of Leadville, CO) operates mines in North Crestone Creek; H.A. W. Tabor, the famed Leadville Silver Baron, is president; [Colo. Hist. Soc. archives]. The company is a subsidiary of the Cassel Gold Extraction Co., Ltd., Glasgow, Scotland. The Crestone Mill is built that winter, but cost twice its original estimate; creditors will not let the mill run until they are paid (Saguache Chronicle, 1881).

1882: The Forest Fire: The "great fire" comes towards Crestone from the north, and burns the foothills for two weeks; it threatens Crestone, and is fought by the miners and everyone else. The fire finally burns itself out at South Crestone Creek, and the town is saved. (*Even 19 years later, the hills near town are barren of trees; see Fig. 10-10*).

1884: The Crestone Mill processes its first batch of ore, yielding an average of $230 of gold per ton of ore, against the cost of milling ($3 per ton). The mill is said to have recovered 90-95% of the assay amount of gold, and yielded $11,389.40 worth of gold bullion (Saguache Chronicle, 1884).

1885: George Adams buys the Baca Grant from Gilpin for $250,000. He had been leasing the grant under Gilpin and raising Herford cattle. Generally, Mr. Adams is much more interested in cattle raising than in mining.

1886: The *Tetons Mining & Milling Co.* operates mines and mills east of Crestone, issues $3,500,000 of stock; President, T.B. Stuart; Secretary, Leonard C. Calkins. A lag in production signals the end of the First Mining Boom in Crestone. (*The company is later sold in 1889 to Scottish company, see below.*)

1887-1903; The Second (Big) Mining Boom

1889: *The Crestone Gold Mining & Milling Co.* operates the Cap Sheaf, Sunbeam, Homestake, Longfellow, and Cleora mines, all in the Crestone Mining District east of Crestone. It was succeeded by *The Saguache County Land & Mining Co.*; President, John McDonald. The company owns the 5 mines listed above as well as The Placer, a 160 acre-area N (or E?) of Crestone; 40 ac was platted as lots (Reed addition).

1890: New deposits of free-milling gold are reported in the mountains near Crestone.

1891: The McArthur-Forrest cyanide process is first used in the USA in 1891 at the Independent Mill between Spanish and Cottonwood Creeks in the El Dorado Mining District. Prior to this, the Mill had been recovering gold by mercury amalgamation on copper plates. The mill had 50 stamps and a daily capacity of 40 tons. [*Small mounds of tailings existed at the mill site (as of 1952) which assayed from $10 to $30 per ton in gold (Parker, 1952, p. 27).*]

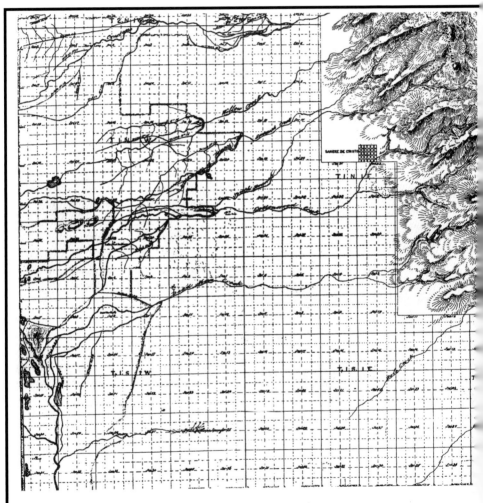

MAP OF THE CRESTONE ESTATE

Fig. 10-7. Map of the streams and ditches in the Baca Grant, as of 1891 (from Pelton, 1891). The solid lines grid lines are 1 mile apart, and define numbered "sections", but these were never officially sections belonging to the General Land Office survey grid; the dashed lines are ¼ mile apart and define 40-acre parcels. Note the mining town of Sangre de Cristo at the mouth of Cottonwood Creek, later renamed Cottonwood.

George Adams divides the Baca Grant into 1 square-mile "sections" (Fig. 10-7), as if it were part of the General Land Office township and range survey grid (but it never was). His reason for doing this is unknown, but the label "Crestone Estate" suggests he was considering subdividing the Ranch. Fortunately, this never happened.

1893: George Adams files suit in Federal Court to have the miners evicted from the Baca Grant.

1897: The Colorado Bureau of Mines summary for 1897 states: "*In Saguache County what is now designated as the gold belt extends along the Sangre de Cristo Mountains from Orient* [Valley View Hot Springs] *to the south lines of the county. This belt has been unusually active during 1897, and the only drawback is a question of title to some of the leading mines near Duncan and south of Crestone, located in the property of Baca Land Grant No. 4. This matter is at present being adjudicated in courts, and when settled a greatly increased rush to this section is anticipated.* " Perhaps the writer was assuming the court would rule in favor of the miners. However, the opposite happened, and in 1900 the Grant owners forced the miners off their claims, essentially ending the gold rush.

1898: The US Supreme Court rules (Shaw v. Kellogg) that Adams owns all the mineral rights in the Luis Maria Baca Land Grant (Baca Ranch).

1900: Adams evicts the miners, including the whole camps/towns of Spanish, Cottonwood, Duncan and Lucky. The miners, their families, store owners, and everyone else moved either north to Crestone, or south to Liberty. Adams sells the Grant to the San Luis Valley Land & Mining Company for $1,400,000. This was a subsidiary of the United Gas Improvement Company of Philadelphia, PA, representing wealthy Philadelphia industrialists interested in the mining potential.

The SLV Land & Mining Co. rebuilds the Independent Mill at Cottonwood, between Spanish and Cottonwood Creeks; "as depth is reached, the free-milling ores change to a sulphide carrying considerable copper" (Henderson, 1926, p. 17). The new 00-stamp mill is rated as the largest stamp mill in the world. However, the Independent Mine was already playing out, and this new mill only treated 60,000 tons of ore in its lifetime.

901: The railroad arrives!
The narrow gauge Sangre de Cristo line of the Denver & Rio Grande Railroad (also known as the Crestone branch) is extended from Moffat to Crestone." *In 1901 the railroad came to Crestone, and soon there were 2000 citizens in the town, and 10,000 in the larger "district" from Villa Grove to the Sand Dunes. As much as $80,000.00 a month in gold was hauled by rail from the stamp mill at the Independent Mine to the eastern slope*" (Source: Town of Crestone website).

The San Luis Valley Bank building is built on the SW corner of Galena Ave. and Alder St. by G.A. Luikart & Co., with a capital of $5,000 (Bankers Magazine, 1901). This building is now the Town Center Building, and hosts the Crestone Historical Museum. [*The Town of Crestone was officially incorporated on March 29, 1901.*]

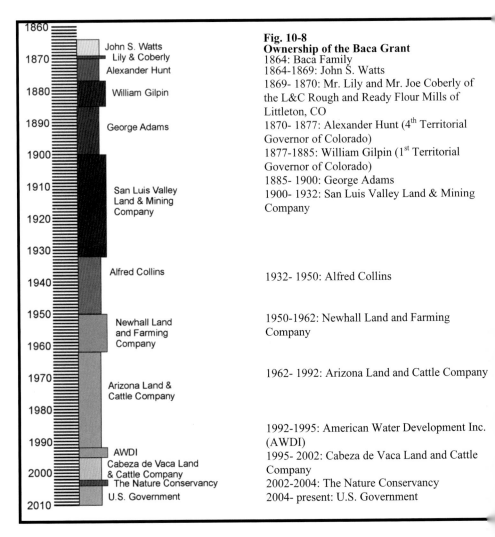

Fig. 10-8
Ownership of the Baca Grant
1864: Baca Family
1864-1869: John S. Watts
1869- 1870: Mr. Lily and Mr. Joe Coberly of the L&C Rough and Ready Flour Mills of Littleton, CO
1870- 1877: Alexander Hunt (4th Territorial Governor of Colorado)
1877-1885: William Gilpin (1st Territorial Governor of Colorado)
1885- 1900: George Adams
1900- 1932: San Luis Valley Land & Mining Company

1932- 1950: Alfred Collins

1950-1962: Newhall Land and Farming Company

1962- 1992: Arizona Land and Cattle Company

1992-1995: American Water Development Inc. (AWDI)
1995- 2002: Cabeza de Vaca Land and Cattle Company
2002-2004: The Nature Conservancy
2004- present: U.S. Government

1902: The D&RG railroad is extended from Crestone to the Independent Mill at Cottonwood. This mill, the largest in either the El Dorado or Crestone districts, eventually processes most of the $7-8 million in gold produced by the El Dorado Mining District. The Cleveland Mill, south of the mouth of Burnt Gulch in the Crestone Mining District, closes down in 1902.

Arthur Lakes publishes a description of the Crestone District in Mines and Minerals Magazine, based on a short visit in 1901. Professor Lakes was instrumental in founding the Colorado School of Mines and was its first geology professor; he taught there from 1869-1893. His description of Crestone and its mines is one of the few contemporary accounts published by a geologist.

"Crestone, although its village and works have the appearance of great youthfulness, is not altogether a young camp, for there are relics of old arrastras and mills and shafts, dating back to the earliest settlement of Colorado. The present camp, however, is quite young. The mines are located on apparently true fissure veins in the granite of the Sangre de Cristo range, near its base. At first these mines showed large bodies of oxidized free-milling gold, which included the erection of large crushing and concentrating mills; but in course of time this rich surface material gave out with depth, and a barren zone was entered which later gave place to a zone of unoxidized high-grade pyrites. In this some of the mines are at present. This ore, from its massiveness, would appear to be a subject for smelting. Copper pyrites occur in some of the mines, yet singularly enough, this ore which is usually rich in gold and silver as well as copper, is here locally barren in gold values.

The great steepness with which the mountains rise, offers considerable attraction for making crosscut tunnels near the base to tap fissure veins which run parallel with the strike of the range. A depth of over 1000 feet could thus be gained readily on them.

Directly east of the village a lofty cliff arises from its talus slope for some 1,500 feet in a vertical wall, known as Banner Mountain [see Fig. 10-9]... On top of this peak a prospect shaft about 70 feet deep, is located on what is called the Banner vein. This vein is a highly mineralized zone in the center of a much larger vein or body of quartz and feldspar, upwards of 500 feet wide, which running north and south, appears to form the backbone of the mountain. This great body is composed of quartz and large white feldspars, and would be called a pegmatite. The Banner vein occupies a little knob or isolated table in this great vein."

"Walking across the huge vein, we come to the edge of a vertical cliff, descending some 300 feet. This cliff is formed of the side or the face of the pegmatite vein, from which the wall of granite has partly been removed. At the base of this first cliff is a bench, and another cliff about 500 feet is of granite to the talus slope. The oxidized vein at the top of the mountain showed good gold values in its free milling oxidized ore, so far as the shaft descended. But it was obvious from the steepness of the mountain, the lack of water, and other inconveniences, that it would be impossible to develop this prospect to any depth, at that far height, and the only way to develop the banner vein, assuming that it continued downwards indefinitely, and at its present steep inclination, would be by a crosscut tunnel at the base of the cliff, on top of the talus slope. From this point it seemed probable that the vein met with at the top of the peak, could be reached by a crosscut within 1,000 feet.

Assuming that the vein keeps down, in what condition would it be likely to find the ore reached by the tunnel? Judging from the experience of the other mines of the district, the ore at this depth would be in an unoxidized state and most likely in the form of white iron pyrites, which elsewhere in the camp, runs well in gold.

From such a tunnel a road could easily be made to the stream where there are good milling facilities. Taking into consideration the fact that the veins of this young camp are true fissure veins and that the unoxidized ore as found of late, runs well in gold, there seems a reasonable hope for permanency for this little burg, which is, as we have said, one of the most charming locations both for residence and mining that we have seen in Colorado, and is well adapted for mining and milling purposes. The climate, considering the high altitude of San Luis park, is remarkably pleasant the year through."

Fig. 10-9. Banner Mountain as seen from just north of the Crestone city limits, looking east; from Lakes (1902). Note the absence of trees both in the floodplain of North Crestone Creek (foreground), and on the gullied slope below the cliffs. Both areas are densely forested today. The trees were probably all burned off by the Great Fire of 1882, which occurred 19 years before the sketch was made.

1903: daily train service to Crestone is discontinued; first oil wells are drilled in the San Luis Valley near Mosca; later wells are drilled in 1924 near Hooper (Reddin, 2007).

1904-1938: Mining Yields Dwindle; Cows Rule

1904: mines in Liberty are all closed, town is abandoned. Independent Mine closes. On the Baca Grant, cattle production is king. The last grizzly bear to roam the Sangres (Old Mose) is killed; see Perkins, 2002. The Adams State College Grizzlies are named after this bear, and there is a life-size (12 ft high) bronze statue of Old Mose on campus.

Fig. 10-10. Grant owners build up herds of Hereford cattle, creating one of the great cattle ranches of the West. From Baca Grant Developmen Company, Inc., 1909

1907: Sangre de Cristo railroad is closed by D&RGRR.

1909: San Luis Valley Land and Development Company is formed.

230

1911; the Great Flood on North Crestone Creek, ravages town. The population of Crestone is 250, according to Gazetteer Publishing Co. (1911).

1914: The Rito Alto Trail, north of Crestone, is built by the US Forest Service. The trail is the first to extend from the San Luis Valley to the range crest, and is for sheep herds to access grazing meadows near and above timberline.

1916: "only assessment and development work was done" in the Crestone- Baca Grant district (that is, no actual gold production); McCaskey, 1919.

Albert Ellington, Eleanor Davis, and a few friends from Colorado College make the first ascents of Mt. Adams, Kit Carson Mountain, Crestone Peak, and Crestone Needle; July 22-24, 1916 (see text box in Chapter 5).

1919-1922: Chief Engineer for the SLV Land & Mining Co. was Royce J. Tipton, who later became famous; he died in 1967. The SLV Land & Mining Co. changes name to San Luis Valley Land & Cattle Company.

1920: Arthur Carhart, the first Recreation Engineer in the U.S. Forest Service, imagines the Sangres as the future home of a "Great Rocky Mountain Summer University, a consolidation of the courses of natural science of all the schools west of the Mississippi and south of the northern line of Colorado" (cited in Wolf, 1995, p. 205). Wolf concludes that the Baca Campus of Colorado College (CC) fulfills Carhart's dream, but CC courses are mainly social science rather than natural science. The latter fields are covered by the Crestone Science Center.

1921: Bill and Venetta Stewart winter on Pole Creek (see Hatheway, 2010)

1923: the last gray wolf in the Sangres is killed (see Wolf, 1995).

1927: the train tracks between the Independent Mine, Crestone, and Moffat are removed.

1930: Alfred Collins, major stockholder of the San Luis Valley Land & Cattle Company, takes over management of the Baca Ranch. He builds up the cattle herd.

From the Mining Journal, vol. 1, no. 15; Colorado Mining News: "*S.A. Keys, president of the Independence Mining & Milling Company at Crestone, Colorado, is hauling ore to the Golden Cycle plant at Colorado Springs, and is considering putting in some machinery. A flotation plant is being built in the Crestone District, and tests have shown that it can extract 92 percent of the metals, as compared with a former recovery of 48 percent. Gold is the principal metal.*"

1931-1937: The Third (and Last) Mining Boom. Grant owners reexamine all earlier workings. "A small pilot mill of 35 tons/day capacity was built at Cottonwood, and was used to test ores from the various discoveries. The metallurgy of this mill was in line with modern advancement; ball-mill grinding, classification, flotation, tabling and amalgamation of certain high-grade products. While this operation was unsuccessful from an investment point of view, it served to re-discover many small openings of potential importance." (Parker, 1952, p. 43).

1935: Ranger F.E. McGraw of the San Isabel national Forest writes: "The only protection afforded these animals (Bighorn sheep) is that of the Baca Grant, and if it were not for this protection the species would become as near extinction as they were several years ago. At the present time their numbers are very limited within three miles of the north side of the Grant." See Wolf, 1995, p. 160.

1938: the Independent Mill is disassembled; marks the end of the mining era that began in 1870 (a 68-year run).

1939-1971: The Baca Ranch and Quiet Years

1943-45: summer grazing of sheep and cows in the National Forest of the Sangres, under grazing leases, reaches its high point.

1950: Alfred Collins sells the Ranch to the Newhall Land and Farming Company of Arizona and California, which was "primarily interested in logging for profit." Collins sells his herd and the cattle dispersal sale breaks all records.

1962: Arizona-Colorado Land & Cattle Company buys the Baca Ranch.

1971: AZL Resources forms the Baca Grande Corporation to develop a 14,000-acre subdivision in the NE corner of the Ranch, called the Baca Grande. The original "target audience" was recent Colorado immigrants (see box below) and military retirees, including those from Fort Carson in Colorado Springs, but including overseas personnel in such faraway places as Hawaii and Guam.

1971-1977: The Baca Grande Subdivision

In 1971 the Arizona Land & Cattle Company created the Baca Grande Corporation and laid out a retirement subdivision of 10,000 lots on 14,000 acres of the pinyon-covered alluvial slopes at the foot of the Sangre de Cristo Mountains. Unfortunately, the planners underestimated the gradient of the piedmont slopes at the foot of the Sangres, and the depth and activity of many arroyos. As a result, erosion has been a continuing maintenance problem. In 1972 they sent out the surveyors to survey the roads, and the bulldozers began to carve out the roads. Roads were surveyed and graded. An airstrip and hotel (Inn at the Baca) were built to fly in and house prospective lot buyers. A commercial strip along Road T was developed with the Inn, a lake, a 9-hole golf course, tennis courts, a gun range, an admin/maintenance building, and Camper Village. Chalets Units 1, 2, and 3 were laid out in the pinyon-juniper forest; the Grants Unit in the grasslands downslope; Mobile Home Estates (Casita Park) west of the Inn.

1972: The Baca Grande Property Owners Association was formed (the de-facto form of government in the Baca Grande subdivision, which lies in unincorporated Saguache County). Mineral rights in the Baca Grant were severed from the surface rights.

1973: The Inn at the Baca Grande and the Golf Course are built, 4 miles west of Crestone on County Road T. A landing strip is built on the opposite side of Road T to fly in prospective lot buyers.

Colorado's population grew slowly before WWII, increasing only 8% between 1930 and 1940. But then growth began to accelerate. Between 1940 and 1950 population increased by 18%; between 1950 and 1960, by 32%; between 1960 and 1970, by 26%; and between 1970 and 1980, by 31%. According to the Colorado Department of Motor Vehicles, the immigration wave peaked in 1972 (based on out-of-state driver's licenses turned in for Colorado ones).

This explosive growth triggered a land boom, and in the late 1960s and early 1970s many historic ranches were bought by developers and subdivided into small lots, awaiting the influx of immigrants. A common sales slogan was "Get a Piece of the Rockies (before it's too late)." Vacant lots were advertised in East Coast and West Coast magazines. In the early 1970s the San Luis Valley was host to many large subdivision schemes, including the Baca Grande in Saguache County, and the Forbes Trinchera and Melby Ranches in Costilla County. Altogether, in the early 1970s as much as 500,000 acres of ranchland was subdivided and offered for sale.

These land developments became highly controversial, because many were poorly planned and/or financed. Many out-of-staters bought their lots sight unseen. Lot buyers were promised amenities and utilities, but when they finally arrived at their lots, the roads were simply bladed bulldozer tracks through the sagebrush, and there were neither amenities nor utilities.

By 1972 so many buyers had complained that the Colorado Legislature passed Senate Bill 35. This bill required Colorado counties to pass regulations to regulate any subdivision of land into parcels smaller than 35 acres. The result of the bill was that any parcel smaller than 35 acres must undergo a County platting/subdivision process and be approved by the Board of County Commissioners, to be a legal parcel. It is not surprising that after 1972 almost all subdivisions in rural Colorado were platted as 35 acre parcels, to avoid triggering the Senate Bill 35 requirements. One might think that 40-acre parcels would make more sense, because 40 acres is exactly 1/16 of a square mile (a section of land in the Township & Range system). But developers soon realized that by subdividing a (say) 640-acre section into 35-acre parcels, they not only avoided the onerous requirements of Senate Bill 35, but they could sell 18 parcels rather than 16.

1977: Maurice Strong, Canadian businessman, obtains majority interest and becomes CEO of the AZL.

1978-1985: The Strongs Reinvent the Baca

1978: Maurice and Hanne (Marstrand) Strong move to the Baca Grant headquarters with their family in October 1978. They are visited by Glenn Anderson, who prophesizes that their job is to reinvent the Baca Grande as a spiritual refuge.

1979: In response to Anderson's statements, Hanne asks elders from nine American Indian tribes to come to the Baca and hold a council on the prophecy. After four days, they tell her that the prophecy is correct.

1981: The Strongs donate 320 acres to the Aspen Institute for Humanistic Studies, to create the Baca campus.

1983: AZL merges with Los Angeles-based Tosco (LA Times, 1989).

1986-1994: The Water War #1 (*Water's for Fightin', Whisky's For Drinkin'*) (for more details, see Martin, 2005)

1986; AWDI (American Water Development, Inc.) is incorporated by a group of investors headed by Maurice Strong. Tosco sells the Baca Ranch to AWDI. AWDI applies for State permission to pump 200,000 acre-feet of water per year to irrigate farmland in the valley and to brew beer, both worthy endeavors.

1986 (August): AWDI amended its application to decrease the pumping to 60,000 ac-ft/year, but would retain the right to pump the other 140,000 ac-ft/year if approved by the court. AWDI admitted that its pumping would affect 256 other wells.

1987 (Aug. 17): The Harmonic Convergence, a loosely-organized New Age spiritual event; included events in Crestone.

1989: AWDI changes its plan and announces that it will sell its water to the highest bidder. This will entail exporting the water out of the San Luis Valley in a pipeline, over Poncha Pass to the Front Range. Citizens for San Luis Valley Water, a nonprofit corporation, is formed to fight water exports out of the valley. Maurice Strong quits AWDI because he "felt it was no longer interested in using the water in a socially and environmentally responsible way" (Crestone Eagle newspaper).

1990: Challenger Gold begins evaluating the Baca Grant for gold mining. They drill 42 exploratory drill holes around Deadman Creek, but gold mineralization encountered was weak and spotty. No mine plan is ever filed with the State of Colorado.

1990 Census: Crestone population is 39 (compared to 195 in the Baca Grande subdivision). Total population of Saguache County is 4602. Gary Boyce publishes a Crestone newspaper named "The Needles", which protests AWDI's plans to export water.

1990 (December): "San Luis Valley voters turn out in record numbers to vote to secure a loan of $472,000 for the Rio Grande Water Conservation District to continue their legal battle with AWDI" (Crestoneeagle.com). Between Oct. 1989 and Oct. 1991, valley residents spend $2.2 million fighting AWDI in court.

1991 (Oct.-Nov.): Lawsuit against AWDI; federal judge rules that the water to be pumped was already tributary to other streams and wells, and thus was not free to be claimed on by AWDI. AWDI appeals to the U.S. Supreme Court.

1992 (Nov.): President George H.W. Bush [with the support of Colorado's senators Hank Brown (R-CO) and Tim Wirth (D-CO)] signs a water bill (the San Luis Valley Water Resources Protection Act) that prohibits export of water from the San Luis Valley unless the Secretary of the Interior determines that such export would not injure the water rights of any Federal preserves such as the Great Sand Dunes National Monument, the

Alamosa and Monte Vista National Wildlife Refuges, and the Bureau of Reclamation's Closed Basin Project. This stipulation forms a large roadblock to AWDI's application.

AWDI purchases a 10% interest in Cabeza de Vaca Land & Cattle Company, a holding company for assorted partners interested in exporting water from under the Baca Ranch (Crestoneeagle.com).

1992 (May): Gary Boyce, a local rancher, had been a vocal opponent of AWDI. Boyce held a public meeting to propose a new water export scheme that relied on shallow well water and surface water. Ranchers would sell or lease their surface water to be exported out of the valley, and let their field revert to natural grass (or more likely, unpalatable rabbitbrush and saltbush). Needless to say, none of the ranchers thought this was a very good idea.

1992 (Oct.): The U.S. Supreme Court agrees to hear AWDI's (plaintiff) case against State of Colorado. Gary Boyce and Jeris Danielson (former State Engineer of Colorado) form Stockman's Water Company.

1993 (June): beginning of "The Building Boom" in the Crestone-Baca area; it lasts until the nationwide burst of the "real estate bubble" in Fall of 2008

1994 (May): the U.S. Supreme Court affirms the ruling of the lower court in 1991, effectively denying AWDI's water rights application.

1995-2003: Water War #2, and "Water is Gold"

1995 (Jan.): Challenger Gold is hired by AWDI to assess the mineral resources of the Baca grant. Challenger finds no gold, but instead traces of oil in 27 of 42 boreholes. In May 1995 Challenger changes its name to Lexam Explorations and applies for County and State permits to explore for oil & gas on the Baca Grant.

1995 (Sept.-Oct.): Lexam drills two test wells 4500 ft-deep and 6500 ft-deep near Deadman Creek. Neither well encountered oil in large enough quantities to be developed economically. In Crestone, Crestone Mart opens a full-service lumber yard to service the Building Boom.

1995 (May): there were a record number of home starts (60+) in the Baca subdivision; the Baca was finally "catching on" 24 years after its inception! Some of the newcomers are retirees, but others are "lone eagle" entrepreneurs dependent on the Internet and UPS/Federal Express deliveries (services not invented yet when the Baca was conceived in the early 1970s). The Kiosk is built to direct the many newcomers (and construction crews) around in the Baca and Crestone.

(June): Cabeza de Vaca Land & Cattle Company purchases the Baca Ranch from AWDI for $13.5 million. (Their offer was higher than The Nature Conservancy's offer, which also wanted to buy the Ranch). Cabeza's managing member is Stockman's Water Company, headed by local rancher Gary Boyce. Other partners included Yale University (a 50% partner), AWDI (10% partner), and Farallon Capital Management of

235

San Francisco, headed by Boyce's father-in-law. Stockman's Water proposes to pump 150,000 acre-feet of water from the Baca and to export it to the Front Range. (However, it never actually files a water rights application for this with the State).

2000 (Nov.): President Clinton signs the "Great Sand Dunes National Park and Preserve Act of 2000." The Act authorizes the Federal government to expand the National Monument into a National Park almost four times its original size. Part of the reason to acquire the Ranch is to acquire its water rights, which would eliminate future water export schemes arising from the Baca Ranch. However, the Act does not authorize the purchase of the Baca Ranch nor appropriate any money for such purchase.
    The Baca Ranch is put up for sale by Cabeza de Vaca Land & Cattle Company.

2001 (Dec.): The Nature Conservancy signs a purchase agreement with Cabeza de Vaca for the Baca Ranch and its water rights (but NOT its mineral rights).

2002: Farallon Management Services, majority owners of the Ranch, want to sell the Ranch to The Nature Conservancy over minority owner Gary Boyce's objection. Farallon's holding company was Vaca Partners, which foreclosed on Cabeza de Vaca Land and Cattle Company on May 9, 2002. "Under the agreement for selling the ranch, signed in Feb. 2002, The Nature Conservancy is holding the Baca ranch in trust until claims to the property are cleared and the ranch can become part of the proposed Great Sand Dunes National Park. However, administration of the property will be through the State Land Board, who loaned $5 million towards the sale, until the ranch formally transfers to the Federal government in 3-5 years." (Crestoneeagle.com).

2003: Binding arbitration awards AWDI $694,000 for its 10% interest in Cabeza de Vaca Land & Cattle Co. Meanwhile, embarrassed by its indirect involvement with Cabeza de Vaca's water-export scheme, the Trustees of Yale University agree to donate their $1.6 million profit from the Ranch sale to The Nature Conservancy, to assist in creating the new National Park.

2004-present: The Feds Buy the Ranch; & Drill, Baby, Drill

2004 (Oct.): The Baca Ranch is sold by Vaca Partners to The Nature Conservancy (TNS) for $31.3 million. Of that price, $14 million was loaned to TNS by the David and Lucille Packard Foundation. The Nature Conservancy acts as a "holding company" until Congress can appropriate the full purchase price. *Note:* Gary Boyce and partners (The Farallon Group, of San Francisco) had purchased the Baca Ranch in June 1995 for $13.5 million; thus they made a profit of $17.8 million in 9 years.

2004 (Nov.): the final Federal appropriation is approved to repay The Nature Conservancy for its $32 million expenditure to purchase the Baca Ranch; full ownership of the Ranch passes to the Federal government (except for mineral rights). After 140 years in private ownership, the Baca Ranch now belongs to the Federal government. In all, 97,000 acres are purchased (excluding the Baca Grande subdivision) and parceled out to Federal agencies as follows: 53,000 acres to Great Sand Dunes National Park; 31,000 acres to the newly-created Baca National Wildlife Refuge; and 13,000 acres to the Rio Grande National Forest.

2006 (August): Lexam Explorations announces its intention to drill two 14,000 foot-deep exploratory oil & gas wells in the Baca National Wildlife Refuge. BNWR officials claim that no environmental impact assessment is required, and say there is nothing they can do to stop the drilling.

2007 (May): the San Luis Valley Ecosystem Council (SLVEC) files suit against BNWR, alleging violations of the National Environmental Policy Act of 1969.

2007 (July): the National Park Service releases the Decision Memorandum on its General Management Plan. The Plan calls for maximizing wilderness in the newly-acquired Park lands

2007 (August): After a firestorm of local protest, BNWR abruptly reverses itself, and announces it will begin an Environmental Assessment (EA).

2008 (Jan.): BNWR releases its Draft EA, which concludes the proposed drilling will have "no significant impact."

2008 (Nov.): U.S. Fish and Wildlife Service (FWS) issues the final EA for BNWR, and concludes that the proposed drilling at BNWR will have "no significant impact." In their ongoing court case, SLVEC claims the EA is fundamentally flawed, both scientifically, and due to conflict of interest (Lexam attorneys controlled the EA before release).

2009 (Sept.): U.S. District Court judge issues an injunction against the drilling, until the SLVEC lawsuit of May 2007 is settled.

2010 (June): in an arbitrated agreement, FWS capitulates to SLVEC and agrees to "start all over again" on the Environmental Impact process for the BNWR, 2.5 years after it issued the draft EA. SLVEC says that the preferred path forward is to purchase the mineral rights from Lexam, preventing any further drilling attempts.

2011 (Jan.): FWS releases the Draft of its second EA for gas drilling

2011 (March): the 2010 Census reports a population of 127 for the Town of Crestone, an increase of 54 (+74%) over the 2000 population. There are 107 housing units, which includes many summer cabins. In Census Tract 9776, 2011 population grew to 3,143 and houses to 2,509, an increase of 23% in population and 41% in houses compared to the year 2000. In contrast, the population of Saguache County as a whole grew little from 2000 (5,917) to 2010 (6,108), an increase of only 3%.

2011 (April): FWS issues a Finding of No Significant Impact for the second EA concerning oil & gas drilling by Lexam; this clears the way for drilling.

APPENDIX 1. HIKING & CAMPING CHECKLISTS

These lists don't mention "normal" clothing items that one would wear, or any food you might want to take along. An asterisk means there should be one such item in the hiking party, but not everyone in the party needs one.

A. FOR A LEISURELY SHORT HIKE (ENDING WELL BEFORE SUNSET)
Clothing:
1—Comfortable lightweight boots or running shoes/cross-trainers. You can break in new boots or shoes on a short hike.
2—Hat with a brim.
   In your pack (a small day pack):
3— **June and first half of July**: Insect repellant; avoid large aerosol cans; individual-size pump-spray bottles give more reliability & flexibility.
4—Sunscreen, but not a lot (you'll be in the trees on most short hikes).
5—Water; 2 liters per person (1 for the way up, 1 for the way down).
6—Lightweight rain gear (poncho, water-resistant shell), *especially* if you will be out in the afternoon, or after the start of the July-August "monsoon."
7*—A map showing your route; those in this book will do; or other topo/trail maps
8—Camera.
9*—A cell phone or pre-tested radio (i.e., some way to communicate).

B. FOR AN ALL-DAY, UP-AND-BACK HIKE (ENDING NEAR SUNSET)
Clothing (in addition to the stuff in List A):
1-- Comfortable shoes or boots you have hiked in before, which did not give you blisters. DON'T try to break in a new pair on an all-day hike.
2—Layers of clothing; you're going to start an all day hike early in the morning when it's cool, but you'll need to shed layers by mid-day, and maybe even put them back on during the afternoon storm.
   In your pack (a medium-size day pack) in addition to the stuff in List A:
3*—Knife or multi-tool.
4*—Fire kit (matches or lighter).
5—A space blanket.
6—Toilet paper, and knowing how to dig and cover a "cathole".
7—A trekking pole or two (your option), in case you knees get wobbly on the way down.
8*—A flashlight; the kind that generates its own electricity via a crank; OR a headlamp with charged-up batteries. Just in case you're still on the trail when it gets dark…

C. FOR OVERNIGHT CAMPING IN THE BACKCOUNTRY
Clothing (in addition to the stuff in Lists A and B):
1—Some moccasins or other lightweight shoes for in-camp.
2—Fleece vest, jacket, or something else warm for sitting around.
3—A warm hat and pair of gloves.
4—A new pair of socks for each day out.
5—Moleskin for blisters.
   In your pack (a high-volume pack) in addition to the stuff in Lists A and B:
All the items in your pack are grouped into ziplock freezer bags of various sizes. For example: tools, food, cooking items, small clothing, larger clothing, etc. The bags don't

weigh anything, and by using them you won't have to hunt in the bottom of your pack for those small "disappearing" items. If you're really obsessive, label the bags. Squeeze the air out of them before closing. On the way out you can put your trash in the empty food bags.

6—Tent or other shelter (set it up before you go, to make sure all the pieces like stakes are there, the poles aren't broken, the fabric isn't mildewed, etc.).

7—Sleeping bag or bivvy sack.

8—An extra stuff sack. You can make a pillow by stuffing it with spare clothes.

9—Sleeping pad; inflatable or semi-inflatable.

10—Personal overnight toiletries (toothbrush, toothpaste, washcloth, beauty cream, etc.)

11—20 feet of lightweight, strong nylon cord (like parachute cord).

12- Everyone needs a headlamp or flashlight, WITH CHARGED BATTERIES, and extra batteries for it and anything else electronic.

13—Entertainment; book, playing cards, star chart.

14*—A backpacking stove, a way to light it, and pots/plates/bowls/cups/utensils. Make sure your fuel bottle is full.

15*—A water filter or iodine tablets.

16*—Cleanup items; soap, scrubby, dish towel.

17*-- A folding shovel, for latrine duty and putting out fires..

18—A communal light source like a lantern, unless you are building a fire

19*—IF IN BEAR COUNTRY: 50 ft of nylon cord and a hanging bag for all food and food trash. Hang it from a high tree branch, at whatever distance from camp makes you comfortable. [In Alaska, typically a party's cook tent is 100 yards from their sleeping tents].

20*—IF YOU BUILD A FIRE: Once you break camp you need to drown the fire it so it's OUT, OUT, OUT. This means *gallons* of non-potable water. A folding canvas bucket is good for this. In a pinch you can carry water in your largest cooking pot, your hat, AND/OR bury the ashes with dirt, using the folding shovel.

OPTIONS:

21*—A GPS.

22*- A satellite phone, or some other fool-proof method of communicating with the outside world.

APPENDIX 2—Recent Accidents on the Crestone High Peaks;

Source is *listsofjohn.com*, unless otherwise noted.

Challenger Point

26-Jul-2003; man and woman from Slovakia; 2 hit by Lightning on trail 1 mile above Willow Creek Trailhead; one died.
23-Jun-2008; 52 yr-old man from Littleton, CO; lost control glissading Kirk's Couloir; broke hip; helicopter rescue; Voluntary glissade- Not Fatal; Source=Lowers, 2008b
7-Jul-2009; hiker fell 1500 ft; helicopter rescue by Colorado National Guard; flown to Pueblo hospital; Fall- Not Fatal; Source=Crestone Eagle

Kit Carson Mountain

21-Jul-1990; man, previously climbed all Fourteeners, fell while soloing; Fall-FATAL
1999; man fell; Fall-FATAL
28-Jun-2003; CMC climbing instructor on North Ridge; Rockfall-FATAL
3-Jul-2003; unknown; Fall-FATAL
11-Jun-2005; man glissades down Kirk Couloir without ice ace; loses control; FATAL
10-Jun-2006; 34 yr-old man from Cheyenne, WY; Fall- FATAL

Crestone Peak (including the Needle-To-Peak traverse); incomplete list.

17-Aug-1981; 68 yr-old man struck by rock dislodged from above; Fall - FATAL
1987; unknown; Lost/Stranded
16-Sep-2000; man fell on Needle-To-Peak traverse; Fall- FATAL
11-Sep-2001; man broke ankle, was lowered 250 ft; Rescued
15-Sep-2001; 46 yr-old woman, injured on Needle-To-Peak traverse; Fall - Not Fatal
25-Jul-2004; 29 yr-old man from Denver, fell on Needle-To-Peak traverse; Fall- FATAL
19-Aug-2006; two 60 yr-old climbers caught on ledge, spent night; rescued next day; Lost/Stranded; also Quillen, M., 2006
24-Aug-2006; 60 yr-old man from St. Louis, on Needle-To-Peak traverse; Fall- FATAL

Crestone Needle (excluding the Ellingwood Arete route; incomplete list).

1978; Young woman in guided school group, slips off snow-covered ledge; Fall- FATAL; Source=American Alpine Club
12-Aug-1982; man fell soloing Standard Route; recovered from injuries in 3 weeks; Not Fatal
11-Sep-1982; man fell 160 ft; Fall- FATAL
12-Oct-82; man fell 250 ft while descending Standard Route; slipped on snow, unroped Fall- FATAL
15-Sep-1991; woman slipped and fell 180 ft ascending Standard Route; serious head injury; rescued 2 days later by helicopter; Fall - Rescued
12-Aug-92; man fell 100 ft; Fall- FATAL (woman in same party suffered head injuries)
22-Aug-92; man hit in head by rock knocked loose by his partner above; fell 40 ft; Fall- FATAL
22-Aug-92; man who knocked loose rock injured; Fall - Not Fatal
20-Aug-93; man (Missouri Pastor) fell twice on Standard Route; Fall- FATAL
2-Jul-01; unknown climber injured on Standard Route; Fall
28-Jun-08; 49 yr-old woman from Denver; experienced climber; Fall- FATAL; Crestone Eagle
9-Aug-08; 44 yr-old man from Texas; Fall- FATAL; Source=Lowers, 2008a

APPENDIX 3—Hunting Near Crestone

The western side of the Sangre de Cristo Mountains, as well as the valley floor to CO 17, is in big game Game Management Unit (GMU) 82. (see http://wildlife.state.co.us/Hunting/GMUnitMaps.html). Big game species hunted in GMU 82 include (in order of popularity) elk, deer, pronghorn, bighorn sheep, bear, and mountain lion. There are no mountain goats or moose in GMU 82.

Elk (*Cervus elephus*)

The Crestone area is quite popular for elk hunting, due to the 4000-head elk herd that winters in the BNWR. In the autumn hunting seasons much of the herd is still outside of the Refuge in the rugged lands National Forest, where it can be hunted. Due to the rugged nature of the terrain, the skittishness of the elk, and the difficulty in approaching them undetected, hunter success is relatively low (22-26%).

HARVEST FOR ALLL MANNERS OF TAKE, 2005-2008				
YEAR	MANNER	TOTAL HARVEST	TOTAL HUNTERS	PERCENT SUCCESS
2008	Rifle	348	1328	26%
	Muzzleloader	10	38	26%
	Archery	23	321	7%
	TOTAL	**381**	**1687**	**23%**
2007	**TOTAL**	**376**	**1617**	**23%**
2006	**TOTAL**	**393**	**1755**	**22%**
2005	**TOTAL**	**322**	**1729**	**19%**

Hunting Licenses: (2009-2010 prices)
Colo. Resident: $49; Colo. Youth Resident: $13.75
Nonresident, Bull or either sex: $549; Nonresident, cow: $254; Youth Nonresident: $103.75

Deer (Rocky Mountain Mule Deer, *Odocoileus hemionus*)

Mule deer in the Crestone-Baca area, like all deer in the Urban-Wildland Interface, have slowly become tolerant of humans and can be termed semi-domesticated. They graze in lots only tens of feet from houses, or alongside the roads, seemingly oblivious to passing cars. Not a few people in Crestone feed them, although this is against all advice and regulations of the Department of Wildlife. Deer have thus come to think of themselves as 'members of the family", like the pet dog or cat. They probably cannot fathom why homeowners, who feed them on some days (or whose neighbors feed them), object to them eating every flower, vegetable, shrub, or small tree planted outside.

Having tried to grow things outside, I understand how much worse the problem would be if the deer population were allowed to grow unchecked, like the elk population has in the Baca Ranch. Since humans have mainly eradicated their natural predators, the only thing that is keeping their numbers in check is hunting. Hunter success rates for deer (42-76%) are considerably higher than for elk, because the deer are less wary of humans, and they can be hunted at lower elevations where the terrain is not so rugged.

Fig. A3-1. Mule deer bucks looking for trouble. Photo by NPS/Great Sand Dunes NPP.

Hunting Licenses: (2009-2010 prices)
Colo. Resident: $34
Colo. Youth Resident: $13.75
Nonresident: $329
Youth Nonresident: $103.75

HARVEST FOR ALLL MANNERS OF TAKE, 2005-2008				
		TOTAL	TOTAL	PERCENT
YEAR	MANNER	HARVEST	HUNTERS	SUCCESS
2008	Rifle	139	184	76%
	Muzzleloader	19	49	39%
	Archery	0	29	0%
	TOTAL	**158**	**262**	**60%**
2007	**TOTAL**	**115**	**248**	**46%**
2006	**TOTAL**	**81**	**125**	**65%**
2005	**TOTAL**	**66**	**156**	**42%**

Pronghorn (*Antilocapra americana*)

The pronghorn is often called an antelope, but it has no relationship to the antelopes of the Old World. It is a member of the goat family, hence its nickname, the "speed goat." Pronghorns live on the grasslands of the valley floor (BLM land), where there is no place to hide from the hunters. Hunting success rates are higher even than for deer, although there are fewer hunters.

Fig. A3-2. Pronghorn on the valley floor; female at left, male at right. Photo courtesy of NPS/Patrick Myers.

Hunting Licenses: (2009-2010 prices)
Colo. Resident: $34
Colo. Youth Resident: $13.75
Nonresident: $329
Youth Nonresident: $103.75

HARVEST FOR ALLL MANNERS OF TAKE (Pronghorn, 2005-2008)				
YEAR	MANNER	TOTAL HARVEST	TOTAL HUNTERS	PERCENT SUCCESS
2008	Rifle	97	106	92%
	Archery	6	20	30%
	TOTAL	**103**	**126**	**82%**
2007	**TOTAL**	**134**	**169**	**79%**
2006	**TOTAL**	**120**	**172**	**70%**
2005	**TOTAL**	**81**	**127**	**64%**

Bear (Black Bear, *Ursus americanus*)
The grizzly bear (*Ursus arctos*) was fairly common in Colorado before 1900, based on historical accounts. Geary says (p. 88) "In 1904, a professional hunter hired by ranchers killed the last grizzly bear in the Sangres." (Wolf, 2002). There were no grizzly bears killed in Colorado between 1952 and 1979, and they were thought to be extinct in the state (http://wildlife.state.co.us/WildlifeSpecies/SpeciesOfConcern/Mammals/GrizzlyBear.htm). However, in 1979 a grizzly was killed by a hunting guide in the San Juan Mountains (see account in Wilkinson, 2008). No grizzly bears have been killed since 1979, so it is unknown whether any are in the state. The grizzly is an endangered species in Colorado. The number of bear hunters on the western side of the Sangres, and their success rate, is not recorded by Colorado DOW, although the total harvest is. In GMU 82 that amounted to 10 in 2008; 1 in 2007; 5 in 2006; and 1 in 2005.
Colo. Resident: $44; Nonresident: $254

Mountain Lion (*Puma concolor*)
Colorado DOW has no statistics on mountain lion hunting in GMU 82. We know they are here, because one was spotted running across the road in the Baca subdivision on Jan. 20, 2004, by (now mayor) Ralph Abrams. Other evidence is the occasional disappearance of suburban pets left out overnight, but that could be ascribed to coyotes as well. Harvest Quota in GMU 82= 6 (2009-2010 Hunting Season).
Colo. Resident: $41; Nonresident: $251

Rocky Mountain Bighorn Sheep (*Ovis canadensis canadensis*)
In Colorado, bighorn sheep and mountain goats are managed differently from other big games species. There are no mountain goats in the Sangre de Cristos, but bighorn sheep are common. The Sangres make up game management unit S09. According to the Division of Wildlife (quoted in Keno, 2007), there are 250-300 sheep in the mountains east of Crestone and the Baca.

HARVEST FOR ALLL MANNERS OF TAKE				
YEAR	MANNER	TOTAL HARVEST	TOTAL HUNTERS	PERCENT SUCCESS
2008	Rifle	7	10	70%
	Archery	2	6	33%
	TOTAL	**9**	**16**	**56%**
2007	**TOTAL**	**7**	**17**	**41%**
2006	**TOTAL**	**7**	**12**	**58%**
2005	**TOTAL**	**7**	**19**	**37%**

APPENDIX 4. REFERENCES

Anderson, Peter, 2005, First Church of the Higher Elevations: Ghost Road Press, Denver, CO, 184 p. (available from author, P.O. Box 904, Crestone, CO, 81131).

Aspen Times, 2005, The Aspen Institute's new idea: The Aspen Times, July 3, 2005. www.aspentimes.com/article/20050703/ASPENWEEKLY/107030004

Baca Grant Development Company, 1909, The Camera in the Sunny San Luis Valley and on the Famous Baca Land Grant in Colorado: Baca Grant Development Company, Inc., Colorado Springs, CO.

Bairstow, Diane, 2006, Experienced climber dies on Kit Carson Peak: Crestone Eagle newspaper, Crestone, CO, July 2006.

Bankers Magazine, 1901, New banks: vol. LXII, January to June, 1901: Bradford Rhodes & Co., New York, NY.

Barnford, C., 1994, Homage to Pythagoras; Rediscovering Sacred Science: Lindisfarne Books, 304 p.

Beckwith, E.G., 1855, Report, by Lieutenant E.G. Beckwith, Third Artillery, Upon the Route Near the Thirty-Eight and Thirty-Ninth Parallels, Explored by Captain J.W. Gunnison, Corps Topographical Engineers, *in* Reports of Explorations and Surveys to Ascertain the Most Practicable and Economical Route for a Railroad from the Mississippi River to the Pacific Ocean, Made Under the Direction of the Secretary of War, In 1853-54: Vol. II, Beverly Tucker, Printer, Washington, D.C.

Bergland, E., 1877, Executive and descriptive report of Lieutenant Eric Bergland, Corps of Engineers, on the operations of Party No. 1, Colorado Section, field season of 1876, *in* Wheeler, G.M., Annual Report, upon the Geographical Surveys West of the One-Hundredth Meridian in the States and Territories of California, Oregon, Nevada, Texas, Arizona, Colorado, Idaho, Montana, New Mexico, Utah, and Wyoming, being Appendix NN of the Annual Report of the Chief of Engineers for 1877: Government Printing Office, Washington, D.C., p. 1250-1252.

Bryant, Kimberly and Haines, Steve, 2007, Lightning starts 20-acre brush fire: Crestone Eagle newspaper, Crestone, CO, August 2007.

Bueler, W.M., 2000, Roof of the Rockies, 3rd Edition: Colorado Mountain Club Press, Golden, CO, 256 p.

Carey, Kip, 2003, Official Colorado Fishing Guide, 2nd Ed.: Kip Carey Publications, www.fishingcolowyo.com, 416 p.

Chernin, Roni, 2003, Inventive team plants sphere in Baca Grants: Crestone Eagle newspaper, Crestone, CO, Dec. 2003.

Cooper, J.K, 2003, The search for the Central Railroad Route to the Pacific through the San Luis Valley in 1853: The San Luis Valley Historian, v. XXXV, no. 2, p. 9-60.

Crestone Eagle, 2003, Fuel reduction project begins near Crestone: Crestone Eagle newspaper, Crestone, CO, September 2003.

Darnell, Marcia, 2000, Roy Gould; Sculpted in Intensity: Colorado Central Magazine, September 2000 issue (http://cozine.com/2000-september/roy-gould-sculpted-in-intensity/).

Del Amor, Jo, 2003, Creating a sustainable local food supply: Crestone Eagle newspaper, Crestone, CO, April 2003 (www.crestoneeagle.com/archives2003/apr03_b1.html)

Denver Post, 2009, Colorado cow mutilations baffle ranchers, cops, UFO believer: Dec. 9, 2009.

D.I., 1875, The Sangre de Cristo mines: Colorado Weekly Chieftain, Mar. 11, 1875.

Doty, Herman Jr., 2007, Bones in a Boxcar; The Investigation of Snippy the Horse: Morris Publishing, Kearney, NE, 134 p.

Eliis, C.E., Hannigan, B.J., and Thompson, J.R., 1983, Mineral investigation of Sangre de Cristo Wilderness Study Area, Alamosa, Custer, Fremont, Huerfano, and Saguache Counties, Colorado: U.S. Bureau of Mines, Open-File Report MLA 65-83, 190 pp.

Erdman, Jim, 2004, Jim Erdman talks with Crestone 'old timer Bob King'—a treasure house of local lore: Crestone Eagle newspaper, Crestone, CO, July 2004, p. B-13.

Fremont, J.C., 1886, Memoirs of My Life, Including in the Narrative Five Journeys of Western Exploration during the years 1842, 1843-44, 1845-47, 1848-49, and 1853-54: Belford, Clarke & Co., Chicago and New York (reprinted in 2001 by Cooper Square Press, 696 p.).

Frank, Buddy, 2008, The Healing Arts Guild, in Pearson, C. (ed.), Crestone; A Sacred Earth Journal: Cindy Pearson, P.O. Box 356, Crestone, CO 81131, p. 78-79.

FWS, 2005, Conceptual Management Plan, Baca National Wildlife Refuge: U.S. Fish and Wildlife Service, Alamosa, CO, May 2005, 71 p. (www.fws.gov/alamosa/baca NWR.html)

Garratt, M. and Martin, B., 1992, Colorado's High Thirteeners; A Climbing and Hiking Guide: Cordillera Press, Evergreen, Co, 260 p.

Gazetteer Publishing Co., 1911, The Colorado State Business Directory, with A Complete Classified Directory of the Entire State, Including Mines, Reduction Works, Etc.: 37th Annual Volume, The Gazetteer Publishing Co., Denver, CO. (http://files.usgwarchives.org/co/saguache/directories/1911-crestone.txt)

Geary, M.M., 1997, Ramparts of Sand: An environmental history of Great Sand Dunes National Monument and the San Luis Valley: M.A. thesis, Colorado State University, Fort Collins, CO, 160 p.

Gilpin, Wm., 1860, Mission of the North American people, geographical, social, and political: reprinted 1873 by J.B. Lippincot & Company, Philadelphia, PA, 217 p. [facsimile edition from University of Michigan Library, Historical Reprint series (www.lib.umich.edu)].

Gilpin, Wm., 1869, The San Luis Park, in Blackmore, Wm., Colorado: Its Resources, Parks and Prospects as a New Field for Emigration ; With An Account of the Trenchera and Costilla Estates, In the San Luis Park: privately printed by Blackmore in London, 188 p.

Grissino-Mayer, H.D., Baisan, C.H. and Swetnam, T.W., 1998, A multicentury reconstruction of precipitation for Great Sand Dunes National Monument, southwestern Colorado: unpublished report submitted Laboratory of Tree-Ring Research, University of Arizona, Tucson, to the Mid-Continent Ecological Science Center, Ft. Collins, CO for the Great Sand Dunes National Monument, 32 p. (http://web.utk.edu/~grissino/downloads/GSD%20Final%20Report.pdf)

Grudowski, M., 2011, Crestone, CO; Live Off the Grid, in "The West's Best Places to Live": Sunset Magazine, Feb. 2011.

Gulliford, Andrew, 2009, Historic Utes leave legacy of peeled pines: Gulliford's Travels, Cortez Journal newspaper, Cortez, CO, 18-July-2009 (www.cortezjournal.com)

Halverson, A., 2000, The National Elk Refuge and the Jackson Hole elk herd; Management appraisal and recommendations, in Clark, T., Casey, D. and Halverson, A. (eds.), Developing sustainable management policy for the National

Elk Refuge, Wyoming: Forestry & Environmental Sciences Bulletin 104, p. 23-52, Yale University, New Haven, CT. http://environment.research.yale.edu/documents/downloads/0-9/104Halver.pdf

Harlan, G., 2002, Postmarks and Places: Adobe Village Press, Monte Vista, CO, 190 p. plus appendix. (see the book review by Quillen, E., 2002).

Harlan, Noel, 2010, Broken dreams; The history of Duncan mining camp: The San Luis Valley Historian, v. XLII, no. 3, p. 5-21.

Hart, J.L.J., 1931, Fourteen Thousand Feet; A history of the naming and early ascents of the high Colorado peaks, 2nd Edition: Colorado Mountain Club, Denver, CO, 48 p. (reprinted 1972).

Hart, Kelly, 2003a, The Wonders of Aerblock: Crestone Eagle newspaper, Crestone, CO, June 2003 issue (www.crestoneeagle.com/archives2003/jun03_b1.html).

Hart, Kelly, 2003b, What is the truth about papercrete?: Crestone Eagle newspaper, Crestone, CO, September 2003 issue (www.crestoneeagle.com/archives2003/jun03_b1.html).

Hatheway, Beth, 2010, Wintering on Pole Creek, 1921 & 1922: Crestone Eagle newspaper, Crestone, CO, Dec. 2010, p. B-12 to B-13.

Hayden, F.V., 1877, Geological and geographical atlas of Colorado and portions of adjacent territory: Jules Bien, Washington, DC, 16 map sheets.

Henderson, Charles W., 1926, Mining in Colorado; A History of Discovery, Development, and Production: U.S. Geological Survey Professional Paper 138, Washington, D.C.

Hyman, Sidney, 1976, The Aspen Idea: University of Oklahoma Press, 402 p.

Jacobs, R, and Ormes, R.M., 2000, Guide to the Colorado Mountains: Colorado Mountain Club Press, Golden, CO, 366 p.

Jones, Finn-Olaf, 2008, For Many a Follower, Sacred Ground in Colorado: New York Times, Jan. 11, 2008. (http://travel.nytimes.com/2008/01/11/travel/escapes/11crestone.html?pagewanted=all)

Julyan, Robert, 1996, The Place Names of New Mexico (revised edition): University of New Mexico press, Albuquerque, NM, 403 p.

Kahn, 2000, Uses and valuation of the national Elk Refuge, Wyoming, in Clark, T., Casey, D. and Halverson, A. (eds.), Developing sustainable management policy for the National Elk Refuge, Wyoming: Forestry & Environmental Sciences Bulletin 104, p. 139-170, Yale University, New Haven, CT.

Kempfer, W.H., 1911, Preservative treatment of poles: U.S. Department of Agriculture, Forest Service Bulletin 84.

Keno, 2004a, Bears are a problem again; several homes broken into by bold bruins: Crestone Eagle newspaper, Crestone, CO, August 2004 (www.crestoneeagle.com/archives2004/aug04_a1.html)

Keno, 2004b, The magnificent Baca elk herd: Crestone Eagle newspaper, Crestone, CO, Jan. 2004 (www.crestoneeagle.com/archives2004/nov04_b1.html)

Keno, 2005a, Tornado hits above Crestone: The Crestone Eagle newspaper, Crestone, CO, May 2005 (www.crestoneeagle.com/archives2005/headlineA1.may05.html)

Keno, 2005b, Moffat/Crestone hit by powerful wind storm—blows roof off of school: Crestone Eagle newspaper, Crestone, CO, July 2005 (www.crestoneeagle.com/archives2005/headlineA1.july05.html)

Keno, 2006, Flash flood hit the Crestone area: Crestone Eagle newspaper, Crestone, CO, August 2006 (www.crestoneeagle.com/archives2006/headlineA2.aug06.html)

Keno, 2007, Bighorn sheep—a symbol of power & agility: Crestone Eagle newspaper, Crestone, CO, July 2007 (www.crestoneeagle.com/archives2007/jul07_b1.html)

Keno, 2010, Diverse mountain habitats support birds of many feathers: Crestone Eagle newspaper, Crestone, CO, February 2010 (http://crestoneeagle.com/?p=1242)

Kerouac, Jack, 1958, The Dharma Bums: Harcourt Brace, New York, 256 p.

Kessler, Ron, 1998, Old Spanish Trail North Branch and its travelers: Sunstone Press, Santa Fe, NM, 384 p.

Koko, Sigi, 2005, The big picture; Strawbale trends and defining "Eco-sensible" design: Crestone Eagle newspaper, Crestone, CO, April 2005 (www.crestoneeagle.com/archives2005/headlineB1.apr05.html)

Kongtrul, Dzigar, 2006, It's Up To You: The practice of self-reflection on the Buddhist path: Shambhala Publishing, 160 p.

Kongtrul, Dzigar, 2008, Light Comes Through: Buddhist teachings on awakening our natural intelligence: Shambhala Publishing, 144 p.

Krall, Angie and Martorano, Marilyn, 2011, The Old Spanish Trail; tracking down a trail: Part 2: Crestone Eagle newspaper, Crestone, CO, April 2011, p. B-1. Crestoneneagle.com/2011/04/01/the-old-spanish-trail-part-2/

Kucin, L. (ed.), 2000, Crestone; An Illustrated Guide to the Significant Attractions of the Crestone/Baca Area; with illustrations by J.J. Roderick: The Way Productions, Crestone, CO (for sale in local restaurants and grocery stores).

Lakes, Arthur, 1902, Crestone mining district in San Luis Park, Colorado; A region containing some good veins favorably situated for economical mining: Mines and Minerals, Scranton, PA, vol. xxii, p. 467-468.

LaMarche, V.C. Jr. and Stockton, C.W., 1974, Chronologies from temperature-sensitive bristlecone pines at upper treeline in western United States: The Tree Ring Bulletin, vol. 34, p. 21-45. (www.treeringsociety.org/TRBTRR/TRBvol34_21-45.pdf)

Lawlor, Robert, 1982, Sacred Geometry; Philosophy and Practice: Thames & Hudson, London, UK, 112 p.

Lindsey, D.A., 2010, The geologic story of Colorado's Sangre de Cristo Range: U.S. Geological Survey, Circular 1349, 14 p. (http://pubs.usgs.gov/circ1349/)

Lindsey, D.A., Johnson, B.R., Soulliere, S.J., Bruce, R.M., and Hafner, K., 1986, Geologic map of the Beck Mountain, Crestone Peak, and Crestone quadrangles, Custer, Huerfano, and Saguache Counties, Colorado: U.S. Geological Survey Map MF-1878, scale 1:24,000. (http://ngmdb.usgs.gov/Prodesc/proddesc_7435.htm).

Lindsey, D.A., Soulliere, S.J., Hafner, K. and Flores, R.J., 1985, Geologic map of Rito Alto Peak and northeastern part of Mirage quadrangles, Custer and Saguache Counties, Colorado: U.S. Geological Survey Map MF-1787, scale 1:24,000. (http://ngmdb.usgs.gov/Prodesc/proddesc_7426.htm).

Long, Haniel, 1986, Pinon Country: University of Nebraska Press, 337 p.

Lowers, Mary, 2007, Bears are back—and so are reports of bear damage: Crestone Eagle newspaper, Crestone, CO, September 2007 (www.crestoneeagle.com/archives2007/sep07_a2.html)

Lowers, Mary, 2008a, Climber dies in 1700 ft fall near Crestone Needle: Crestone Eagle newspaper, Crestone, CO, September 2008 (www.crestoneeagle.com/archives2008/sep08_a2.html)

Lowers, Mary, 2008b, Injured climber rescued from Challenger Peak: Crestone Eagle newspaper, Crestone, CO, July 2008 (www.crestoneeagle.com/archives2008/jul08_a1.html)

Manitou Foundation, 2005, Manitou Institute—Spirit & Nature: Crestone Eagle newspaper, Crestone, CO, April 2005 (www.manitou.org/MI/mhcp.php)

Martin, Helen, 2005, Water resources and rights in the northern San Luis Valley, Part II: The San Luis Valley Historian, v. XXXVII, no. 4, p. 5-42.

Marvin, U.B. and Marvin, T.C., 1966, A re-examination of the crater near Crestone, Colorado: Meteorics [now Meteorics and Planetary Science], v. 3, no. 1, p. 1-10.

May, Peter, 2008, Magical moments creating the *Crestone* album, *in* Pearson, C. (ed.), Crestone; A Sacred Earth Journal: Cindy Pearson, publisher. P.O. Box 356, Crestone, CO 81131, p. 55-57.

McCalpin, J.P., 1982, Quaternary geology and neotectonics of the west flank of the Northern Sangre de Cristo Mountains, south-central Colorado: Colorado School of Mines Quarterly, vol. 77, no. 3, 97 p. (http://geohaz.com/downloads/MONOGRAPHS/1982%20Sangre%20de%20Cristo%20LowRes.pdf)

McCaskey, H.D., 1919, Mineral Resources of the United States, 1916; Part 1, Metals: U.S. Geological Survey, Washington, D.C., 871 p.

McDonald, Marci, 1994, The new spirituality; Maclean's Magazine, Canada, Oct. 10.

Merriam, C.H. and Steineger, L., 1890, Results of a biological survey of the San Francisco Mountain region and the desert of the Little Colorado, Arizona: North American Fauna Report no. 3, U.S. Department of Agriculture, Division of Ornithology and Mammalia, Washington, D.C., 136 p.

Messoline, Judy, 2005, That Crazy Lady Down the Road: Earth Star Publications, Box 522, Hooper, CO, 81136, 250 p.

Milanovich, N.J., Rice, B. and Ploski, C., 1990, We the Arcturians: Athena Publishing, Scottsdale, Arizona, 319 p.

Mills, C.I., 1994, The social geography of New Age spirituality in Vancouver: M.A. thesis, University of British Columbia, Vancouver, BC, 320 p.

Moore, Jason, 2003, Hiking Colorado's Sangre de Cristo Wilderness: A Falcon Guide, Globe Pequot Press, Guilford, CT, 257 p.

Muir, John, 1894, The Mountains of California: The Century Company, New York, 381 p. (www.yosemite.ca.us/john_muir_writings/the_mountains_of_california/)

Muir, John, 1912, The Yosemite: The Century Company, New York; reprinted 1962 by Doubleday & Company, New York, 225 p.

Nealson, Christina, 1994a, Alternative building styles sprout in Saguache County: Colorado Central Magazine, July 1994 issue (http://cozine.com/1994-july/alternative-buiding-styles-sprout-in-saguache-county/).

Nealson, Christina, 1994b, The edifice complex: Colorado Central Magazine, November 1994 issue (http://cozine.com/1994-november/the-edifice-complex/).

Nininger, H.H., 1963, unpublished manuscript on the Crestone Crater: Denver Museum of Natural History, Denver, CO.

O'Brien, C., 1996, The Mysterious Valley: St. Martins Press, NY, 300 p.

O'Brien, C., 1999, Enter the Valley: St. Martin's Press, NY, 339 p.

O'Brien, C., 2007, Secrets of the Mysterious Valley: Adventures Unlimited Press, Kempton, IL, 441 p.

O'Hanlon, Michael, 1999, The Colorado Sangre de Cristo: a Complete Trail Guide, 3rd Ed.: The Hungry Gulch Press, 71 p.

Paine, Jeffrey, 2007, A Spiritual Community Takes Root: U.S. News & World Report, Nov. 16, 2007. www.usnews.com/articles/news/sacred-places/2007/11/16/a-spiritual-communitu-takes-root.html

Parker, C.O. Jr., 1952, A history of gold mining in the Sangre de Cristos: Mines Magazine, v. 42, no. 5, p. 25-27, 43.

Pearson, C. (ed.), 2008, Crestone; A Sacred Earth Journal: Cindy Pearson, publisher. P.O. Box 356, Crestone, CO 81131, 90 p., email: asacredjournal@fairpoint.net

Peattie, D.C., 1991, A Natural History of Western Trees: Houghton Mifflin, 768 p.

Pelton, A.R., 1891, San Luis Valley Illustrated: privately printed in Salida, Colorado; reprinted in 2003 by Adobe Village Press, Monte Vista, CO, 188 p.

Perkins, J.E, 2002, Old Mose; The King of the Grizzlies: Adobe Village Press, Monte Vista, CO, 106 p.

Quillen, Ed, 2002, Book Review: Colorado Central Magazine, August 2002 issue (http://cozine.com/2002-august/drillin-loadin-and-firin-by-gladys-sisemore-postmarks-and-places-by-george-harlan/)

Quillen, Ed, 2004, Regional Roundup: Colorado Central Magazine, September 2004 issue (http://cozine.com/2004-september/regional-roundup-9/)

Quillen, Ed, 2008, Regional Roundup: Colorado Central Magazine, August 2008 issue (http://cozine.com/2008-september/regional-roundup-52/)

Quillen, Martha, 1994, The Great Pyramid of the Arcturians: Colorado Central Magazine, no. 1, p. 4 (www.cozine.com/archive/cc1994/00010043.html)

Quillen, Martha, 2006, Regional Roundup: Colorado Central Magazine, October 2006 issue (http://cozine.com/2006-october/regional-roundup-31/)

Rae, Allison, 2002, Shambala of the Rockies; The Mythos & Power of Crestone: Four Corners Magazine, Sedona, AZ. www.crestonecolorado.com/shambala.html

Reddin, Paul, 2007, Early exploration for oil in the San Luis Valley: The San Luis Valley Historian, v. XXXIX, no. 3, p. 12-16.

Refsnider, K.A., Brugger, K.A., Leonard, E.M., McCalpin, J.P. and Armstrong, P.P., 2009, Last Glacial Maximum equilibrium-line altitude trends and precipitation patterns in the Sangre de Cristo Mountains, southern Colorado, USA: Boreas, v. 38, no. 4, p. 663-678.

Richmond, P.J., 1992, Trail to Disaster: Colorado Historical Society, Denver, CO, 117 p.

Rinpoche, Tsoknyi, 2003, Fearless Simplicity: The Dzogchen way of living freely in a complex world: North Atlantic Books, 260 p.

Rinpoche, Tsoknyi, 2004, Carefree Dignity: Discourses on training in the nature of mind: North Atlantic Books, 240 p.

RMPBS, 2000, Mi Casa es Su Casa: *Spirit of Colorado* series; VHS video cassette, Rocky Mountain PBS (Public Broadcasting System), Denver, CO.

Roach, G., 1999, Colorado's Fourteeners; From Hikes to Climbs: Fulcrum Publishing, Golden, CO, 306 p.

Roach, G. and Roach, J., 2001, Colorado's Thirteeners; From Hikes to Climbs: Fulcrum Publishing, Golden, CO, 367 p.

Robertson, Janet, 2003, The Magnificent Mountain Women; Adventures in the Colorado Rockies: University of Nebraska Press, Lincoln, NE,

Rubin, Julia, 1989, Colorado site called "a place of power"; Spiritualists, environmentalists find haven in the Baca: Associated Press article; appeared in the Los Angeles Times, Aug. 20, 1989 (http://articles.latimes.com/1989-08-20/news/mn-1144_1_gathering place)

Rychlik, W., 2009, Lakes of the Sangre de Cristo Mountains: Pikes Peak Photo, 228 p. (e-book; www.pikespeakphoto.com/sangres/sangre_lakes.html)

Saguache Chronicle, 1881, Some of "Faith's" assertions denied: Saguache Chronicle newspaper, Nov. 4, 1884 issue, p. 1. (www.coloradohistoricnewspapers.org).

Saguache Chronicle, 1884, report by mill proprietor Mr. Wm. Edge: Saguache Chronicle newspaper, July 4, 1884 issue, p. 8. (www.coloradohistoricnewspapers.org).

Schoenecker, K., Lubow, B., Zeigenfuss, L. and Mao, J, 2006, 2005 Annual Progress Report: Elk and Bison Grazing Ecology in the Great Sand Dunes Complex of Lands: U.S. Geological Survey Open-File Report 2006-1267, 45 p. (www.fort.usgs.gov/Products/Publications/pub_abstract.asp?PubID=21779)

Schulte, Kent, 2009, Sangre de Cristo and Great Sand Dunes Trail Map, 3rd Edition: Sky Terrain, P.O. Box 808, Boulder, CO, scale 1:60,000.

Shellabarger, A.W., 1923, Recollections of early days in the San Luis Valley: unpub. manuscript, San Isabel National Forest (reprinted 1997, The San Luis Valley Historian, v. XXIX, no. 3, p. 5-19.

Sherer, Paul, 2005, In The Shadow of the Mountain; A History of Crestone, Colorado: published by the author, P.O. Box 54, Mullinville, KS, 235 p.

Sisemore, Gladys, 1983, Drillin', Loadin', and Firin'; In Crestone With the "Old Timers!"; B&B Printers, Gunnison, Inc., Gunnison, Colorado 81230, 136 p. (see the book review by Quillen, E., 2002).

Slattery, D.P., 2004, Grace in the Desert: Jossey-Bass Publishers, San Francisco, 176 p.

Slaughter, M., 2007, Looking at the history of Duncan: The Hourglass, newsletter of Friends of the Dunes, Vol. 18, no. 3 (Nov. 2007), p. 1, 3. (www.friendsofgreatsanddunes.org/Newsletters/Hourglass%2018-3color.pdf)

Smith, P.J., 2005, "Rock of Ages", the Crestone Conglomerate: Crestone Eagle newspaper, Crestone, CO, August 2005 (www.crestoneeagle.com/archives2005/headlineB1.aug05.html)

Sovell, J., 2006, Baca Grande biological assessment 2005; consulting report prepared for the Crestone/Baca Land Trust, Crestone, CO by the Colorado Natural Heritage Program, Colorado State Univ., Ft. Collins, CO (www.cnhp.colostate.edu), 95 p.

Sri Aurobindo, 2010, Savitri: A Legend and a Symbol, 4th Edition: Sri Aurobindo Publications, Pondicherry, India, 825 p.

Stegner, Wallace E., 1987, The American West as Living Space: University of Michigan Press, Ann Arbor, MI, 89 p.

Stegner, Wallace E., 1997, The Sound of Mountain Water; The Changing American West: Penguin Books, NY, 288 p.

Stegner, Wallace E., 2000, Angle of Repose: Penguin Classics Series, Penguin Books, NY, 592 p. (paperback reprint).

Stegner, Wallace E., 2002, Crossing Into Eden, in Where the Bluebird Sings to the Lemonade Springs; Living and Writing in the West: Random House, NY, p.34-44.

Strong, Maurice, 2001, Where On Earth Are We Going": Texere Publishing, New York, hardback, 431 p. (also published in paperback by Vintage Canada).

Tejada-Flores, Lito, 1990, Beyond climbing games; Alpinism as humanism: Summit magazine, Fall 1990 issue.

Torkelson, Jean, 2001, Colorado's Sanctuaries, Retreats, and Sacred Places: Westcliffe Publishers, Englewood, CO, 256 p.

USDA Forest Service, 2010, Species; Pinus edulis; USDA Forest Service website, www.fs.fed.us/database/feis/plants/tree/pinedu/all.html; accessed Feb. 2010.

U.S. General Land Office, 1866, Map of Public Surveys in Colorado Territory, to accompany the report of the Surveyor General, 1866: General Land Office, Department of the Interior, October 2, 1866; printed by Major & Knapp Engraving, Manufacturing, and Lithographic Company, New York, NY. Scale 1:1,140,480. http://www.davidrumsey.com/maps445.html

Wangyal, Tenzin, 2000, Wonders of the natural mind; The Essence of dzogchen in the native Bon tradition of Tibet: Snow Lion Publications, Ithaca, NY, 224 p.

Wangyal, Tenzin, 2007, Tibetan Sound Healing: Sounds True, Inc., 104 p.

Wangyal, Tenzin, 2011, Awakening the Sacred Body: Hay House, Carlsbad, CA, 200 p.

Welsch, Chris, 2009, Crestone; Colorado's Spiritual Crossroads: Special to the Minneapolis Star Tribune, Travel Section, Dec. 12, 2009 (also San Diego News Network, Jan. 25, 2010)(www.startribune.com/lifestyle/travel/79139502.htm).l

Wheeler, G.M., 1877, Annual Report, upon the Geographical Surveys West of the One-Hundredth Meridian in the States and Territories of California, Oregon, Nevada, Texas, Arizona, Colorado, Idaho, Montana, New Mexico, Utah, and Wyoming, being Appendix NN of the Annual Report of the Chief of Engineers for 1877: Government Printing Office, Washington, D.C.

White, Wm. Edward, 1881, Crestone Peak; What can be seen from there—An Eloquent Description: Saguache Chronicle newspaper, Saguache, CO, July 1, 1881 issue, p. 4 (www.coloradohistoricnewspapers.org).

Wilkinson, Ernest, 2008, Colorado Outdoor Living; Eighty-Plus Years: O&V Printing, Alamosa, CO, 158 p.

Winger, C. and Winger, D, 2003, The Essential Guide to Great Sand Dunes National Park and Preserve: Colorado Mountain Club Press, Golden, CO, 239 p.

Winson, Robert and Sagan, Miriam, 1999, Dirty Laundry; 100 Days in a Zen Monastery: New World Library, Novato, CA, 2nd Ed., 202 p.

Winter, Paul, 2010, CRESTONE; A Celebration of the World of Crestone: liner notes to the Album, Web version; (http://paulwinter.bandcamp.com/album/crestone); accessed 03-MAR-2010.

Wolf, Tom, 1995, Colorado's Sangre de Cristo Mountains: University Press of Colorado Press, Niwot, CO, 339 p.

Wood, Daniel, 1990, The Wizard of the Baca Grande: West Magazine, Alberta, Canada, May 1990 issue.

Wyckoff, William and Dilsaver, L.M. (eds.), 1995, The Mountainous West; Explorations in Historical Geography: University of Nebraska Press, Lincoln, NE, 422 p.

APPENDIX 5: SUBJECT INDEX

253

James McCalpin moved to Colorado in 1972 for the rock and snow climbing, and then discovered the laid-back mountain high lifestyle of the day. In 1979 and 1980 he spent summers in Crestone, and hiked all the valleys of the western Sangre de Cristos while mapping its glacial geology and recent fault history for his PhD at the Colorado School of Mines.

He also met many strange and wonderful local characters. In Crestone these included Maurice and Hanne Strong, who with their family had just moved to the Baca Ranch in 1979. Many of those characters are no longer with us: Preacher Bo from Cotton Creek; Ed Riegel from Wild Cherry; Billy Hutchinson, Jack Dempsey, and Frank Snider from Crestone.

After a varied career as a government geologist, professor, and consultant, Dr. McCalpin bought the McAlpine Ranch at Crestone in 1996 and founded the Crestone Science Center in 2000 (www.crestonescience.org). Although he continues international consulting (www.geohaz.com), the Sangres have always managed to pull him back home.

Anyone pretending to be a guide through wild and fabulous territory should know the territory. I wish I knew it better than I do. I am not Jed Smith. But Jed Smith is not available these days as a guide, and I am. I accept the duty, at least as much for what I may learn as for what I may be able to tell others.

An appropriate sentiment from Wallace Stegner, 1987, *The American West As Living Space*

Other Guidebooks by the Crestone Science Center:

No. 1: *The active geologic environment of Central Colorado; Aspen-Glenwood Springs-Silt, Colorado (1997)*; Friends of the Pleistocene trip, Rocky Mountain Cell, Sept. 12-14, 1997: 92 p.

No. 2: *Neotectonics of the Rio Grande Rift in Colorado (2008)*; Guidebook to Field Trip 8, Geological Society of America 2002 Annual Meeting, Denver, Colorado: 115 p.

No. 3: *Finding Fault in the San Luis Valley-- A Geology Field Trip Along the Sangre de Cristo Fault and Geothermal Sites (2007)*: July 14, 2007, 18 p.

No. 4: *Central Rio Grande rift, Neotectonics and Volcanism (2008)*-- Field Trip #2, Part 1, Seismological Society of America Annual Meeting, Albuquerque, NM, 19-April-2008: 36 p.

No. 5: *Quaternary Happenings in the Overthrust Belt, Western Wyoming (2008)*; 2008 Friends of the Pleistocene Field Trip—Rocky Mountain Cell, Sept. 6-8, 2008: 92 p.

No. 6: *Quaternary Geology and Geochronology of the Uppermost Arkansas Valley—Glaciers, Ice Dams, Landslides, Floods (2010)*; Guidebook to Field Trip 405, Geological Society of America, 2010 Annual Meeting, Denver, CO: 35 p.